MOVING TO A
SMALL TOWN

ALSO BY THE AUTHORS

Simple Living: One Couple's Search for a Better Life

The Singular Generation

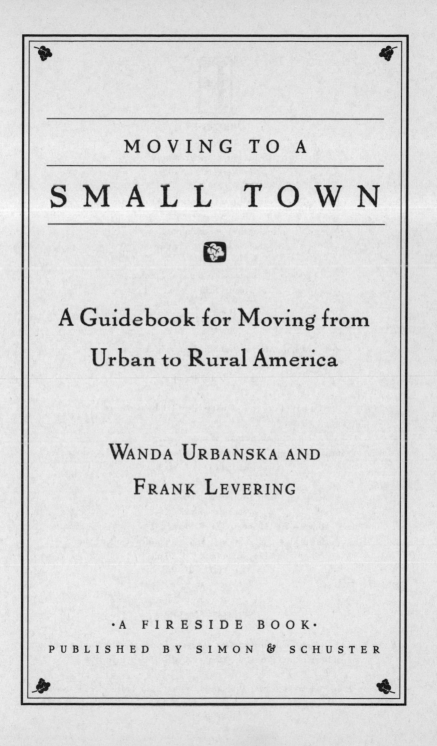

MOVING TO A
SMALL TOWN

A Guidebook for Moving from
Urban to Rural America

WANDA URBANSKA AND
FRANK LEVERING

·A FIRESIDE BOOK·
PUBLISHED BY SIMON & SCHUSTER

FIRESIDE
Rockefeller Center
1230 Avenue of the Americas
New York, NY 10020

Copyright © 1996 by Wanda Urbanska and Frank Levering
All rights reserved,
including the right of reproduction
in whole or in part in any form.

FIRESIDE and colophon are registered trademarks
of Simon & Schuster Inc.

Designed by Jessica Shatan

Manufactured in the United States of America

1 3 5 7 9 10 8 6 4 2

Library of Congress Cataloging-in-Publication Data

Urbanska, Wanda, date.
Moving to a small town : a guidebook for moving from urban to rural America / Wanda
Urbanska and Frank Levering.
p.   cm.
"A Fireside book."
Includes index.
1. Cities and towns—United States.   2. Relocation (Housing)—United States.
3. Quality of life—United States.   4. Country life—United States.
I. Levering, Frank.   II. Title.
HT123.U77   1996
307.76'2'0973—dc20   96-1615
                                                                                         CIP

ISBN 0-684-80223-6

Excerpt from L. Robert Kohl. *Survival Kit for Overseas Living,* reprinted with permission
of Intercultural Press, Inc., Yarmouth, ME. © Copyright 1996

Excerpt from Thomas H. Naylor, William H. Willimon, and Magdalena R. Naylor.
The Search for Meaning, reprinted with permission of Abingdon Press, Nashville, TN.
© Copyright 1994.

To Edmund Stephen Urbanski,
a citizen of the world,
who grew up in the small town
of Ostrow, Poland

Contents

Introduction

"Whatever you can do or dream you can, begin it. Boldness
has genius, power and magic in it."

—GOETHE

In 1986, we moved from within one mile of the busiest intersec-
tion in Los Angeles to bucolic splendor just north of Mount Airy,
North Carolina, a town of 7,157 tucked in the foothills of the
Blue Ridge Mountains. We had big-city tastes, sophisticated
friends and fast-track careers. One writer friend cautioned that
in the hinterlands our minds would "turn to mush." And, she
warned, "there'll be nothing to write about in the middle of
nowhere."

Her dire predictions proved false. Since then, our professional fortunes have soared. Singly and jointly, we've published
four books along with countless magazine and newspaper articles, turned around an unprofitable family orchard, thrown ourselves into community life and watched our lives change
profoundly under the small-town watch. For us, the move has
reconfigured our lives dramatically and "taken" beyond our
wildest dreams.

Making the move from the big city to a small town* can work for you, too. This book will show you how.

So you think you want to leave the city and start life over in a small town. You have a strong sense that life would be better there. When on vacation in the country, you relish the slower pace. While tooling through towns off the beaten path, you're struck by the lower costs of everything from BLTs to oil-and-lube jobs and moved by the friendliness of the locals. You find yourself sleeping easier. Your body's looser. Your soul soars higher. If you could figure out a way to earn a living, you'd make the leap in a heartbeat.

Your children could be your impetus for wanting to put down roots in a small town. Maybe you'd like them to be free to ride their bikes around town, play ball in the park or in friends' backyards without fear and attend safe, quality public schools. You'd like them to have a secure base from which to take risks later in life—perhaps following in the footsteps of the many American leaders, from presidents to writers to captains of industry, who are small-town bred, whose success is often attributed to the opportunity to try everything. (Mark Twain once said of his hometown of Hannibal, Missouri: "All of the *me* in me is in a little Missouri village halfway around the world.")

Or maybe you'd like to start a new business, develop another side of yourself. Perhaps you're at retirement age and would like to get out of the city and settle into a community where you know your doctor as a friend and tradespeople as neighbors, where you're comfortable strolling the streets and feel that someone would care if you had a medical mishap. Or perhaps you'd simply like more time to do the things that matter most to you.

Your yearning for a new life in a small town is not at all unusual. In fact, for a whole host of social, demographic and economic

---

*We define a small town as a nonmetropolitan area with a population of less than 50,000. However, most of the small towns we write about are in the 25,000-or-under category.

reasons, countless Americans are picking up and leaving the cities for new lives in the country. In a kind of reverse migration of the Okie exodus from the 1930s Dust Bowl, Californians are now heading back to places like, well—Oklahoma. And Idaho, Ohio, Oregon, Utah, Colorado and North Carolina. The list goes on.

This book will shepherd you through the process of planning and executing such a move, right down to advising newcomers how to avoid the faux pas common among big-city people once you've unpacked your boxes, hooked up your telephone and been visited by the Welcome Wagon.

It will help you decide if you're right for small-town life; offer a systematic approach to scouting a town whose culture and lifestyle jibe with your own; give advice about how to recast your career; show you how to plan and make the move as well as how to figure the costs; and advise you on how to make a place for yourself in a small town. It will take you by the hand, walking you through the steps of making the sometimes tricky but ultimately rewarding transition of moving to a small town.

WHY THE YEN FOR THE SMALL TOWN?

> "In a city, [people's] huge number ensures that it will not only be more crowded than other places, but also more restrictive, competitive, bureaucratic, hectic, and just plain arousing; the quietest times in New Yorkers' apartments are louder than the noisiest in small towns."
>
> —WINIFRED GALLAGHER,
> *The Power of Place*

Moving to a small town has become a major fantasy of the 1990s, beckoning Americans the way California living did a generation ago. Even those of us who aren't planning a move, it seems, are fantasizing about one. Our most popular TV shows have come from the datelines of such fictional pinprick towns as Cicely, Alaska; Evening Shade, Arkansas; and Cabot Cove, Maine. The hippest Hollywood celebrities now live in places like Whitefish, Montana, and Schuyler, Virginia—anywhere but Beverly Hills. And the public seems to agree. While four out of five Americans live in or around major metropolitan areas, the director of strategic planning and research at DDB Needham Worldwide, Chicago, recently told *Advertising Age* that two-thirds of all Americans—if given their druthers—would live in a small town.

Tribune Media columnist Donald Kaul, an unabashed urban partisan, grudgingly arrived at the same conclusion when he poked fun at *Money* magazine's annual list of America's ten most livable locales. *Money,* he wrote recently in his nationally syndicated column, always selects as its top location "some burg where they pull in the skywalks at 10 P.M. and think that 'espresso' is Italian for the commuter lane on the freeway." He challenged his readers to define livability in small-town or big-city form.

When the responses rolled in, Kaul conceded defeat. "It turns out there are two kinds of people: those who like big cities and those who like small towns. It also turns out that the people who like small towns are in the vast majority."

Small Towns: The Promise of a Simpler Life

For many, the yearning for a small town coincides with a stage of life—the middle-aging of the 76-million-member Baby Boom generation, for example, coupled with the desire for a comfortable, middle-class lifestyle that for many may no longer be within reach in major metropolitan areas. Rearing families, putting kids through college and anticipating retirement, members of this key population segment are now more interested in root-laying than thrill-seeking, in maintaining their health rather than maintaining the many options that city life offers. Many would prefer peace of mind to a piece of the pie and would rather build a good reputation than a great fortune.

Our yen for a slower-paced small-town life is also a reaction to the yuppie-treadmill syndrome of the 1980s with its single-minded devotion to getting and spending. Indeed, some cultural analysts say that a national spirit of getting back to basics is taking hold, which they attribute to a paradigm shift we are making from consumers to conservers.

Increasingly people have come to regard the place where they live (and the community of which they're members) to be as important as what they do for a living. Today, people are more likely than they were even five years ago to accept Winifred Gallagher's notion that our everyday perceptions "spring from a collaboration between our brains and our environments." And, in the minds of many, small towns represent the best possible environment for well-being, harmony and creative, proactive living.

A Longing for Community

But perhaps the most significant reason for moving to a small town is the desire for community, for real-life interaction with genuine people whom you come to know over time.

"When you're longing for a small town, it's an amorphous thing," says Ken Munsell, executive director of the Small Town Institute in Ellensburg, Washington (population 12, 361). "People are missing something and they don't know what it is." What "it" is, is community life—something more easily found in a small town than elsewhere, something to anchor the millions of Americans (especially the Baby Boomers and Generation Xers) who grew up emotional transients. According to Munsell, there are millions living in both the city and the suburbs who don't "have a sense of community; they don't even have a vocabulary for it."

The desire to be idealistic about local government, to be an active participant in its workings (escaping the noxious effects of urban cynicism) and to see the results of one's efforts is another key reason for gravitating toward small towns. "While small towns lack economies of scale, they enjoy economies of scope—i.e., fewer people do more things and know more about what is going on," writes Dr. Philip M. Burgess, president of the Denver-based Center for the New West, a think tank studying economic-development issues, in his case study of Brush, Colorado (population 4,165). As a result, "action is less constrained by institutional fragmentation," allowing small communities to make "speedy decisions." "Although personalities and political conflicts can and do play a significant role in small towns," he writes, "conflicts are managed and often resolved through personal rather than institutional methods."

What's more, small towns offer an attractive alternative to an increasingly chaotic and overwhelming urban world filled with too many choices. Just as studies have shown we're overwhelmed with selections in supermarkets, so too are we overwhelmed by myriad offerings and the mass of people in the cities.

Small towns offer life on a human scale—the opportunity to live life "small" and at a slower pace, to pay attention to details, to elevate ordinary events to the level of sacred experience. In part, too, the quest for small-town life is a quest for reconnection to the sensuous world, one freer of technology and the impersonal and mechanistic bustle of the city.

The Changing Image of Small Towns

Indeed, the image of small towns has undergone a major metamorphosis over the last ten years, almost completely shaking off Sinclair Lewis's damning 1920 portrait of small-town America, *Main Street*. That book, more than any other single source, was the basis of the long-held view of small towns as populated with smug, complacent, narrow-minded and mean-spirited people who would willingly stifle any free spirit who happens along—a portrait (and a stereotype) that would linger for generations.

But social changes in the form of high-tech computers with on-line services, cable television and satellite dishes have shattered the isolated, insular reality of Lewis's small-town prototype. Electronic culture has made small towns more tolerant of diversity—of sexual orientation, life situation and ethnic and racial origin—than in the past. Few small towns remain stuck in the cultural backwaters. "Those living in small towns today are far more sophisticated than they were a generation ago," says Munsell. In terms of information, he says, "people who live in small towns today have access to virtually everything that city dwellers do."

There's Got to Be Something Better than This

The allure of the small town is compounded by a growing disenchantment with America's cities. Once irresistible destinations for the ambitious, many cities are now riddled with drive by shootings, rampant drug use, racial tension, spiraling costs, deteriorating infrastructures and inadequate, unsafe public schools. "Urban apartheid"—the term coined by David A. Heenan, author of *The New Corporate Frontier: The Big Move to Small Town, U.S.A.,* referring to the growing, palpable chasm between rich and poor in our big cities—may well be the root of this deterioration. But whatever its source, many overworked urbanites, living with an unhealthful level of stress, are questioning the price tag of their city lives. For many, the dream of the big city is being displaced by the nightmare.

Crime hitting close to home can level the final blow, sending urbanites packing. Drs. Thomas and Magdalena Naylor were so traumatized by the killing of the seventeen-year-old son of close friends outside the Richmond (Virginia) Coliseum that they headed for the Vermont hills with their seven-year-old son. The jobs they left were hardly insignificant: He resigned as a tenured full professor of economics at Duke University and she quit her nearly $250,000-a-year psychiatric practice.

Many urbanites have begun to fear not only for their physical safety but for their physical health. Indeed, a recent Duke University study indicates that residents of so-called "hostile cities"—that is, cities in which people exhibit high levels of cynical mistrust, anger and aggression—are more likely to suffer fatal coronary heart disease and death from other causes than do those living in more pleasant places. (The study found the nation's most "hostile" cities to be: No. 1 Philadelphia; No. 2 Cleveland; with New York City and Detroit tying for No. 3.)

A DEMONSTRABLE DEMOGRAPHIC TREND

Two experts who specialize in rural demography, Dr. Kenneth M. Johnson, professor of sociology at Loyola University in Chicago, and Calvin Beale, a senior demographer at the U.S. Department of Agriculture, recently completed a study that documents what Johnson calls the "rural renaissance" of the last part of the twentieth century.

"This rural turnaround was first evident in the 1970s when rural or nonmetropolitan areas grew more rapidly than metropolitan areas for the first time since 1810," says Johnson. Though the numbers have fluctuated since then, Johnson has gone so far as to predict a renaissance of small-town and rural life over the next two decades.

Dr. Jack Lessinger, professor emeritus of real estate and urban development at the University of Washington, seconds this opinion in his book, *Penturbia: Where Real Estate Will Boom After the Crash of Suburbia*. The next major growth wave, he writes, "will include selected small towns across the nation. . . . This migration is away from the suburbs to new and old towns distant from our great metropolitan areas. In the coming transformation, a skein of small towns within a large region will form a cosmopolitan, urban-rural complex."

Although it will take time to see whether this bold forecast materializes, experts in such fields as corporate relocation and van-line moving are already pointing to smaller trends that might seem to presage it—migration patterns from the urban population centers on the East and West coasts of our country to more remote points inland in the Midwest, Pacific Northwest, Southeast and Southwest.

"In terms of people moving, Southern California is cold," says the president of a Global Van Lines affiliate in California. "So is Seattle. What's hot today is the Midwest from Ohio to Illinois, including Michigan. In the West, it's a corridor stretching from eastern Nevada starting with Las Vegas into western Utah up through western Wyoming and Montana, all of Idaho and central Washington and Oregon."

The Rust Belt states are experiencing in-migration after two decades of decline. "The Midwest lost 700,000 jobs between 1970 and 1985, driving thousands of the region's people to relocate to more prosperous areas in the Sunbelt. But since 1985, more people are now moving *from* California and Texas *to* places like Ohio than the other way around," reports *The Washington Post.*

The Freedom to Move

While some people are forced to choose between urban careers and bucolic settings, professionals are now more than ever able to have their cake and eat it, too. Because of the revolution in telecommunications, "knowledge workers," such as freelance stockbrokers, analysts, software designers, manufacturers' reps and writers, no longer have to choose between profession and place.

"For the first time in American history, people across a wide range of professions can continue to pursue their work while moving to the place of their choice," says Dr. Philip M. Burgess of the Center for the New West. Indeed, Burgess has identified nine million Americans for whom he's coined the term "lone eagles," who either have moved from urban to rural settings, carting their professions with them, or have the potential to do so. These telecommuters will continue to transplant themselves and their jobs to more livable, physically appealing and less-crowded locales. This migration—just now getting under way—Burgess predicts, will comprise the nation's most far-reaching life/work-style change since the emergence in the 1970s of the two-wage-earner family.

In this book, you'll meet a number of dynamic ex-urbanites who have followed precisely this path and have shared their secrets for building successful lives in a small town. Among those who pulled up stakes from urban asphalt and transplanted them into small-town soil are:

◉ **Frank Crail,** founder and CEO of the Rocky Mountain Chocolate Factory, Durango, Colorado (population 12,439), moved from San Diego in 1981, to open his own business, though he had nothing specific in mind. Crail settled on a chocolate shop, which has since grown into a $20-million-dollar-a-year, multinational company with 202 stores in the United States and Canada. In 1995, *Money* magazine named the company's chocolate the best-tasting in the United States, and *Success* magazine listed it as the No. 7 best franchise opportunity in America. The business was started, Crail says, "by the seat of my pants on $50,000 in borrowed money. In the beginning, we did everything ourselves. Today, we're Durango's largest employer, from the manufacturing point of view."

◉ **David and Mary Jo Burnett** moved in 1989 from Long Island, New York, to Alliance, Nebraska (population 9,920) with an eye toward lowering operating costs for Burnington's Inc., their international, railroad- and diesel-parts export business, which specializes in supplying customers with hard-to-obtain parts for older equipment. To help get the business established, the couple sold their Long Island home and pumped the equity into a 4,000-square-foot former Sears building, purchased for $10 a square foot—a price unheard of in their old city.

"One of my primary reasons for leaving New York was the high cost of housing," says Mary Jo Burnett. "Our mortgage for a small house one hour outside of New York was $1,400 a month. Our real estate taxes were $4,800 a year. It cost me several hundred dollars monthly to commute to Brooklyn each work day. In Alliance, our mortgage is $325, and we are eight blocks from our office. The boys walk two blocks to school. We get so much more done in a day because of more time."

◉ **Art and Dee Dee Rosenberg** moved from San Diego to Galax, Virginia (population 6,700), when they felt crime at the doorstep of their "decent neighborhood." What pushed them to move wasn't the time their son, Aaron, came home from preschool and drew a gang sign in his coloring book. "The thing that finally did it," says Dee Dee Rosenberg, "was a fatal shoot-out in the mall where we shopped."

So in March of 1993, Art Rosenberg, then an assistant postmaster in Carlsbad, California, made what some might consider a rash move. After scouring a government flyer of nationwide employment opportunities in the U.S. Postal Service, he spotted a listing for the position of postmaster in Galax. He made a call and, when offered the position over the phone, snapped it up—before even locating the town on the map. He was given one week to report to work.

"The night before I left for Galax, I had a dream that the post office was a little wooden shack," he recalls. But once Rosenberg drove into town, his anxieties vanished. "It was beautiful, like an angel was riding in the car with me," he recalls. "I drove into town, and people started waving at me. I did a double take. You don't wave in San Diego, because people might shoot you.

"Moving to Galax has changed me. I don't care about material things anymore. Now I go into work on Saturdays because I love it so much. It's stuff I *want* to do instead of something I have to do."

The material side of the Rosenbergs' life has also improved. They purchased twice the house for half the money, have added a new baby to the family and have discovered the meaning of the word "neighborly."

"I don't own a lawn mower, but our yard always gets mowed. Our neighbor, Gary, mows it for us. I remember the first time he did it. I said, 'Gary, what are you doing?' I didn't know if I should offer to pay him or what. Now we share the lot and have gardens together. His daughter baby-sits for us."

🎣 **Chris and Lynn Murray** moved in 1984 from suburban Philadelphia to coastal Castine, Maine (population 517), with their two young sons, Keith and John. As a result of the lower cost of living, Chris Murray was able to turn what was once a hobby (carving waterfowl) into the family's primary source of income, while having more time to spend with his sons. In Philadelphia, the family was "spending no time together, going crazy," he says. Now Chris Murray volunteers as a golf coach at George Stevens Academy in nearby Blue Hill, while his wife keeps busy raising funds for the town's historic society and selling real estate part-time.

"A parent has more—I don't want to use the word 'control'—but more access to her child's life in a small-town environment," asserts Lynn Johnson Murray. "It's easier to keep tabs on them while they gradually spread their wings. Life here reminds me of life along Main Line Philadelphia when I was a young girl. It's a more *real* existence. You walk everywhere. It's a safe haven, particularly for children. Our younger son has been able to remain a child at school, instead of feeling like in the second grade he had to be a man, sent off with his briefcase."

❂ **Drs. Linda and Len Lastinger,** who moved to Galax in 1980 after graduating from Duke University Medical School and doing their residencies there, find that their lives have been enriched through frequent contact with people. "I can go on a bike ride and stop at every single block and visit with people and catch up with their lives," says Linda Terry Lastinger, a native of Miami. "Friends say, 'You know everyone here.' In fact, I may know 10 percent of the people, but that's enough. Wherever you go, you find friends. You're aware of the currents passing through people's lives. You've experienced the death of a spouse with them, the leukemia of a niece. Knowing everyone's story adds a certain drama to life; it personalizes people. You find you're living not only with your own dramas and traumas, but with other people's. It gets you outside of yourself."

At its best, small-town America—with its time-honored code of community and continuity, of safety and civic pride—offers an environment where money can matter less than character, where a premium is placed on long-term interest over short-term gain. Small towns promote a slower pace and simpler living; in them, one person can make a difference.

Just as moving to a small town has transformed the lives of

Linda and Len, of Art and Dee Dee, of David and Mary Jo, of the two of us, the same can happen to *you*—provided you plan your move well and play your cards right.

Our goal in *Moving to a Small Town* is to help you find a glittering gem among our nation's 35,320 small towns. Here, in this heads-up small town, you can create a satisfying new life for yourself and your family, full of both pleasures you may have never before experienced and obligations that will ground you and lend new meaning to your life.

CHAPTER ONE

Are You Right
for Small-Town Life?

This chapter will help establish whether your attraction to small-town life is a mere passing fancy or the basis for a true commitment. We'll pose a series of questions as a way of predicting if you'll fit into—or, even better, whether you're likely to *thrive* in—a small town. By the answers, you'll be able to identify those who might be better off left to the anonymity and highbrow culture of an urban setting (for instance, those for whom privacy and the right to unbridled freedom of expression are of utmost concern). And you'll also see the characteristics of those who'll take right away to small-town life.

"If you're not right for small-town life, you're going to have a hard time making it," warns Mike Goldwasser, a former Philadelphia resident who in 1973 moved to rural Carroll County, Virginia, to open a cattle ranch. A big-city person needs to have the right "orientation," he says, in order for the move to take. This orientation includes a "respect for hard work and caring for your neighbors" in addition to a giving, easygoing personality; an affinity for all kinds of people, regardless of socioeconomic status, educational attainment and level of sophistication;

the desire to give freely of your time and a communal (rather than singular) approach to living.

In this chapter, we'll help you determine if you're good small-town material. In the process of deciding whether you are, don't be dismayed to discover a few urban wrinkles. We'll show you how to smooth them out later on in the book (see Chapter Six), so don't assume that their presence means you're poorly suited for small-town life.

To find out if you're right for small-town life, you'll first need to look inward. In the space below or on a separate sheet, list five things that are currently lacking (or slighted) in your life that you'd like to devote more time to. (Add on if there are more than five.)

1. _____

2. _____

3. _____

4. _____

5. _____

If your answers include any, some, or all of the following, you've passed the first round, making you a good candidate for small-town life:

🖐 Spending more time with family.

🖐 Knowing neighbors better.

🖐 Getting to know people in multiple contexts, over time (for example, the man who sells you a car may also be your daughter's soccer coach).

🖐 Having more time for community life or simply becoming part of a community.

🖐 Feeling that you—one person—can make a difference.

❧ Yearning for more time in which to tap into and develop your creativity.

❧ Doing work that has an immediate, tangible impact on the local scene.

❧ Feeling safe in public places, such as your neighborhood, your children's schools, church, downtown and shopping areas.

❧ Spending more time out-of-doors/being in better and more regular touch with nature.

❧ Having time to explore the spiritual dimension of life.

❧ Leading a more harmonious and organic—less fragmented— life.

❧ Slowing the pace of your life.

Read through the following questions and answers, answering them as truthfully as possible. Realize that the accompanying answers are optimum responses and by no means constitute a definitive checklist for small-town "fitness." But they should give you some idea of what plays in Palmyra—and whether or not you will!

Q. *Do you have an open mind or are you quick to form judgments about people, places and institutions?*
A. Although it's a good quality in any context to have an open mind, it's especially important in your role as a newcomer to— and resident of—a small town. It's wise never to make assumptions about people, places and institutions. Never assume, for example, that the school system is inferior or that small-towners hold benighted attitudes about politics or social issues. Leave yourself open to new discoveries.

Although you're likely to encounter folks who are less well-educated than you, you're also likely to meet some who'll make *you* stretch to keep up. (And, yes, they may even be less well-educated than you.)

"There's this assumption that when you move to a small town, you're moving out to where all the people have third-grade educations, and all they know how to do is walk behind a mule that pulls a plow," says Dr. Jeffrey L. Tate, a psychiatrist who moved with his wife, Ellen Hillis Tate, and their two children, Andrew and Elizabeth, from Houston to Rogers, Arkansas (population 24,692), in 1993. "I've not found that to be true at all. People here are bright, educated and well read. They know history, politics. We have stimulating discussions—more than we did in Houston, in part because we have more time."

Like Tate, we've found that small-towners are often *better* informed about current events than their urban counterparts because they have more time during which they read, process, absorb and retain information. Likewise, they tend to have more time (and inclination) to volunteer in the schools, for civic projects, to attend conferences and keep up with late-breaking changes in their fields.

Q. *Are you an elitist?*

A. There's a good place in this world for elitists, but it's almost never small-town America. Like emus, elitists are better suited to congregate with their own kind in rarefied centers of culture—namely, major metropolitan areas, universities and capitals of government, commerce and the arts.

Indeed, small-town snobs are insufferable. Because every personality stands out in bas-relief against the small-town backdrop, snobs will be known, disdained and disliked. And by virtue of their snobbishness, they'll find few peers (from their perspective, no one in town is educated, refined or discerning enough to match wits with them) and will live in a perennial state of discontent. Such uppity malcontents would be better off staying in the city.

This is not to say that *accomplished* people should not or cannot make a place for themselves in a small town. It's just that touting your wisdom or credentials, or attempting to hold yourself above others will estrange you from your community. If you're down-to-earth and approach small-towners with the attitude that you have more to learn than teach, you should do well—and learn lots—in the process.

Q. *As you set your personal and professional goals, do you wish to focus on one thing or many things?*

A. Living in a small town will provide the opportunity to step out of the narrow box of specialization. It will allow you to stretch to reach different parts of yourself, both professionally and personally. If you're a writer, it's assumed that you're also a public speaker, a teacher and a storyteller. For instance, we've been asked to teach, write for or consult with disparate employers ranging from an electrical supply company to city hall to a local arts agency—everything from award applications to health-advocacy plays.

In a small town, attorneys, physicians and other professionals similarly may be called upon to broaden their scope. A commercial real estate developer may branch out into residential work. Freelancers often piece together incomes from differing skills. You're likely to encounter a gutterer/piano tuner and VCR repairer under the same hat. A shoe repairer may run a silk-screening press as a sideline. Many small-towners find this variety stimulating and fun.

On the extracurricular side, you may star in a local theatrical production, organize a blood drive and run for the school board. The challenge—and delight—of small-town life is in how many aspects of yourself will be called upon and employed. Just as putting dormant muscles in your body to use improves your body's metabolism and overall function, tapping into your many talents should help you become a happier, better-integrated individual.

Although specialists may find a place for themselves here, the small town provides an atmosphere in which the generalist thrives.

Q. *Would you like to settle in one place for the rest of your life?*

A. Your move is more likely to work out if you make a genuine commitment to your new town right from the get-go. The greater your commitment, the more you'll get out of the community. If, on the other hand, you view yourself as a transient (or voyeur) in town, your connection to the community won't be as meaningful—and sensing this, townsfolk will be less likely to devote time and energy to you.

The Tates made the move with the right attitude. "The way it feels to me right now—and what we were hoping for before we moved—is that we're putting down life-long roots," says Jeff Tate, who as an Air Force brat grew up all over the country. "I don't think either of us wants to uproot and be 'new in town' again."

Becoming "joiners" is the cornerstone of the Tates' campaign to fit in. Indeed, setting down roots is not only a matter of putting them down in your own backyard, but growing them into the town's "civic infrastructure." You need to be involved with the town's clubs and organizations, church and school groups, volunteer organizations, fund drives and local businesses. Ellen Tate is president of the PTA at Elizabeth's elementary school, is active in their Sunday school and was elected to Leadership Rogers, a chamber of commerce–sponsored program that introduces participants to the workings of the town's civic life. Jeff Tate is active in Sunday school, the chamber of commerce, the Boy Scouts, a weekly book club and, of course, his rapidly growing business. "We've achieved that sense of community we were looking for, which is what I have enjoyed the most about the move," he says.

Making a commitment to a small town means that you "invest" in it, explains Chicago native Jane Shiley, who, in the fall of 1994, moved to Saratoga, Wyoming (population 1,969), with her husband, Bob Shiley. After six short months in Saratoga, the Shileys (who are preparing to open a nearby mountain dude ranch for small-plane pilots) have already decided to become "lifers." Jane Shiley says: "Bob's ready to go down and buy cemetery plots."

While it may not always work out that you end up staying for life (or beyond), going in with a "putting down roots" frame of mind will expedite your integration into the community.

Q. *Do you like studying the details of people in the passing parade and speculating on what makes them tick?*

A. Part of the pleasure of a slower-paced, small-town life involves taking in the "scenery" of other people—noticing details, ruminating about the lives, loves and aspirations of others. It involves noticing who wears loud ties; who's always punctual and who's usually late to meetings. Bill Clinton is said to have developed his political personality as a child growing up in the small town of Hope, Arkansas (population 9,643), where he was a "sponge"—always observing the attitudes and mimicking the behavior of those around him.

In *The Bridges of Madison County,* when Francesca notices that her lover's silver bracelet needs polishing, she chastens herself for being "caught up in the trivia of small-town life she had silently rebelled against through the years." As if trivia were such a bad thing. We argue that it is precisely this "trivia" that makes small-town life significant. Indeed, it is our disregard for details—for the rituals of life, the nuances of living small—that has gotten us into trouble in the cities. The devil is not in the details. The angel is in the details, the angels of significance that constitute our lives, that make everyday life sacred, mystical and holy.

If you're in a hurry, on the move and on the make, with little time and less patience for what you might view as social patter and subtleties, if you've got a bull-in-a-china-shop mentality (meaning that you know what you want and are single-minded about going for it, not caring about what trinkets or people you knock down along the way), then you're not ideally suited to small-town life.

Q. *Do you enjoy telling stories and hearing them told?*

A. "We are interrelated in a small town, whether or not we're related by blood," writes Kathleen Norris, in *Dakota: A Spiritual Biography.* "We know without thinking about it who owns what car. . . . Story is a safety valve for people who live as intimately as that; and I would argue that gossip done well can be a holy thing. It can strengthen communal bonds."

Storytelling is a critical part of the social fabric—the life-blood—of a small town. If you want to immerse yourself in the oral tradition, if you find that you naturally remember details about people and enjoy hearing their stories and letting knowledge about them accumulate as time marches forward, you make a good candidate for small-town life.

Q. *Do you treasure your anonymity?*

A. If you really treasure your anonymity, think long and hard about moving to a small town. "You must realize you're going to be under a lot more scrutiny [than in a city]," says Ken Munsell, executive director of the Small Town Institute. "The smaller the place, the greater the scrutiny."

If you shudder at the thought of becoming public property, of people observing your moves—even noting such "inconsequential" things as the fact that you left fifteen minutes early to work on a given day, or that you're having a new awning put on your porch—then you might not be happy in a small town.

But don't be too quick to dismiss small-town life for such offenses as what Sinclair Lewis in his 1920 classic *Main Street* described as the disapproving "triple glare" of three old women watching his lighthearted heroine gallivant down the street. If you decide you cannot stand being too closely watched but have never experienced loving community, you may be throwing away the glory of the baby with the grit of the bathwater.

"We may want to be anonymous because we may not understand the virtues of *not* being anonymous," says Munsell. Anonymity is generally purchased at the price of community. "You sit alone in your room," he says. "No one's bothering you but your life may not be very fulfilling, either."

And while neighbors may pry, they can also protect. When you're away, they may get your cat to the vet after it's been hit by a car, saving its life. They may call the police if they see someone unfamiliar poking around your home. They may call you at work to report that your daughter didn't show up at the usual time after school today.

Q. *Are you prepared to roll up your sleeves and go to work for the community?*

A. It is essential that you be a giver rather than a taker in a small town. If you view every situation—indeed every hour of your workday—exclusively as an opportunity to make money (and every hour in which you don't do so as a loss), it may be hard for you to establish a foothold in the community. If the idea of volunteering, or "gift work" (as writer Christopher Day referred to it in *Building with Heart*) doesn't appeal to you, you'd better think twice about your move. Giving to the greater good is the goal among small-towners, and community-mindedness is the ultimate compliment.

"If you're not willing to say, 'OK, here I am; put me to work,' you're letting down your friends and neighbors," says Norman Crampton, author of *100 Best Small Towns in America*. If you resent being asked to pitch in or do things, perhaps you should say no to a small town before you put yourself in the awkward position of being asked.

Q. *Are you willing to accept the fact that your life is not entirely your own?*

A. If you want to make a successful adjustment to small-town life, you must understand that you will do things for others because they ask you to (often even if you don't want to). Just as when you belong to a family, you're expected to play a designated role and fulfill certain obligations, when you're a member of a small town, you belong to the community (in addition to belonging to yourself and your family). If you're the type who would shirk community duty, it's probably not a good idea to thrust yourself into the midst of it.

Q. *Are you prepared to rub elbows with and have continuing contact with people who don't always mirror "sophisticated" city tastes?*

A. In all but university towns, you may encounter many people who are less cosmopolitan than those you hobnobbed with in the city. Often (but not always), small-towners are more "middlebrow" in cultural tastes than urban refugees. If it pains you to associate with people whose political views are unlike your own, who may speak ungrammatically or who may reach for Judith Krantz and Sidney Sheldon rather than Anne Tyler or Walker Percy, you may not fit into small-town life as well as you do in your city circle. (However, do remember that in a small town, with time, others on your wavelength will gravitate your way. In actuality, such people exist in every pocket of America.)

Your attitude toward cultural tastes can serve as a kind of Rorschach test as to whether you actually *belong* in a small town. "My city friends are very concerned that they don't want to deal with rednecks," says one former New Yorker now living in rural New England. "To me, that's like making a racist statement. Once you get to know them, you stop seeing them as rednecks."

Q. Are you willing to stretch your conception of what a good friend should be and what he or she might do?

A. In the city, people tend to be friends with professional peers, colleagues, old college or school classmates and family members. In a small town, you're more likely to "generalize" in friendship (just as you do in work), in part because the pool of potential friends is considerably smaller. If you're one of only a handful of accountants in town, for instance, and aren't particularly drawn to your professional peers, you may need to branch out and make friends with others. In a way, the town serves as a kind of outsized Rotary Club for the entire community, mixing people by professions, so that it's not unusual for a pest-control expert to become tight with a banker or an internist to pal around with a broker.

Ann Moltu Ashman, who moved to Elkin, North Carolina (population 2,858), from Stamford, Connecticut, in 1983 (having previously lived in San Francisco and Washington, D.C.), says that she and her husband have "a different set of friends than in San Francisco." Ashman co-owns an independent insurance agency. "If we lived in San Francisco," she says, "I would probably not have as a close friend a doctor's wife. We'd be in different leagues. We would probably have more friends from our own business—people we worked with."

Always closely identified with Democratic politics, Wanda has found herself forming unexpected and first-time friendships with Republicans in Mount Airy, shattering some long-held and unkind stereotypes about the nature of the "Republican beast." Perhaps most surprising to an unabashed political partisan, Wanda has found these Republicans to be principled, truthful, even idealistic—not unlike the best of her Democratic friends.

Q. *Would you like to mingle with a cross-section of society?*

A. Although the assumption is that you encounter a wider cross-section of humanity in cities, the reality is that you are more likely to have *significant interaction* with a greater gamut of people in small towns. Because there are fewer people to choose from, you're more likely to get up close and personal with a greater range of individuals of varying ages, occupations and levels of socioeconomic status than in the city.

When we lived in Los Angeles for seven years, we never once attended a funeral. Why? Because everyone we knew then was like us—young, well-educated writers. In Mount Airy, we regularly attend funerals simply because we know a number of older folks. And though the percentage of minority members is significantly smaller here than in L.A., we count as good friends a number of African-Americans. We also have close dealings with an illiterate person, an ex-con, people on welfare and disability as well as millionaires.

"In small communities, it's hard to escape the reality of different kinds of people," according to *Small Town,* March/April 1992. "When townspeople must constantly interact with the impaired, share their lives and experience their joys and tragedies, it is exceedingly difficult to cast them aside or condemn them."

Q. *Are you likely to adopt—or resist—the view that your new community is the best town anywhere?*

A. In an on-the-ball town, there's significant local boosterism and continuous-feed reinforcement of local values. And although this may sound hokey, it actually serves a useful purpose. Boosterism—even grandstanding about the superiority of your town—helps to instill community pride and reinforce its unique identity; it also provides that intangible "oomph" that keeps the community perking. If you give yourself over to such feelings (rather than holding yourself at a cynical distance), you can rest a cornerstone of your own personal identity on a strong identification with the place where you live.

"The belief in the superiority of local ways of living actually conditions the way of life," write Arthur J. Vidich and Joseph Bensman in *Small Town in Mass Society: Class Power and Religion in a Rural Community*. "Springdalers 'make an effort to be friendly' and 'go out of their way to help newcomers. . . . ' By this constant focus on warm and human qualities in all public situations, the public character of the community takes on those qualities and, hence, it has a tone which is distinctly different from city life."

When you become a part of the town's inner circle, you'll find yourself a "true believer" in the preeminence of your Springdale. (Just like religious converts, many nonnatives end up among a town's most zealous advocates.) You come to believe that life in your particular small town *is* superior to its big-city predecessor and that your town is more wonderful than the town twenty-five miles down the road. This feeling of pride shouldn't cause you to act smug, but it should be sincere.

Q. *Are you an earnest person?*

A. As a rule, small-towners are less ironic and cynical about their lives than their big-city cousins and express greater enthusiasm and earnestness than you'd typically find in a hard-bitten city dweller. This is certainly true with regard to local institutions such as the PTA, the police force and town hall, on which small-towners can have an enormous impact. "We can be as active in shaping the future of the community as we want to be through local government and organizations," says former Houstonite Jeff Tate of Rogers, Arkansas.

For example, if the trash delivery were inadequate in the city, a resident might throw up his hands in despair, thinking it was useless to try to complain, whereas in a small town, he might call the mayor and find himself chairing a task force to study the problem.

Wanda learned how much difference one opinion can make when, as an eleventh-grader attending high school in Orono, Maine (population 10,578), she expressed concerns to her high school principal about the experimental class that passed for American history. The class—in which students accomplished such self-guided feats as pasting together collages and assigning themselves class grades—was funded through a federal educational grant. Not long afterward, the principal asked her if she would like to serve as a full voting member on the Maine Advisory Council for Title III, representing all the students in the state. In effect, she was given the chance to deny funding to the very program about which she'd complained.

This earnest approach not only colors the small-towner's approach to government and institutions but affects personal behavior as well. Effective small-towners are team players. You earn "points" if you can be counted on to show up at friends' lectures, presentations and fund-raisers, to serve as an example for youngsters and the community, to volunteer to help and to sincerely try to improve your own performance. Small-towners are constantly pushing to better themselves by such objective measures as perfect attendance at club meetings, showing up on time and promptly returning phone calls.

In the small-town context, you can be sure that your good behavior will not go unnoticed and will accrue to you—not only by the good karma it engenders but by the positive notice you'll receive in the community. So, if you're by nature earnest, you're pre-adapted to small-town life.

Q. *Are you a joiner?*

A. You need to be. In a small town, churches, civic organizations and clubs are the lifeblood of society. If you hate the thought of being a member of a club or organization and detest attending meetings and handling projects, you'd better think twice about moving.

Small-town clubs are meaningful meeting grounds for improving community, interacting, socializing and networking. Studies show that their presence is of unquestionable importance in the social fabric of the town. If a town lacks clubs and organizations or the ones that exist are weak, that red-flags a serious deficiency. (You'll learn more about how to tell a desirable small town from a less-desirable one in Chapter Two, "Scouting a New Location.")

"If you're going to move," advises Jennifer Vyvey, town clerk of Saratoga, Wyoming, "you should be gregarious and get involved with the small-town life. If not, you may get bored."

Q. *Have you always hankered to be a celebrity—but have had no luck getting on* Jeopardy?

A. If you have always wanted to be a celebrity, here's your chance! You will be one in a small town—especially when you first move. And unless the town has a large transient element or a significant number of big-city transplants, the fact that you've moved from a big city will qualify you as a person of elevated status. Even after your novelty has worn off, you're likely to remain a "celebrity." With fewer people, more attention is paid to each one, just as the child who has seven toys instead of 147 will know and treasure his seven better, most likely remembering each of them the rest of his life.

Q. *Are you hungry for more contact with others?*

A. This is a key point when considering moving to a small town. Because the tempo in small-town life is slower than in the city, you'll achieve greater casual contact with others, such as neighbors, acquaintances and individuals you know only slightly. Sitting out on the porch, meeting up in the grocery stores, walking along tree-lined streets, biking and jogging and confabbing in public places such as parks, libraries and restaurants are but a few of the ways small-towners come into contact with one another. To make the most of these interactions, you'll want to give your wristwatch the cold shoulder.

Q. *Are you able to keep your thoughts to yourself, or do you find yourself saying the first thing that comes to mind?*
A. Discretion is of paramount importance in a small town. If you're the kind of person who has a lot of opinions and has a hard time keeping them to yourself—and if what comes out of your mouth can sound critical or negative—consider this a strike against your fitness for small-town life. If, on the other hand, you can train yourself to zip your lip, you may find yourself breaking the nasty habit of negative thinking and its uglier, more damaging cousin, negative talking.

After going through this series of questions, you should have an idea as to whether or not you're right for small-town life. You may have decided that it *will* suit your personality and inclinations to a T, that you're ready to put on your walking shoes and hang out a shingle on Main Street. Or perhaps you think you'd better stay on in the city.

If you've decided that you're right for small-town life, or if you have been unable to make a final determination, read on. The rest of *Moving to a Small Town* develops important themes and concepts introduced here. For instance, the next chapter, "Scouting a New Location," will give you the tools with which to choose among potential small towns—that is, to separate the small-town wheat from the chaff.

CHAPTER TWO

Scouting a New Location

"A city is the physical manifestation of an invisible reality, the souls of its people."

—JOHN OSMAN
Citizens Planning Conference on the
Future of the American Community, 1957

So, you've decided that you're right for small-town life but don't know where to go. And chances are, you're not one of the lucky few with family ties to a place where you'd like to live. There's no Uncle Clem in Pleasant Point eager to usher you into the family business or find you a deal on a Victorian home. Or perhaps you do have a hometown you'd consider going back to, but would like to view it with fresh, analytical eyes while at the same time evaluating other options.

To find your own piece of small-town paradise, you'll want to make an assessment of your personal needs and then zero in on a particular geographical area. Once you've done this, you can evaluate a number of towns before narrowing your field. After you've determined your finalists, you'll want to do in-depth, on-site research, carefully studying the communities before settling on your new hometown.

This chapter will give you the tools to conduct your own town search in much the same way that professional relocation companies do when making corporate searches for client companies. You'll take into consideration a variety of factors, such as the town's growth rate and potential, the quality of its housing stock, infrastructure and educational system, the cost of living and the tax code. You'll be able to fill out an environmental checklist and evaluate community character.

Though you may stumble upon your dream town during a pleasure trip, be careful about confusing a vacation with a scouting trip. The pleasant glow of holiday travel will invariably cloud your purpose—and your findings—when you are looking for a new location. A scouting trip is serious business.

ASSESSING YOUR NEEDS

Personal/Family Quality-of-Life Checklist

The first step in the process that will lead you to a scouting trip and, eventually, to your new hometown is making up a personal quality-of-life checklist. Set aside a quiet evening to commit to paper what's important to you. If you're married, sit down with your spouse and do it together. If you have kids and they're old enough to harbor strong opinions, include them as well. Make up a checklist of preferences and needs, listing all the factors that seem crucial to your health, happiness, career and education—in short, your quality of life.

Don't censor yourself. Include quirky particulars, even if they seem trivial in the greater scheme of things. Put in anything that comes to mind, such as a deli where pastrami sandwiches aren't served on Wonder bread; an ocean view; proximity to a zoo, a foreign-film theater or horseback-riding trails. If you're a swimmer and need a year-round pool, write it down; if you regularly see a chiropractor, include it on your checklist. If wildflowers send you soaring in the springtime or you take special delight in selecting your Christmas tree from a cut-your-own farm, add these factors to your preference sheet.

Remember, this is a personal/family quality-of-life checklist. Evaluation of a town's assets, character and civic infrastructure as well as its economic climate will come later. When drawing up your list, consider such crucial "intangibles" as:

🌑 Climate; specify preferences, such as arid, sunny or cold weather.

🌑 Geographical terrain.

🌑 Aesthetic, architectural considerations.

🌑 Art, music, food.

🌑 Ethnic or racial mix of people.

🌑 Specialized medical services or needs.

🌑 Educational needs.

🌑 Religious needs; specify denomination of church, or need for mosque or synagogue.

🌑 Recreational resources (i.e., skiing, golfing, boating).

🌑 Access to spectator sports (i.e., Major, Minor or Little League).

🌑 Access to child care or elder care.

🌑 Proximity to immediate or extended family.

🌑 Proximity to public transportation.

Each family member should make an individual list, numbering from one to ten his or her priorities. Then combine them into a master family list, placing priorities in order of importance. Keep this list handy for when you conduct your town studies. You may not find a town in which you get everything you're looking for, but consider yourself fortunate if you get most of what you want.

Pittsboro, N.C.: "Everything We Hoped for—and Then Some"
Steve Durland and Linda Burnham boiled down their list to four crucial factors. The Los Angeles couple scouted several locations nationwide before deciding on Pittsboro, North Carolina (population 1,436), to which they moved in July 1993. Among their criteria were: having a "critical mass" of colleges and universities nearby with cultural offerings about which they could write for *High Performance,* the magazine they edit for performance artists;

being able to find affordable, wooded acreage in the country; a reasonable cost of living and having easy access to a "decent" airport.

In their new locale, all their needs have been met. They live in the country between bustling Chapel Hill, North Carolina, and tiny Pittsboro, just a forty-five-minute drive from the Raleigh/ Durham International Airport. After renting for a year and a half, they've made a move toward permanence by purchasing some country acreage.

Because their work could be conducted from anywhere and because they were not averse to a cold climate, they considered a number of far-flung locations before settling on Pittsboro. They looked at Durland's hometown of Britton, South Dakota, in the Black Hills; Boulder, Colorado; and the Amherst, Massachusetts, area.

"The most important thing was finding something that appealed to both of us," says Durland. "We visited places one of us would like and the other wouldn't. We were scoring things. Pittsboro came out with the highest score."

Erasing any doubts about Pittsboro for the Southern California–raised Burnham was her discovery of a "wonderful" house to rent that in Los Angeles only could have been found on a Hollywood set: "a two-hundred-year-old log cabin by a stream, near a gristmill, on the National Register of Historic Places," says Durland. The house seemed an omen, leading the couple to believe that not only were there other exceptional properties out there for the plucking (and eventual purchase) but a wonderful life awaiting them.

"We came here hoping for the best but were cynical about getting what we wanted," says Durland. So far, the reality has *exceeded* their expectations. "It's been everything we'd hoped for— and then some."

Geographical Search

Unlike Burnham and Durland, most people don't have the geographical flexibility to view the entire country as their open canvas. For most of us, geography will be the *first* consideration in narrowing the field from America's 35,320 small towns, townships and municipalities with populations under 50,000 to just three and eventually one.

With master list in hand, pull out a map or atlas of the United States and determine a region in which you'd like to focus your search. If, for instance, you'd like to be within driving distance of your family, most of whom live in northern California, this will focus you in on a quadrant in northern and central California, southern Oregon and western Nevada. If you'd like to be within an hour's drive of the ocean, this will eliminate Nevada and further circumscribe your field.

Perhaps your spouse needs to be near a major medical center for treatment. In this case, you'll be looking for a small town within an hour's drive of Sacramento, San Francisco or Eugene. In order to set up a state-of-the-art home office, you'll require access to one-party, voice-grade, touch-tone 9,600 baud, so this capability will figure prominently on the checklist. Maybe you anticipate having to care for your great Aunt Delilah, who's approaching ninety and has no other living relatives. If so, the town will need to have adequate elder care and long-term geriatric living facilities. Your teenage daughter's highest priority is being able to pursue drama, and your son's, his soccer, so you'll be looking for a town with an active community theater and a soccer league for elementary-school-age Peles. Don't overlook your own happiness, which would be placed in serious peril in the absence of a Thai restaurant, as would your spouse's if deprived of the services of a shiatsu masseuse. Your final personal needs assessment would take into account all of these factors.

CONDUCTING A TELEPHONE SEARCH

Once you've arrived at a field of, say, eight to twelve towns, your goal is to narrow it to three contenders. Take the checklist you've made up along with the supplementary question list below and make a series of telephone calls. Take notes to which you can refer later on.

Call the town clerk, mayor or town manager; someone at the chamber of commerce; the economic-development director for the town or county (if one exists) and a newspaper editor or reporter. If their answers are satisfactory and you feel like proceeding (meaning nothing you've learned has knocked the town out of the running), try a second round of calls to a school employee and someone at a long-standing business like a bank. And, finally, ask for the name of a newcomer to whom you could speak.

Milan Wall, co-director of the Heartland Center for Leadership Development in Lincoln, Nebraska, recommends requesting names of clergy members who are new to town. Because they're "in a position to observe social and cultural behaviors in town," he says, coupled with their personal experience as new arrivals, they're likely to have a good perspective on how newcomers are treated in the community. Call one up.

From these people you'll want to glean general information about the health and well-being of the town. When you have them on the phone, if other questions occur to you and they have the time to answer them (or they're in an expansive mood), go with the proverbial flow. But remember, you have a lot of calls to make, so don't try to be exhaustive at this stage. When you actually *visit* the towns, you'll be conducting a more comprehensive study.

Of course, not everyone you reach will have the time to talk when your call comes through. Small-town people are busy, too. If someone's rushed, ask when would be a convenient time to call back. If you reach someone who seems reluctant to talk or doesn't have much to say, ask for the right person. If you try a number of people in town and continue to hit a brick wall or encounter a guarded or suspicious attitude, take it as a warning sign.

"If you get a sense that people aren't receptive, outgoing and open, keep going," says David Savageau, co-author of *Places Rated Almanac* and principal-in-charge of PreLOCATION, a personal relocation consulting firm based in Gloucester, Massachusetts. "Just move on."

Be forewarned. The following set of questions does not constitute a litmus test. Ideal responses to every question could be found only for some imaginary small town. You're not looking for all the "right" answers so much as for a viable community with high quality of life.

"If you learn that none of a town's major employers is owned locally, for instance, that shouldn't be enough evidence to strike that community from the running," says Milan Wall, "but simply weigh that fact against all other evidence."

Although you may need to sprinkle some salt on the answers you get, the experts say that it's unlikely that people will depart too radically from the truth. After all, you're not representing a BMW plant looking to relocate; you're a private citizen and they've never heard of you. "For the most part, you can count on people to give you their perception of an honest representation," Wall says.

TELEPHONE ASSESSMENT
Questions to pose, followed by interpretive suggestions.

1. Town Clerk/Mayor/Town Manager
What are the top accomplishments in the last three years for your community?

Any town official should easily be able to recite three civic accomplishments, such as a building project, an added recreational program, an innovative public-private partnership. In a terrific, proactive community, the list may include five to ten. If he draws a blank or the accomplishments seem *truly* trivial—make a note of it. However, don't expect the Taj Mahal to go up every year in Mudville.

Do you have much turnover on your town council or local governing body?

Leadership turnover suggests an infusion of new ideas and perspectives into government. If the answer is: "The same six guys have been on the council forever," that is a sign that it's business as usual without much innovation.

Are women and people of color represented in positions of leadership? (If the town has no significant minority population, ask only if women hold positions of leadership.)
If there are no women (or people of color) in positions of leadership, this suggests the town is in the social rear guard and unlikely to be receptive to newcomers of either gender.

How does your town demonstrate community pride?
An official of even a very small town should be able to point to an annual festival, parade or celebration. If none exist, this suggests a cultural vacuum.

2. Chamber of Commerce Director/Assistant
What is the annual budget for the chamber of commerce?
You'd like to see as fat a budget as possible (and the larger the membership, the better). Although no precise measuring stick exists for how large an annual chamber budget should be in a town of a given size, Art Sutty, manager, local chamber programs for the U.S. Chamber of Commerce, says that if *any* town with fewer than 10,000 residents has a chamber with a paid staff, it's ahead of the game.

In the towns of that size that do, he cites a recent nationwide survey showing that the average annual budget is $120,000. But, he cautions, because not every small-town chamber answered the survey, "the averages here are more exceptional than rule-of-thumb."

What that means is that if you find that the chamber's budget in a town of 10,000 or less approaches or exceeds $120,000, you're looking at an unusually dynamic chamber; chalk that up as a plus.

Consider the following numbers, taken from the same survey, in the same light:

❸ For chambers in towns with populations of 10,000 to 20,000, the average annual budget was $140,456.

❸ In towns with populations between 20,000 and 30,000, it was $214,872.

❸ And in towns with populations between 30,000 and 50,000, it was $225,243.

How would you describe the main street, or downtown, in your community?

A vital retailing community (housed in a strong, attractive downtown) is what you're looking for. If the response is, "We're doing all right," try to pin down specifics by asking how many vacant store fronts exist on Main Street and how many new stores have opened there in the last year. If he or she says, "There's a new Wal-Mart fifteen miles away, and it's killing us," ask how local business is responding. If they're organizing to draw business back downtown, that's a good sign. If all they're doing is grousing and grumbling, it's not.

Is retail activity up or down over the last three to five years?

The answer you want to hear is up.

What are the three major retailers in town?

If there are three auto dealers, that would indicate that people buy big-ticket items here (a plus for the local economy). If the answer is a feed shop, a tractor store and a tackle shop, that will show the town's agricultural character. If the answer is a 7-Eleven, a Pizza Hut and a Dollar General store, that tells you there's not a lot of indigenous retailing going on.

3. Economic Development Director/Assistant
Who are the three biggest private-sector employers? How long have they been in business and are they locally owned?

Ideally, you'd like to see three diverse industries, such as an agricultural processing plant, a value-added manufacturer (such as furniture, textiles or a mail-order business) and something in high tech or telecommunications. The longer they've been in business the better, and if they're locally owned, this will indicate a stronger commitment to the community than if company ownership is absentee.

Are the town, county and region growing, staying the same or declining?

The best answer is slow steady growth in town, as well as countywide and regionally. Slow, steady growth sidesteps the problems associated with boom-and-bust economies. A boom economy can be as bad as—if not worse than—a stagnating one.

What efforts are you making to grow business and industry locally?

Too many towns put all their effort into attracting outside business, thus neglecting home-grown small businesses and cottage industries that could be significant players in the future. In some cases, they even neglect the needs of major businesses facing expansion.

4. Newspaper Editor/Reporter
What were the top three local stories in the last year?

This will give you insight into local tempests and tensions, and how problems are resolved.

Has your circulation gone up or down over the past three years? How about ad revenue?

You'll probably get an answer about circulation but not about ad revenue (although the latter is more indicative of the health of the local economy than the former). However, answers to either question should shed some light on the town's economic strength.

How would you rate the town's government?

This will give you a valuable second opinion.

5. Bank Employee

Are your financial institutions locally owned or branches?

Although their numbers are dwindling nationwide, locally owned banks are positive influences in communities in which they remain.

If the bank or banks are primarily branches, who has loan approval— the local manager or his or her supervisor at headquarters?

When evaluating a branch bank, you're seeking maximum local autonomy. You'd like for the bank manager to be able to approve loans, and ideally for the management to be stable—not merely a training ground for young Turks who'll be shipped out as soon as they've learned the ropes.

Are your bank deposits up, down or holding steady over the last five years?

You'd like to see an upward trend.

6. School Employee

How would you characterize the morale of teachers, administration, staff and students?

Clearly, positive morale is most desirable.

Is the physical plant well tended?

The answer you're looking for is yes. You'd like to hear that students and staff take pride in the buildings and grounds.

Typically, how do your students stack up in standardized test scores?

High student performance on standardized tests is one of the best indicators of a superior school system.

7. Newcomer

How receptive have town residents been to you?

A town with friendly, welcoming residents is the best possible response.

Have you been invited to join clubs and participate in civic activities?
The answer you're looking for is that the newcomer has been deluged with invitations and opportunities to participate.

Do you often hear disparaging references to outsiders or a characterization of other people in terms of "us" versus "them"?
If outsiders are kept at arm's length from the local community or viewed as interlopers, this identifies the community as closed and insular—and not a good one to which to move.

In addition to questioning these seven people, you'll want to run through your personal/family quality-of-life checklist with the person who was the most forthcoming.

After you have made these rounds of calls, more than likely your three favorite towns will have emerged. Perhaps you may even have a hunch as to which your eventual hometown will be. Sometimes just one remark or telling anecdote about a town will give it an edge over other places. Other times, a feeling or a composite of positive responses will make the difference.

If, however, you've been unable to decide on three towns to pursue, you'll need to make additional telephone calls, ask more follow-up questions and gather as much information as you can until you can make a selection. Making a case aloud for each of the contending towns, using another person (or persons) as a sounding board, can sometimes help crystallize your own feelings. After your presentation, ask for a vote. Then cut your list to three.

TOWN STUDIES

Scouting Trips

After narrowing your field to one to three contenders, you're now ready to proceed to the next phase of your search. In this phase, you'll make in-person visits to the towns you've selected. If you're married, it's best to travel with your spouse. If you can't swing that, one spouse can be the designated "investigative reporter" and make the trip alone.

Thoroughly document your peregrinations, even if you and your spouse are both along, but especially if you're traveling by yourself and plan to report back to a spouse and family. Be sure to pack several notebooks and a camera. If you prefer talking into a tape recorder to taking notes, bring one along or leave it back at your motel so that you can record your thoughts, observations and bits of dialogue when you get back to your room, before you lose them. Bring rolls of film and shoot pictures liberally—of Main Street, pedestrians, houses, parks, monuments, recreation areas, the schools, the post office, pretty places and ugly ones—in short, photograph anything that strikes your fancy.

Plan on spending a *minimum* of three days in each town and, if possible, a full week.

If you're visiting three towns, it's better to make noncontiguous trips so that you can digest each new experience, go home and report back before venturing out again. But if you have to fit your three towns into one long trip over a two-week period, for instance, there are advantages to that, too. Once you're on the trip, you'll fall into an investigative rhythm. You'll learn the kinds of questions to ask and you'll become emboldened about approaching strangers.

"Windshield Survey"

Naturally, your first impression will be the look and feel of the town. Indeed, some say that you can tell the most essential things you need to know from the basic "windshield survey"—that is, a slow, neck-craning drive through town.

"You can sense coming into a small town whether it's a success or a failure," says Dr. David Henzel, professor of economics and director for the Center for Economic Education, University of Missouri, Rolla. "Success breeds success. It isn't like a big city where you can't tell what the hell you've got. They all look alike; they smell alike. Small towns are different."

If you're like most of us, though, you'll want something concrete to back up your first impressions. "Go in and talk to merchants, because they're accessible. They're put on the spot. So are librarians," says Monica Hinton, director of human resources, Center for Improving Mountain Living, Cullowhee, North Carolina. "Go to civic meetings, the hospital auxiliary. Tell them: 'I've got a six-year-old with attention-deficit disorder.' See what resources they have available."

As you ask questions and dig deeper into the lifeblood of the community, the same subjects will keep coming up: political or civic controversies, points of interest and pride. The more you learn, the more insightful your follow-up questions will be. Take copious notes. Record hard data. Each town is specific and idiosyncratic, so you'll need to use your judgment as to whether to pursue a line of questioning or move on to a new one.

TRADING PLACES: WHAT TO LOOK FOR

What follows is a comprehensive evaluation to fill out about the town and its prospects for the future. You'll want to make several photocopies of the questions so you'll have a fresh set of sheets to fill out for each town you visit.

When going through this list, remember that you'll need to view these questions and lines of inquiry as benchmarks and avenues of comparison—not absolutes. No one yardstick can tell you everything you need to know about a place, just as no set of facts (such as age, marital status, educational attainment or occupation) about someone will give you total insight into his or her heart and soul. There are certain intangibles about towns, like people, that you'll have to use your intuition to discern. But taken together, the answers to the following questions will help you form a composite picture of the town that should help you decide objectively if it's right for you.

What's more, certain factors will weigh more heavily for different people. For instance, while educational quality is of vital interest to every would-be resident, as it demonstrates the town's interest in its future, the quality of education will be far more important to a family with school-age children than to a retired couple. Only you know which aspects are most important to you and your family, so when you are making the rounds to complete this survey, keep your keenest interests at the front of your mind.

Condition of the County

The economic condition of the county and the region is a key factor to bear in mind when choosing a new hometown. No town is an island, and although some towns may appear to perform well in isolation, this is partly illusion. When a county or region does poorly, the towns located therein also lose. "If the county's not doing well, the town becomes less desirable," says Dr. Vaughn L. Grisham Jr., director of the McLean Institute for Community Development at the University of Mississippi. "I would say that you consider that the community almost never corresponds to corporate limits."

Oxford, Mississippi, the university's home base, is a prime example. It's "a nice place to live but LaFayette County is not," Grisham says. "Twenty-five percent of the county lives in poverty. We're about to have a new bakery in Oxford, but you have to have a critical mass of people who buy bakery goods to make it succeed. If the economy is not healthy in the whole county, it's less likely to succeed. I'm trying to sensitize merchants by telling them: 'You have an obligation to support economic development throughout the county. It's in your self-interest.'"

The spring 1993 issue of the *National Civic Review,* a publication of the Denver-based National Civic League, put it more apocalyptically: Those communities that focus on "forting up" to exclude "undesirables" and "those regions that fail to learn how to function as units are very likely to face accelerated decline." However, those regions that work collectively and cooperatively to attract industry, resolve conflicts, tackle regional problems and share visions will be prepared to take on the future in an increasingly global society.

ECONOMIC CONDITIONS/PHYSICAL INFRASTRUCTURE/INSTITUTIONS

1. TOWN'S ECONOMIC PERFORMANCE

Visit the town hall (or in the case of a very small town, the county courthouse) and make an appointment with, or ask to see, the mayor, town or county manager, planner or finance director to ask questions about growth and economic performance. Often individuals will be able to answer only some of the questions and will refer you to others to answer the rest. Some questions can be answered by a chamber of commerce employee.

A. *Steady Growth*
Is the town experiencing steady growth, boom growth or stagnancy?

Ideally, you'll want to find a town that's experiencing steady, but not booming, economic growth. Your best bet is to find a town in which property values, personal income, building starts and population are on a gradual upswing.

"A town should grow like a tree—not rapidly and not all in one direction," says Mount Airy, North Carolina, commercial developer Burke Robertson, himself a recent transplant from Charlotte, the state's largest city.

Slow, steady growth assures a healthy tax base that can keep up with demand on local government services. By contrast, in a boom town, there are tremendous, costly needs (for the expansion of schools and water and sewer lines) without an adequate tax base to finance them; there's also the danger that the boom could turn to bust. In a no-growth area, while real estate prices may seem incredibly cheap to a city dweller, they could fall *even lower*. And with a depreciated tax base, the infrastructure is likely to continue deteriorating.

B. *Gross Retail Sales Receipts*
What are the gross retail sales receipts for the town and/or county for the last three years? Is the increase at or above the rate of inflation?

Again, the best answer is a slow, steady increase in gross retail sales just above the rate of inflation. If gross retail sales receipts are growing, this indicates that the economy is steadily expanding. The chamber should be able to provide you with year-end totals for the last three years. (If you're looking at monthly numbers, be sure to compare them to the year before, not the month before; for example, due to seasonal variations, January sales will be lower than December's.)

For a per-capita figure, divide the gross retail sales receipts for the year by the population. Do this for each of the three towns you visit and you'll be able to compare the level of retail activity and the degree to which residents (and those coming in from surrounding areas) spend money in town.

C. New Construction
How many commercial and residential building permits were filed for the last year data is available compared to each of the three years before?

These figures are perhaps more telling than gross retail sales receipts, which represent one-time, in-and-out sales. If the trend is upward, this suggests that local residents and businesses have enough confidence in the area's future to make sizable investments in it. If you see a significant dip in building permits, ask why. Unless we are in a recessionary period, this may be cause for concern.

D. Government's Fiscal Health
What is the fiscal health of town government?

Ask the town's finance officer or another official an open-ended question about the fiscal health of local government. From the answer, you may be able to discern the town's budgetary priorities. If he or she trots out the fund balance but says nothing about the operating budget, you can tell the emphasis is on saving, not spending (or vice versa).

Then ask to see the town's operating budget. Inquire about the capital reserve available (if any). Ideally, a local government should have *at least* two months' operating capital on hand for emergencies. (You can calculate how far its reserve will stretch by dividing it by the monthly budget.)

If the town has ever issued a bond, it will have a bond rating from that year given by such companies as Standard & Poor's Corp. or Moody's Investors Service. Unless it's more than five years old, this rating will be a good indicator of the town's fiscal health. Bond-rating companies evaluate the credit risk a town faces vis-à-vis its tax base and water and sewer customers, while analyzing its budgets, operating statements and tax rates in relation to other communities.

The ratings will range from the top mark of AAA all the way down to a D rating. Investment-grade ratings of AAA, AA, A and BBB give you a green light. If a mark slips below BBB—and the town gets anything from a BB to a C—however, the town has received a "speculative-grade" rating, which should concern a town-shopper. Even worse is the CI rating which is reserved for income bonds on which no interest is paid. A rating of D indicates payment is in default.

Another indicator of the town's fiscal health is its annual audit (required by most states). Town government is required by law to provide you access to this information. A layman can ask to examine that audit report, but be forewarned: they're lengthy and hard to read. If a compressed report was issued, it will be more accessible.

A good fiscal report card—encompassing the operating budget, the bond rating and the audit—suggests (though it doesn't guarantee) sound fiscal management.

Make a note of the town's operating budget and the number of citizens it serves. This will provide a good benchmark for comparison between various towns. But don't necessarily assume that the town with the higher budget is doing the better job. Town A may be more frugal while Town B may be the municipal equivalent of a high liver. What's more, you'll need to compare services provided as well as the level of service.

2. ECONOMIC DEVELOPMENT ACTIVITY

Does an active economic-development program or entity exist in the town or county with what the Heartland Center calls a "realistic appraisal of future opportunities (and an) awareness of competitive positioning"? Ask to see the plan if one exists.

Scrutinize the economic-development plan to see where the emphasis lies. (If no plan exists, quiz the director about the program's philosophy.) Communities that are chiefly looking for what Janet Topolsky, associate director of the rural economic policy program of the Aspen Institute, Washington, D.C., calls the "big cookie"—or, salvation in the form of a major company coming in from the outside—are standing at the wrong oven. "The best economic developers should be looking to grow home-grown businesses," she says. "If all a community is trying to do is attract wealth from outside, it's not a good sign."

Indeed, towns that seek to expand their wealth by increasing the value of what's already there are termed "high-performance" communities. This measure has become increasingly popular as many small towns sign onto what Philip M. Burgess of the Center for the New West calls the "slow-growth movement." "To borrow from Tom Peters, high-performance communities stick to their knitting," says Burgess. "They add value to existing activities and build on their strengths."

What communities need to do is anticipate change and the landscape of the future. Signs that economic developers are doing things right include: an emphasis on job training, especially in the area of high technology, computer technology and repair; the identification and funding of home-grown cottage industries through "microloan" programs from banks or venture capital clubs; helping grow small businesses; collective efforts at community marketing; making the promotion of tourism an economic-development goal and targeting for relocation such prosperous and proactive individuals as upscale senior citizens and home-based businesspeople who can work anywhere.

Even with a vigorous local economy, economic developers

need to pursue new jobs continuously. According to the University of Mississippi's Dr. Vaughn L. Grisham Jr., most communities lose between 6 to 8 percent of their jobs annually. "You've always got to work on job replacement," he says. "You can't sit still."

3. TAXES

At the town hall, check out the governmental entities with taxing authority, including the state, county and locality. A town finance officer will help you determine what (if any) taxes are levied on income, retail sales, real and personal property. Ask if there's an intangibles tax on the value of your stocks and bonds.

Specifically you'll want to figure the following:

A. *Property tax rate*. Figure the cost of the tax on the price of an average three-bedroom home. (Refer to question 10B on page 63 for the cost of a three-bedroom, single-family home.)

B. Are there any *special tax districts,* such as a special school tax, water-district or hospital tax? If so, what are their rates? Again figure the tax against the cost of a three-bedroom home.

C. *State and local sales tax*. (Some counties impose a sales tax on top of state sales tax.)

D. *Income tax*.

E. *Personal property tax*.

F. *Intangibles tax on the value of your stocks and bonds.*

4. ECONOMIC CONDITIONS

A. *County median household income*

You can obtain this annually updated figure from the county, which gets it from the state planning department. Get the state figure and compare.

B. *Per capita income*

You can get this figure from town hall or the county courthouse.

C. *Average bank deposit per capita*

The FDIC issues an annual report of money on deposit that includes data for every town and county in the nation. (This data includes deposits from all FDIC-insured commercial banks and savings banks regulated by the FDIC, barring all credit unions, according to Frank Gresock, an FDIC spokesman.) To obtain this information, look up the numbers for the town you're checking into in *The Data Book,* an eight-volume set of FDIC data at a research or business library. Or you may write for a free copy at: Publications Office; FDIC, 550 17th St. NW; Washington, D.C., 20429. (If you need the information in a hurry, call the FDIC's Office of Research and Statistics at (202) 898-3940.)

To determine a state average as a benchmark of comparison, ask for the total bank deposits in the state and divide by state population. (Likewise, you'll have to divide the gross deposits per town or county by the population to get bank deposits per capita.)

If one community has significantly higher bank deposits per capita than another, this will give you a reading about the level of wealth in the community. But be forewarned, this is just *one* indicator and the numbers may be inflated by an employer with a sizable payroll on deposit, for example. What's more, the numbers could be skewed downward in a place like millionaire-thick Aspen, Colorado, where many residents may not park *any* of their money in local banks.

D. *Workforce distribution by industry*

This will reveal the diversity of the economy. The ideal workforce is as diverse as possible, so that if one sector falls on hard times, the others can help prop it up. Supply these categories with percentages obtained from the town hall, the chamber of commerce, or the economic development director so that you can compare workforce diversity among the communities you're considering.

Manufacturing

Trade (retail/wholesale)

Services

Construction

Agriculture

Mining

E. *The unemployment rate*

Compare the current rate to national and state averages, also to the annual average for the town or county for previous three years. (If you look at monthly figures, watch out for unseasonably high rates in January and February and unseasonably low rates in December, June, July and August.)

F. *The percentage of families below poverty level*

Compare this to national, state and local averages, and also to numbers for the previous three years. (At press time, the latest figures available from the Census Bureau showed that in 1991, the incomes of 14.2 percent of all Americans fell below the government's official poverty level.)

G. *The rate of births to teen-age mothers*

According to Zero Population Growth's Urban Stress Test, in model communities, the teen-age birthrate is below 9 percent of all births and the infant-mortality rate is less than 8.5 deaths per 1,000 live births.

H. *The demographic profile of the town, including median age*

You'd like to see a town in which there is a "healthy percentage" of residents between the ages of twenty and forty-five, according to Milan Wall of the Lincoln, Nebraska–based Heartland Center for Leadership Development.

5. BUSINESS CONDITIONS

A. *What is the proportion of locally owned businesses in town?*

Although you may have a hard time pinning down a precise figure, the rule of thumb is that the greater the proportion of locally owned businesses, the greater the strength of the local economy. When more businesses and industries are locally owned, the tax base is larger and more revenues are pumped back into the community. What's more, if a company or plant is locally owned and an economic downturn occurs, owners will be more reluctant to cut back on the hometown plant than to scale back distant locations. If chamber officials don't have a breakdown of locally owned vs. outside-owned businesses, they can give you an idea. Ask which are the top twenty businesses in town and who owns them, and you'll get a sense of how much business is locally owned.

B. *The median age of business owners*

You'd like to find a community with significant business ownership by people age forty-five and younger. "The healthier small towns will have a substantial number of younger people in business ownership," says Milan Wall.

Ask someone at the chamber to guess the median age of business owners on Main Street. You'd like to hear that the median age is forty-five or younger. Younger business owners are desirable because they tend to be more innovative than their older counterparts in their approach to business and community problem-solving, and they are also more likely to make a greater commitment to the future of the community. "They're in an investment mode," says Wall. "It's tragic but true that in many small towns, older business owners will drain a company of its assets before they retire, leaving nothing to sell."

C. *Is there a strong downtown?*

No single indicator will reveal the viability of the town so quickly and effectively as the look, feel and vitality of the downtown. The downtown functions as the welcome mat to—and heart of—the community.

If the downtown is forlorn and neglected, the community has lost its way. "If downtowns die, so will the region," says Dale Doyle, director of communications and program development of International Downtown Association.

The small-town downtowns that are ahead of the game are ones in which businesses have banded together and structured and organized to make themselves economically viable. Five key principles are in play when downtowns are working:

1. They need to look good and authentic. "Phony Swiss Chalet themes won't work," says Betsy Jackson, program manager for the National Main Street project.

2. Graphics and signage should reinforce the idea of unity and quality in the district.

3. A program of vigorous promotion is pursued to establish (or reestablish) a favorable image of downtown.

4. Good organization. "Most downtowns faltered in the sixties and seventies because they weren't competitively organized," Jackson says.

5. Downtown development. Business development should be stressed in concert with all these other components.

Indeed, a vivid downtown—one that's enjoying something of a renaissance or one that never withered to begin with—is an indicator of a red-blooded town. This will be one of the easiest factors for you to judge because all you need to do is stroll down Main Street. If it looks battered and unkempt, if a large number of the store fronts are vacant, if parking spaces are ubiquitous and unclaimed, if no important tenants are downtown, make a note of it; you have reason to be concerned about the strength of this town.

6. INFRASTRUCTURE

The condition of the town's infrastructure is an indicator of its optimism about—and willingness to invest in—the future.

A. *How many schools serve the town? How old are they? And in what condition?*

Although new school construction is impressive, well-maintained, updated older schools can be just as good. In rural areas especially, you'll want to know where the schools are. Be wary of too *few* schools in an area, which may suggest overconsolidation. Better to have a small school—even one with mixed grades—than a school that's thirty miles away with no hometown identification for the students.

If the high school is in a neighboring town, find out how many miles students will be bused to get there (and how long this will take). Clearly, it's better to have a high school in town. Further, you'll want to determine if the classrooms are filled to capacity. If the school-age population is expected to grow, find out what plans are being made to accommodate the numbers: new construction or classroom additions.

B. *What are the age, condition and capacity of roads, water-treatment and sewer plants?*

Again, this will demonstrate the town's preparedness for the future and desire to grow. Has a new sewage-treatment plant been completed with significant additional capacity (that would allow for industrial expansion and population growth) or is the town just getting by with what it has? What about water treatment? Roads?

Each of these major components of a town's infrastructure—roads, water and sewer treatment plants and lines—has a life expectancy. Ask the town planner how much "time" is left on the clock for each of these and what plans exist for expansion. If the water or sewer components need serious attention or replacement in the near future, you're likely to be hit with increases in respective rates. If the roads need substantial improvement, you're likely to see an increase in property tax rates.

C. *How many parks, public places and recreational facilities exist and what is their condition?*

Jot down the number and types of public parks and recreational facilities in town. Remember, the more there are and the more varied, the better. There are no benchmarks for how many parks and recreational facilities a town of a given size should have, but you can ask people how happy they are with existing facilities and judge for yourself whether the facilities seem adequate, superior or wanting for a town of that size. Towns that are recreational in nature, such as resort towns on the coast or in ski areas, should be better endowed with recreational offerings.

D. *What private recreational facilities are available?*

Find out if there's a country club in town and what facilities it has: golf course, swimming pool, etc. What's the price of membership?

7. QUALITY OF EDUCATION

One of the best expressions of how good a community is, is its willingness to invest in its children's education. "A community that's not willing to put money into education is not worth going to," says community development expert Dr. Vaughn L. Grisham Jr.

To evaluate the quality of public education, you'll need to visit (or call) the school superintendent's office and also go directly to the schools. Reluctance (or refusal) on the part of school officials to disclose such things as test scores and graduation rates raises a red flag, says Jack Wimer, editor of *Expansion Management* magazine.

A. *What is the per-pupil expenditure?*

It's easy to compare the figure you get against the national average of $5,193 per pupil. But this benchmark is limited in its usefulness. Before putting too much stock in it, take into account the local cost of living. If you're scouting low-cost southern or northern Plains states, for instance, a lower-than-average per-pupil expenditure should not automatically set you against the school system. By the same token, a higher-than-average per-pupil figure in a small town near a pricey urban corridor may tell nothing more than the fact that local teachers command high salaries.

"There's a regional approach to education and a seriousness of lifestyle that translates into educational quality," says Wimer. In a "bang-for-your-buck" analysis conducted for *Expansion Management,* Wimer found several instances of small towns with low per-pupil expenditures and surprisingly high performance.

One such community was Nampa, Idaho (population 28,365). "Their per-pupil classroom spending was at 20 to 30 percent below the national average, yet the kids all test in the top 2 percent," he says. In general, he says, "You get the most bang for your buck in the cold northern states. In Minot, North Dakota, kids don't quit school for jobs, because most likely they'd be out there with an ice pick."

B. *What is the student/teacher ratio?*

The national average is 17.2 to 1. Conventional wisdom among educators is that the fewer pupils per teacher, the better. In most cases, this is true. However, there are exceptions—especially in the northern Plains states—where large class size doesn't seem to affect student performance or high school dropout rates. In general, however, a low student/teacher ratio is a good indicator of how the community values education.

C. *What's the high school graduation rate?*

The national benchmark for comparison is that 71.2 percent of all high school students get their high school diploma. You can look unfavorably at graduation rates that fall significantly below that and more favorably at rates above it.

D. *How do high school students fare on national standardized tests? Fill in average SAT and ACT scores.*

The experts say that this is probably the best single indicator of educational quality in the school system. "The layman is far better off looking at average test scores than at per-pupil spending or student-teacher ratio," says Wimer. The national average in 1993 for the Scholastic Aptitude Tests (SAT) score was 902 and for the American College Test (ACT) was 20.6. If the test scores tend to exceed these numbers, you're likely to have stumbled onto a small town with a superior school system.

However, be sure to ask what *percentage* of the student body took the tests. The national average is 55.5 percent taking SATs and ACTs. If a significantly lower percentage (that is, a more elite group) took the test, you would expect the scores to be higher, and consequently that would diminish the significance of higher average scores. If a higher percentage of students took it, you'd expect the average scores to be lower and this should mitigate against judging lower numbers too harshly.

E. *Do many parents and community members serve as in-school volunteers?*

In communities with strong schools, you invariably find a significant level of volunteerism—that is, parents, grandparents or community members offering to serve in such roles as teacher's aides and special tutors, just pitching in for whatever jobs need to be filled.

F. *Is there a community college, college or university in town or close by?*

Having an institution of higher learning in town will certainly benefit the community at large—even if your child's heart is set on going to college elsewhere. Most colleges and universities attract visiting speakers, put on film series and concerts and offer continuing education classes—programs to which the entire community is welcome. And campus facilities such as a library, swimming pool, tennis courts or football stadium may also be beneficial to you.

Job training programs most often offered through community colleges will help strengthen the economy locally.

8. QUALITY OF HEALTH CARE

The following questions can be answered by a staffer at the town or county health department and by visiting or calling the local hospital and speaking to someone in the administrator's office.

A. *How many primary-care physicians are there? How comfortable do you feel with them?*

In rural areas, that is, counties with populations of less than 50,000, the average number of primary-care physicians per 100,000 population is 55.6, according to Robert Quick, communications director of the National Rural Health Association. (This compares with an average of 96.2 per 100,000 population in urban areas.) If the town you're looking at has more than 5.56 primary-care physicians per thousand population, it would be above the national average for rural areas. (Primary-care physicians include general and family practitioners, doctors of osteopathy and physicians whose specialties include pediatrics, internal medicine and obstetrics/gynecology.)

After you determine the number of physicians, visit the doctors in their offices to find out what their services and philosophy are. Most rural physicians will take a few minutes to talk with you, Quick says.

B. *What are the doctors' affiliations?*

Find out whether they are linked with managed-care plans, health-maintenance organizations or larger regional medical centers. If they are, according to Bill Erwin, spokesman for the American Hospital Association in Washington, D.C., "that means they have strong referral networks. If they need backup, they can get it."

If potentially you will be working for an employer who requires you to participate in an HMO, you'll want to know which doctors in town would be yours.

C. Is there a local hospital and what is its condition?

For major care, such as open-heart surgery or major trauma, you'd doubtless be going to a tertiary-care regional medical center—not a small community hospital. However, having a good local hospital in your town that offers primary care and such services as oncology treatment, outpatient surgery and access to an emergency room is a big plus for any community—from a medical-care perspective as well as for the local economy.

There is no list of criteria that everyone should seek when evaluating a small hospital. Visit the facility and see if it meets your needs. If you're planning on starting a family and anticipate a normal pregnancy, see whether it has a maternity unit; if you have a heart condition, determine what services are available locally and which ones you'll have to be referred for.

Find out if the hospital is accredited by the Joint Commission on Accreditation of Healthcare Organizations. By early 1997, every accredited hospital in America—which includes the overwhelming majority of the nation's 6,600 hospitals—will have received a performance report from the commission detailing its quality in twenty-eight key performance areas from infection control to patients' rights. You can ask at the hospital to see this reader-friendly report, or purchase one directly from the commission for $30 a copy by calling (708) 916-5800.

D. What percentage of the hospital's physicians is board-certified?

Slightly over 60 percent of all physicians nationally are board-certified in their specialty or some other, according to the American Medical Association. Considering that more board-certified specialists would tend to be located at major medical centers and teaching hospitals and among younger physicians, any number approaching this benchmark or exceeding it would be impressive for a small-town hospital. (Physicians who are board-certified have had extra training and have passed a rigorous test in their specialities.) Although achieving board certification is not necessary, it's a desirable credential.

E. *How good is the hospital's emergency room?*

Emergency care should be of paramount concern when you are evaluating a local hospital. When judging a hospital's emergency room, ask whether a physician is on duty twenty-four hours a day. Not every rural emergency room will have one, but it's better if it docs.

You might also ask if the E.R. physicians are board-certified through the American College of Emergency Physicians—the seal of approval for advanced training in emergency medicine. (Bear in mind that this is a relatively new certification, so you'll find many perfectly competent older E.R. physicians without it.)

F. *What is the financial condition of the hospital?*

You should be able to see a general financial report if the facility is publicly funded or held, although, if it is part of a chain, you may have to go through headquarters. Some private hospitals, however, may be reluctant to divulge financial information. "The thing you have to remember when talking to representatives of a hospital is that they're selling their services," says Robert Quick of the National Rural Health Association. "They'd rather not tell you things they don't want you to know."

G. *What is the mortality rate at the hospital?*

Although no figures are kept on the national average mortality rate for the general patient population, according to a spokesman at Consumers' Checkbook, a Washington, D.C., medical-information publisher, figures are kept on the mortality rate of Medicare patients within thirty days of hospital admission. *Consumers' Guide to Hospitals* reports that the national average mortality rate for such patients was 8.7 percent in 1991, the last year for which figures were available from the Health Care Financing Administration. The guide, which rates all hospitals accepting

Medicare patients, also describes the total number of Medicare cases treated, gives a breakdown of diagnostic categories and presents a three-year mortality trend. For one measure of how well a particular hospital stacks up against others, you can inquire about the mortality rate for Medicare patients, to see if it is above or below the national average. You can order your own copy of the guidebook for $12 by calling (800) 475-7283.

And you can certainly ask a hospital spokesperson if its *overall* mortality rate has risen or fallen over the past three years. Clearly, you'd like to see a declining rate. "If a hospital has an extremely high mortality rate, I'd raise my eyebrows and wonder," says Quick.

However, experts caution that the mortality rate should never be the deciding factor when evaluating a hospital. Certain other factors, such as rough terrain, poor roads, high alcohol consumption per capita and being situated in areas that are either extremely rural, have a disproportionately high elderly population or a concentration of low-income residents, may inflate a hospital's mortality rate, while having little or no bearing on the quality of care.

H. *How is the delivery of Medicare services?*

All states have peer-review organizations that monitor and review Medicare treatment in every participating hospital in America. To find out the name and number of the peer-review organization overseeing the hospital you're evaluating, call the main Medicare number at (800) 638-6833. An operator there will refer you to the appropriate peer-review outfit, which will give you the lowdown on a particular hospital. From this, you'll be able to get a reading from medical peers on how a particular hospital treats its Medicare patients.

I. *How is the morale of the nursing staff?*

One way to determine the morale of the nursing staff is to ask about the turnover among nurses. Do nurses come and go in turnstile fashion? Low turnover indicates that working conditions, including employee morale, are good.

You might also inquire what percentage of the hospital's nurses are RNs (registered nurses). The national average is more than four RNs to every LPN (licensed practical nurse), according to the American Hospital Association. Also ask how many nurses are employed per patient. Traditionally, there's been one nurse for between three to six patients in an acute-care hospital and one nurse for every one or two patients in intensive-care units.

J. *If there is no local hospital, how long does it take to get from your town to general health-care facilities?*

Access to health-care facilities is especially important for senior citizens but is a factor for everyone. "We recommend trying to keep the drive for routine care to an hour," says Quick. "Anything much above an hour, and you don't get the preventive care you need."

K. *Who operates the emergency medical services (EMS) unit? How effective is it?*

For emergency care, a crucial factor to consider is response time—how quickly the EMS team would answer an emergency call in the area to which you're considering moving. Call the service, give your intended location and ask what the average response time might be. The ride to an emergency room, Quick says, should be "no more than thirty minutes."

Also, you'll want to look at whether EMS workers are employees or volunteers. If the EMS is professionally staffed twenty-four hours, then the response time is likely to be faster and the service more competent.

If the town you're considering is especially remote, you might inquire whether the local hospital has helicopter service. Most small hospitals do have landing pads.

L. *Does the public have access to free medical services through county health departments or free public clinics? Do physicians in town accept Medicaid and Medicare patients?*

Although *you* may never need to use these services, it's important for the sake of the community that they be available. If the answer to both of these questions is yes, it indicates that care is there for the medically underserved in town.

M. *Are there chiropractic and alternative medical services in town or close by?*

If alternative medicine—such as chiropractic, acupuncture, biofeedback, Ayurvedic medicine, massage therapy and hypnosis—is important to you or your family members, find out what services are available. If they're not in town, determine how far away they are.

9. QUALITY OF GOVERNMENT SERVICES

Question people on the street about the quality of the town's government, and be sure to inquire at both the town hall and the newspaper.

A. *What type is your government: council/manager, mayor/council, or board of commissioners?*

Probably the most effective form of government in a small town is the council/manager form in which a town council makes decisions that are implemented by a professionally trained manager (as opposed to a political mayor who may not understand or keep up to date on the workings of government). In some cases, the town may have an elected mayor along with a city or town manager. It's better to have a manager in town government, says Milan Wall, co-director of the Heartland Center for Leadership Development, "because that person has gone through training, and perhaps certification training, and is probably active in professional associations, such as the International City Managers Association, that provide a continuous updating of skills."

B. *Is government service delivery efficient, effective, responsive, accountable, equitable and entrepreneurial?*

One way to measure is to note how responsive government employees are to you, a newcomer making inquiries. You'll also want to poll people on the street with this question.

When evaluating local government, an informal measure of effectiveness is to keep track of how many times your call to town hall is transferred before you reach the person who can answer your question; how many minutes you're left on hold; and how many days pass before you receive promised materials in the mail.

C. *How concerned are local government officials with the "customers," its citizens?*

By asking everyone you meet and opening your eyes and ears when you're in town hall, you can get a good reading on how satisfied local taxpayers are with government service and how responsive and friendly government employees are to them. You'll see the degree to which local government has adopted the techniques of "total quality management," that is, a customer-service approach to serving its citizens.

10. HOUSING STOCK

The town or county planner or manager or a member of the local board of realtors should be able to answer the following questions:

A. *What percentage of total housing in town is detached single-family homes?*

1. *What percentage is mobile homes?*

2. *What percentage is apartments, condominiums and duplexes?*

B. *What is the median price of a free-standing, three-bedroom home?*

C. *What is the median rental price of a two-bedroom apartment?*

D. *What is the median rental price of a three-bedroom home?*

E. *How old is most residential housing in town?*

F. *What is the availability of houses or units for rental and purchase around town?*

G. *What is the percentage of vacant lots in town limits?*

This information will help you determine the costs involved in purchasing a home and the relative difficulty of finding vacant lots on which to build. It will also give you some information about the costs of renting—and the difficulties of finding rental units—before you buy.

HOW MYRON AND CARMEN MISIASZEK FOUND
THEIR HEARTS IN . . . NEWPORT, OREGON

❦ ❦

Myron and Carmen Misiaszek had their hearts set on moving to Oregon from the greater Boston area, but it took them several years to decide where to hang their hats. "We were looking for a picturesque, pretty place," says Carmen Misiaszek, a nurse, who together with her husband, Myron, a floor sander, moved to Newport (population 7,519) in 1993 and 1994 respectively. "It took us a number of trips to decide where. We drove around a lot, looking at different properties. We'd go around and look and observe how people were living. We saw Newport for the first time in 1987."

Location: They wanted a place that had a small-town ambience to it but one not so remote that they'd feel hemmed in. They wanted a location "where we had some alternatives," she says. "One of the things that attracted us to Newport was that it is equidistant between Portland and Eugene. We like the fact that we're within two to two-and-a-half hours from three cities: Corvalis, Salem and Eugene. The further north you go up the coast, the closer you get to Portland, but then you lose your access to the other inland cities."

Water and Sewer Rates: When the two were making their initial tour of Oregon, they carefully gathered data about the various towns they visited—including tax and water rates, which they picked up from realtors. "We'd ask for property sheets, fact sheets," says Carmen Misiaszek. "They'd Xerox them for us. We'd tell them we'd spend the afternoon looking and, if interested, would be back in touch."

Climate: Challenging the conventional wisdom that in coastal Oregon an umbrella is as essential to your wardrobe as underwear, the Misiaszeks did their own homework. "People back in Boston were telling us: 'It rains all the time. Do you really want to live there? You'll be deluged,'" says Carmen Misiaszek. "We got one of those topographical map books, which includes rainfall charts, and looked at the Oregon coast. We found that rainfall ranges widely depending on where on the coast you are. It turns out Newport doesn't get much more rain than Boston—80 inches a year. If you go 60 to 70 miles north, you'll get 120 to 130 inches. Newport is a good pocket because it's at the head of the Yaquina River."

Hospitality: Carmen Misiaszek is a convert on the matter of the friendliness of small-towners in the Beaver State. "Outside the big city, people in general are calmer and friendlier and more helpful," says the Philadelphia native. "I'm impressed when I go into a Kmart and people continually come up to me and ask: 'Can I help you find something?' Because I'm short, sometimes I can't reach things on a top shelf. The first time it happened, I was looking for shoelaces for Myron. A middle-aged man of fifty-five or sixty came up and said: 'Can I help you?' He reached up and brought down a package of shoelaces. He said: 'Is that the one you want? Let me bring down some others.' That's happened to me so many times out here."

The Welcome Mat: One good way to find a town that will welcome newcomers, according to the Misiaszeks, is to go to a place where newcomers are numerous. "Very few people have roots in Newport," she observes. "People here are much more eclectic and open to newcomers coming in, joining the crowd. Here, we felt welcome."

THE CIVIC INFRASTRUCTURE

In this phase of your town search, you'll be examining the "civic infrastructure" of a town. The civic infrastructure—a term coined by the National Civic League—refers to the invisible networks connecting the volunteers, civic organizations and government of a community. "Just as the physical infrastructure is made up of roads and bridges and power lines that need to be inspected every so often, so too a community has a civic infrastructure that requires occasional inspection and shoring up to make it stronger," says Christopher T. Gates, National Civic League president.

Factors such as a formalized approach to leadership development, a code of inclusiveness, and a cooperative, win-win approach to problem solving and community building are in place in all successful communities. Towns on top of the game invariably have traditions of self-help, supported by a grassroots ethic of community service.

In order to get a handle on community leadership, an outsider needs to try to pinpoint where the power structure lies. Janet Topolsky of the Aspen Institute says that you should never make assumptions about who's in charge. "It's like walking into a family and figuring out who's the leader. You can't walk in and assume that you'd better talk to the father, because you don't know who's really running the show." The mayor may be the leader or she may be a figurehead; the real power could lie with a business leader or a group of them, or an attorney or a town manager.

The key point, she emphasizes, is that in a "good town," active local institutions and leaders have "a shared vision of future goals. You want to see that everyone's working toward the same end. The point is: Are people working for the same purpose or at cross purposes? And if they are working toward the same end, does that purpose make sense?"

In order to scope out the civic infrastructure in a given town, pose the following questions to local officials, chamber of commerce officers and people on the street. Then you can make up your own mind about how strong it is.

1. CIVIC PARTICIPATION

A. *What percentage of voters turns out for local, off-year elections?*

Call the local board of elections or municipal clerk and ask for the percentage of voter turnout for the last three local off-cycle (nonpresidential and nonstatewide) elections. The national average for such elections is "rarely above 20 percent," says David Lampe, editor of the *National Civic Review*. If the local voter turnout approaches or exceeds that number, consider it a positive sign.

B. *What is the degree of participation at public hearings and council meetings?*

You'd like to hear that there's a healthy turnout at most hearings and council meetings, that citizens don't merely show up to register their concerns about self-serving single issues. If people rarely turn up for public hearings, it reveals a large degree of apathy.

Bear in mind that the greatest number of people *do* come to hearings and meetings when the wolf is at the door (or is perceived to be). But even a community's response to adversity will give you clues about its underlying civic health. Dr. David Hentzel, professor of economics and director for the Center for Economic Education, University of Missouri, Rolla, cites the case of Cuba, Missouri, which in 1984 lost its major plant, a shoe factory.

The first thing that struck the professor about Cuba (population 2,537)—and pointed to its future success in attracting new industry—was the turnout at public meetings. "I would go over to a town meeting. The town hall seats 150. Most meetings would have 250 or 300 people attending. Adults. They represented 10 percent of the population," says Hentzel, who wrote the book *Apples and Shoes: The Economics of a Small Town,* about how Cuba rebounded from economic catastrophe.

Everyone in town was deputized to attract new business. "There's an amazing amount of information that comes out at a dinner-table conversation," says Hentzel. "To a set of trained ears, this information is valuable." From attending town meetings, "everyone knew how to act." Waitresses and truck drivers, he says, began "filtering through conversations they heard and passing along tips" to the head of economic development, who was aggressive about following up leads. Not long after the factory's closing, a couple of new companies opened, including a paint factory and a company that makes automotive door gaskets. Strong, well-attended town meetings had set the stage for Cuba's turnaround.

C. *How many candidates ran unopposed in the last three elections?*

Ideally, you'd like to see that candidates are frequently (if not routinely) challenged and that political campaigns serve as the fulcrum of a spirited, partisan debate about local issues—with a minimum of hard feelings. This, along with a frequent turnover in elected positions, makes for a healthy local political climate.

However, the smaller the town, the greater the likelihood of finding candidates running unopposed. In some towns, elective offices are so poorly paid or thankless that no one but the office-holder would want them. But whatever the size (and budget) of the town, if candidates frequently (or always) run unopposed, this generally indicates one of two things: one, that civic life lacks dynamism and that a cynical, you-can't-change-anything-so-why-bother attitude has set in and/or that what David Lampe calls "a king- or queen-of-the-hill" syndrome exists that effectively stamps out competition. Or two, that the leaders are popular, fair and effective. "Sometimes when someone runs unopposed," says the National Civic League's Gates, "the only person capable of doing the job *is* doing the job. Or everyone likes that person so well, no one would want to run against him or her."

So how can you make this determination?

The best way is to question members of the community about how they feel about their elected officials. In some towns, people will be only too eager for a new set of ears to pour out their grievances to—or sing paeans to. But even if they won't come out and directly criticize, you can hear in people's tones how they feel about their leaders. If there's a resigned or complaining tone, you'll be able to tell that they don't feel well represented.

If, on the other hand, you routinely hear a leader praised for his effectiveness, skill and equanimity—or just that he's "a good fellow" or that he "does his best" or "does well by us"—the fact that he's not being challenged may indicate that he's doing such a good job that everyone wants him to stay.

2. CLUBS/CIVIC GROUPS

How many clubs and civic groups are there and how strong are they? What are the clubs known for—service projects or just gathering for meals and social hours?

Make a note of the number of civic clubs in town and ask around to find out what significant projects they've undertaken. You can usually get a listing of the clubs and their officers, phone numbers and meeting times from the chamber of commerce, office of economic development, local Welcome Wagon group or at the public library. Attend a few meetings. Find out what service gaps volunteer groups fill in the community.

If there's obvious evidence of their work—such as litter-free roadsides adopted by civic or youth clubs, gardens or parks maintained by garden clubs, an annual Kiwanis talent show or a Lions Club once-a-year flea market—or if townsfolk can identify a number of significant projects (either ongoing, annual or onetime), all of this suggests strong, dynamic civic life.

3. COMMUNITY LEADERSHIP

A. *Are leaders willing to share power? Do they attempt to achieve consensus for significant decisions and solicit various points of view—or do they make decisions behind closed doors?*

Experts on community leadership concur that strong, effective leadership is never the dominion of a powerful few, nor is it concentrated in one corridor of power. Rather, leadership at its best is dispersed and democratic and creates an atmosphere in which things get done.

"Leadership is not what happens at the top," asserts the University of Mississippi's Dr. Vaughn L. Grisham Jr. "It's a continuum." Effective leaders empower others to act. What's more, they're constantly building local, regional and national networks that help tie their community into a larger universe. According to a study done for the 1990 book *American Rural Communities,* this "dispersed" form of community leadership is not the norm; it's found in just 10 to 20 percent of small towns with populations under 50,000.

A good way to find out about the quality of leadership is to ask minority members and the less well heeled about local leaders. Ask who they are. If people rattle off a long list of names and you keep hearing different ones, this would indicate dispersed leadership. If the names are always the same handful of people—or even worse, just one—take this as a warning signal.

The worst possible leadership model for a small town is the strong-arm leader. "I would want to avoid the place where you find a single strong leader who can get everything done, who can cut through all the red tape," says Grisham. Unfortunately, even to this day, this archetype is not uncommon in small-town America. When this leader dies, if he's held tightly on to the power cards and cords, there will be a leadership vacuum and a concomitant drop in the town's standing in the region.

B. *To what degree are women and minority members accepted in leadership positions? How many serve in significant capacities?*

You'll want to determine specifically what positions have been and currently are held by women and minorities. Literature published by the Heartland Center for Leadership Development in Lincoln, Nebraska, says that in "thriving" communities women hold roles "that extend beyond the traditional strongholds of female leadership." Among these roles are mayors, presidents of chambers of commerce and heads of health-care facilities.

C. *Are younger leaders on the scene and is training available to them?*

The Heartland Center advocates a "deliberate transition of power to a younger generation of leaders" through such programs as youth-leadership training and leadership-development programs for young adults and future community leaders under age forty. Ask whether such programs exist. Often they're sponsored by the Jaycees, the chamber of commerce or an economic-development outfit.

4. VOLUNTEERING AND PHILANTHROPY

A. *Is there a spirit/climate of volunteerism in town?*

Find out whether there's a clearinghouse for volunteers locally. Such an entity could be a civic organization, a ministerial association or a strong church that prints a community-wide calendar, which includes listings for volunteers. If such a calendar exists, it will provide a quick and easy way for you to plug into community life; it's also a sign that the community's network of volunteers is strong and centrally organized.

You can also gauge the volunteer spirit in a community during your walk-around tour by looking for clues, such as store-window signs or banners across Main Street advertising upcoming tractor pulls, benefit suppers, auctions and fairs. Events sponsored by a coalition of volunteer organizations are especially auspicious, indicating that volunteer groups in town work together harmoniously.

B. *How generous are townsfolk with charitable giving?*

Find out what the major charitable drives in town are, such as the United Way, the March of Dimes or a local community-chest fund. Ask how generously citizens support them and whether giving trends point upward.

C. *Does a community foundation exist? If so, what does it fund?*

A community foundation is a valuable asset to any town, the municipal equivalent of having a rich uncle to lend some bucks when you're in a spot or need to launch a worthy project. Such a foundation may be able to fund a variety of worthwhile projects—anything from granting individual college or professional school scholarships to seeding start-up community ventures.

Only four hundred such foundations exist in big cities and small towns throughout the United States, according to Lampe, making them "very rare." Any small town that's home to a community-based foundation has an enviable asset. If one exists, ask what its focus is and if it has a fund drive. The very best foundations do not rely solely on their endowments, Lampe says, but have ongoing asset-acquisition drives.

Perhaps the nation's premier example of the transformational effect a foundation can have on a town comes from Tupelo, Mississippi, where the Community Development Foundation has been active for more than fifty years. With an annual budget of $1 million, it helps to lure new small- and medium-size businesses to town, to fund employee training and to invest in education, infrastructure and the arts.

The results of its long investment in the community are impressive. On average, the town of 30,685 adds 1,000 new jobs a year, has the second-highest per-capita income in the state, supports its own symphony orchestra and is home to the nation's largest rural hospital. Perhaps its most impressive achievement, however, is that in the traditionally low-scoring Magnolia State, Tupelo's high school graduates outperform their counterparts in both the state and the *nation* on ACT tests.

The key? It's simple, says Dr. Vaughn L. Grisham Jr., author of *It Can Be Done: The Tupelo Model* (Aspen Institute: 1995). "Investing in human infrastructure."

5. ETHNIC AND RACIAL DIVERSITY

A. *What percentage of the population is white, African-American, Hispanic, Asian-American, and Native American?*

If you're looking for diversity, or if you're a minority member and want to be a part of a racial or ethnic community, you'll need to pinpoint the size of each minority group in town. These numbers are collected by the state data center and dispensed to localities. This information can be obtained from town or county hall.

B. *How integrated are people of color into all aspects of town life— from civic groups and government, to churches and school leadership?*

By visiting the town hall and touring the town, you'll be able to see for yourself how many people of color work in various capacities. Ask how many people of color are in civic clubs and churches and how many serve on the school board and in school administration and how many work for local government.

When evaluating how well represented minority members are, be sure to take into account their percentage in the local population. (For instance, there are precious few people of color in some pockets of New England and the Great Plains states.) You wouldn't judge as harshly a town where less than 2 percent of the population was black for having only three African-American town employees as you would a similar-size community in which 45 percent of the population was African-American that employed just six.

"People can focus too much on diversity they can see," says Christopher Gates, "and not enough on what they can't see. In some all-Anglo communities, for instance, the diversity problem may be a division between urban and rural people or old-timers versus newcomers. Race and ethnicity aren't the only polarizing factors when you look for inclusiveness and diversity."

6. CONFLICT RESOLUTION
Do informal dispute-resolution mechanisms exist, or do conflicts always wind up in court?

It's better—and less costly—if informal dispute-resolution mechanisms exist to head off conflicts before they become tangled in court. In a few communities, you'll find court-ordered or court-sanctioned mediation, if only on an adjunct basis.

In some towns, active citizen organizations offer up their expertise to resolve community and individual conflicts *before* they land in court. Sometimes progressive staffers in town hall or elected leaders who recognize the need to seek alternate routes to dispute resolution lead the way by choosing these as the means of first resort.

You might ask small-towners how development disputes and environmental conflicts have been resolved in the past. Do the townsfolk roll over and play dead when developers propose significant and potentially damaging changes? Or is there a forum to air concerns and resolve differences? Such forms of enlightened conflict resolution remain rare for small towns, so if they exist, chalk them up in the plus column for the town.

7. COMMUNITY VISION

Has the community drafted a community-wide vision plan? Is there an ongoing mechanism to update it every five or so years?

The community that has mapped out a vision for itself, like the person who's set down concrete goals, is far more likely to be master of its future than a mere pawn of fate. The community vision plan should have concrete goals.

Vision plans are so common, says Lampe, "I'd be surprised if a community with an organized municipal government didn't have some kind of vision plan." If you find a town in which a vision plan doesn't exist and there are no plans for creating one, make a note of it. This constitutes a curious omission.

For communities that have drafted vision plans, there should be copies at town hall available to you. Reviewing this plan should help you determine if you'd like to move there. Find out if the plan calls for aggressive growth. Is it the kind of growth you agree with? And does the plan address your concerns—environmental and otherwise? Ask how often the plan is to be updated. Experts say that vision plans should be revisited every three to five years, although this may be financially difficult in very small towns.

You might also inquire about how the plan was assembled— whether it was drawn up exclusively by hired outside consultants or whether citizens were involved from the beginning. (The best plans will combine the expertise of the professionals on such arcane matters as zoning and land-use issues with the passion and commitment of community members.)

After you've read the plan, ask businesspeople in the community if they agree with it.

8. INTERCOMMUNITY COOPERATION

To what degree does the town work cooperatively with the county, with other towns in the county and within the region? Is there a large

*disparity between conditions—economic, educational, services, etc.—
in the county and the town?*

Intercommunity relations and cooperation are increasingly
important as residential and commercial development seamlessly
cross boundaries between municipalities and counties, prompting regions to market themselves cooperatively in a global economy.

You'll want to find out how well county and municipal gov-
ernments work together and in regional groups. At the economic
development office, ask about the extent to which business leaders participate in regional planning and economic development
groups. Be wary of towns that adopt a fortress mentality, holding
themselves apart from the county and region.

ARTS AND CULTURE/QUALITY OF LIFE

This round of the town search is about determining the quality
of "everything else." You'll be looking for the poetic and inspir-
ing facets of the town—such intangibles as the friendliness of the
people, their spirit, the town's relationship with its past, how civ-
ilized or rough-hewn it is, the look of the Main Street streetscape,
if caffe latte can be had downtown, if you can walk the streets at
night without having to look over your shoulder and how many
days the sun shines. You'll be trying to determine your comfort
level in town as well as the spirit of the place.

Your ideal town might be a place where people feel about
themselves and each other the way retired Mount Airy hosiery
manufacturer Robert Merritt does: "We're a bunch of ordinary
people doing extraordinary things."

This could well be the most pleasurable phase of the town
search. It involves poking around museums, looking for cultural
clues, strolling in parks and cemeteries, reading up on the area's
history, checking out the community theater, listening to old-
timers spin yarns about how electricity first came to Brownsville
or how Buster's dog, Garrison, once became best buddies with a
domesticated possum.

"Community Character"

Increasingly, "community character" is being deemed a valuable and vulnerable resource by urban planners and citizens; it is definitely something you want to evaluate when judging a community.

"With each passing decade, planners add another issue to their list of responsibilities," writes Gary Pivo in *Small Town*, a bimonthly news journal published by the Small Town Institute in Ellensburg, Washington. "The 1960s saw the inclusion of social equality, the 1970s added the environment, the 1980s added traffic and the 1990s may add *community character*." To prove his point, Pivo cites the town of Shelbourne, Vermont (population 5,871), which recently conducted a community survey during a town-plan debate. "Out of thirty-seven possible community objectives, people ranked 'preserve small-town character' first and 'preserve rural character' third," he reports.

Indeed, a community with a strong, specific identity is one that knows and celebrates its past, understands its intrinsic value and is more concerned about preserving its indigenous culture than embracing the homogeneous national culture as issued from New York and Los Angeles. If scads of newcomers have moved into town waving money and demanding change, you'd like to know that the place has been able to maintain its integrity (and not immediately drop its cultural pants for the new arrivals). The dilution of local culture by aggressive newcomers "has created tension in a lot of places," notes Janet Topolsky of the Aspen Institute. A worthy question to pose in communities that have experienced significant in-migration, is: "How do you maintain your historic, cultural character when a bunch of newcomers arrives?"

A community that lacks pride, self-esteem and a cultural "center," like the aimless person who bounces from cheap thrills to artificial highs, is likely to be isolated, desultory, and suffering a cultural vacuum. This gaping hole is most often filled with the piped-in culture of television, video games and videocassettes.

1. TOWN HISTORY/IDENTITY

Your starting point for research on town history should be the library. Ask the librarian questions about the town and where to go for answers. Request town histories. In some cases, you may be handed a scrapbook with a town history typewritten on a few pages, interspersed with photographs.

If there's no museum in town, often you'll find a local history exhibit at the library or in the visitors' center, if one exists.

A. *Do ordinary people know the history of the town well enough to tell it? How active are attempts to preserve local history?*

You'd like people to know the history of the place: if it started as a railroading town, a logging center, a trading post for farmers or a stagecoach stop. Ask locals how old the town is; for whom or what it was named; who is its most famous (and/or infamous) son or daughter; the mix of its early agricultural and manufactured products and how that compares to today's output. If most people can answer at least some of these questions pridefully and knowledgeably, you can assume that they think highly of their town. The way people answer your questions will be as significant as the answers themselves.

Find out if there's an active historical society and attend a meeting if one coincides with your town trip.

B. *Is there a strong, specific local identity?*

Ask people to sum up in a sentence or two the town's greatest virtues or what it's best known for. You're looking for answers like: "We manufacture the best western saddles around." Or: "Our high school marching band is the state champion and has been to the Rose Bowl five times." Or: "We're like the little engine that could: We all work together."

You might also keep an informal count of the number of references made to the town in local advertisements, bumper stickers and billboards. If people proudly display the town's name (or some affectionate nickname), brag about local accomplishments or promote tourism, that's a good barometer of local identification and pride.

C. *What are the community's sacred spaces and places?*

What's sacred to a community may be an old historical district, a living history farm, a particular building, park or monument. It may be the birthplace of a famous writer, politician or inventor. Or it may be "a web of things—important or mundane," says Ken Munsell, executive director of the Small Town Institute. "It could be a view or a tree in which people have invested memories."

Ask people what their sacred spaces are or, if you want to be more colloquial, "special places." Ask: "What's the most important/memorable place in town? What's the most unusual feature about this town? Are there any town symbols and what do they mean to you?" Often a sacred space cuts to the central myth about a particular small town.

For instance, in Hillsville, Virginia (population 2,008), the central architectural metaphor is the county courthouse where in 1912 the Allen family—one of whom was on trial for what the family felt was a trumped-up charge of resisting arrest—shot up the courthouse, killing five, including the judge. The story made national headlines and continues to be the central myth of the town, suggesting an ongoing fractiousness and an almost Wild West feeling to an otherwise sleepy town in southwestern Virginia.

Once you get a good reading on a town's most sacred place or myth, decide whether it speaks to you.

D. *Are attempts being made to preserve historical buildings in town or have most been razed?*

While anyone representing the town's historical society will gladly answer such queries (perhaps in greater detail than you desire), simple observation will tell you whether there are many historical homes around town and historical buildings downtown and elsewhere. Historical markers and plaques are telltale signs of a concerted effort to preserve local history as well. The presence of older homes and historic buildings is a good indicator that townsfolk recognize the value of preserving the town's heritage and are willing to put money individually and collectively toward historic preservation.

2. THE LOCAL LIBRARY
How many volumes does it have and what are its hours?

Support for the public library is a good measure of the value the community accords books, literature and that most basic form of continuing education—reading. Browse through the shelves and make a mental note of the proportion of new to older books. Look for how much space the library devotes to books of local interest (that includes the town, state and region). Ask the librarian how many volumes the library has. For every thousand residents in town, a top-notch library will carry at least five thousand volumes. To determine if the books just gather dust or if they're heavily circulated, ask how many books are checked out monthly.

Check its hours and see whether it is open on weekends. A decent library (except in the smallest communities) should be open at least forty hours a week, with some of those hours on weekends. Ask whether the hours have been reduced significantly during the belt-tightening 1990s. Small-town libraries are often bolstered by active Friends of the Library groups that help support the library with funds, books, volunteers and programming.

3. THE LOCAL NEWSPAPER
What is the quality of the local newspaper?

You can judge the quality of the local newspaper simply by reading it. See how many locally written news stories, photographs and features it produces. The lazy dailies merely run national news off the AP wire and lace in local press releases and boosterish news. Objective enterprise reporting, which probes local issues and the actions of business and government, is the hallmark of a quality newspaper.

Weekly or biweekly newspapers are much more likely to stick to local news because readers will already have received national news from TV or another newspaper. When judging them, look for a paper that has more substance than a mere community bulletin board and brag sheet.

You may also want to inquire whether you can get same-day delivery of out-of-town papers such as *The Wall Street Journal* and *The Washington Post.*

4. RECEPTIVITY TO NEWCOMERS

A. *How friendly and welcoming are people to you?*

Clearly, you're looking for a place where newcomers are not branded for life as the "come heres" or as "from away" (as some standoffish Mainers call folks who haven't lived there for their entire lives). You want a place where people are as open and receptive to you as they would be to long-time neighbors and friends.

"Some communities are very cliquish," says Jim Schriner, partner of PHH Fantus, a Chicago-based corporate relocation firm. "If you're not a long-term resident, it's very hard to be accepted, let alone get a job."

The best way to gauge the friendliness of the natives is by talking to newcomers. Ask them how they've been received and if their opinions are taken seriously. If there's a newcomers club and you happen to be in town when it meets, by all means attend. If most of the newcomers are desperate to move on—and/or wax nostalgic for their old hometowns—it is a definite warning signal that the town is not particularly warm to outsiders.

If you miss the meeting, call up the club president and chat. Ask for names and numbers of others to whom you might speak.

B. *How many native sons and daughters have returned?*

If a good number have returned to town to raise families, for the quality of life or to start or grow a business, this indicates the town has a staying power that should bode well for you, too.

5. ARTS PROGRAMMING

A. *Is there an arts council, and what does it do?*

Ideally the town will have its own arts council or theatrical guild offering such things as classes in art and dance and in-school programs featuring visiting artists and dancers. But perhaps most importantly, it will stage productions.

"The presence of a theater would be a positive indicator for any town," says Kathie DeNobriga, executive director of Alternate Roots, an Atlanta-based clearinghouse for small theaters throughout the southeastern United States.

If the arts council has its own building or stage so much the better, but don't discount active guilds that put on plays in a variety of locations from high school auditoriums to Elks lodges. The benefits of such efforts extend beyond the arts. Having an active roster of theatrical productions works wonders in building networks of often disparate people. "The act of putting on a show is an incredibly community-strengthening thing," says DeNobriga. "It helps the community immeasurably."

If there's an arts council, ask about the size of its budget and if it has any paid staffers. Arlene Goldbard, an arts and cultural affairs consultant based in Ukiah, California (population 14,632), says that when judging the cultural life of a town, look for significant "public provision" for the arts, which means that groups aren't constantly scrambling for funds through annual fund drives and private donations. With at least one strong funding source in place, arts providers can focus more of their energy on the arts.

B. *Does the arts council have indigenous productions, or are they all imports?*

You'd like to find an arts community that doesn't merely serve the cultured elite, but caters to broader community tastes while honoring local legends. "The ideal is to do work that celebrates a town's own culture," says DeNobriga.

Good small theaters often include local original works in their rosters—often in experimental productions, theater in the round or in annual, original one-act play presentations. Such productions usually employ the minimum of props and play to smaller audiences than main-stage productions; because the payment of royalties and the building of sets are omitted, such productions can be staged for a pittance.

What's more, some communities offer perennial professional or semiprofessional productions in outdoor summer dramas retelling some local legend, such as *The Horn of the West* in Boone, North Carolina, about Daniel Boone's story; *The Trail of the Lonesome Pine* in Big Stone Gap, Virginia, an Appalachian love story; and *The Lost Colony* in Manteo, North Carolina, about the early settlers who disappeared from the coast of North Carolina in the 1600s.

However, the town in which top-quality, locally written and produced plays constitute the entire theatrical fare would be unusual to say the least. The best you can hope for is a mix of local originals with old standbys.

In the absence of locally written plays, regional works of interest or works that speak to a particular cultural or ethnic group are pluses. For instance, in a theater in Choctaw, Oklahoma, you'd like to see productions that celebrate the stories of Native Americans—not the comedies of Neil Simon.

However, culturally sensitive selections may not always be found—especially with pickup theatrical groups. DeNobriga cautions against dismissing a local theater altogether because it only offers such old standbys as *Annie Get Your Gun, The Crucible* or *Our Town*. Almost *any* production is a bonus to a community.

C. *How well-attended are arts council productions? What percentage of their revenues comes from ticket sales?*

When a hefty percentage of an arts council's revenue comes from ticket sales (rather than institutional support), it indicates that programs are widely attended.

THE SURRY ARTS COUNCIL: A STAR IS BORN IN
THE FOOTHILLS OF THE BLUE RIDGE

🍇 🍇

Ask people in Mount Airy to name the town's strongest cultural point of pride, and the answer is easy. Skipping right over the fact that legendary television star Andy Griffith was born here in 1926, they will invariably point to the Surry Arts Council. Established in 1969, the arts council excels by every measure—from varied and innovative programming (traditional, experimental and indigenous) to aggressive fundraising.

What's the secret?

Dynamic leadership, a strong commitment to the community and the tapping of local veins.

"We've worked very hard to be responsive to the whole community," says Surry Arts Council Executive Director Tanya B. Rees, a former Miss Mount Airy who has funneled her prodigious energies into helping build the council into one of the most successful in the nation serving a town its size. (Indeed, the council's annual budget has risen from $65,000, when Rees came aboard in 1989, to an unheard-of $600,000-plus for the fiscal year 1995-96—25 percent of which comes from program income/ticket sales and 25 percent from grants.) "I've observed communities where the arts council staff dictates to the community what they think it should have," she says. "But what's the point in having a classical series concert and entertaining the twelve people in Mount Airy who want to come?"

Instead, the Surry Arts Council sponsors everything from local bluegrass and old-time music to jazz and theatrical performances, to writing, art and dance workshops; it provides in-school programming and programs for seniors, people of color and special needs. It puts on Act Too, an original one-act play revue for local aspiring playwrights and Arts Alive, a two-week summertime arts enrichment program for children under age twelve. Every September, it hosts Mayberry Days, a down-home weekend for fans of *The Andy Griffith Show.* Working closely with the county's three school districts, the arts council sponsors or co-sponsors after-school programs for "at-risk students" both at the junior high school and in a nearby government housing project. ("At-risk students" are candidates for juvenile delinquency, teen pregnancy and dropping out of school.) The arts council has snared grants to write and produce original plays on social issues, such as teen pregnancy and STDs. (One locally generated award-winning play was professionally filmed and is being made available to schools and health departments in each of the state's one hundred counties.) The council runs two art markets in which local artists can display and sell their creations and has received partial funding to build an amphitheater.

With three full-time staffers and three hundred-some volunteers working out of headquarters in the Andy Griffith Playhouse (the former Rockford Street Elementary School), the council must have some rich benefactors somewhere . . . right?

Wrong.

"We do not have *any* extremely high givers," says Rees. "A consultant came to check us out. He said, 'You must have a single source of income from one corporation. If that corporation pulls it, you'll die.' But he found out that our median gift is ten dollars. That's really good. We have a membership of 1,500, and our mailing list goes out to 2,000." The rest of its money comes from ticket sales, grants, fund-raising events, local government and consignment sales for artists.

"When I was looking for other arts councils to compare budgets with," says Rees, "I came up with a city of 260,000 in North Carolina. It had a similar budget to ours, but we get $6,000 annually from the county and they get $450,000." (The Surry Arts Council also receives $40,000 annually from the city of Mount Airy.)

The arts council's most recent enterprise has been acquiring a forlorn, 1930s-vintage downtown theater—vacant for twelve years—spiffing it up and opening it to the public for dollar-a-seat, second-run movies. (Rees and others managed to persuade the owner of the 5,800-square-foot cinema to donate the structurally sound property and the shell of a projector to the arts council.) The enterprise has helped to bring in revenues for the arts council, revitalize that portion of downtown and knit the community together by providing a new and much-needed "people place" downtown.

"We have an incredible socioeconomic range of moviegoers," says Rees enthusiastically. "Everything from housing-project folks who come up and grab my arm and say they've never been able to afford to go to the movies, to the millworkers who say, 'This is the first time my *whole* family has been able to go!' to someone from a higher-income bracket who says, 'I can bring six kids to the movies and get out for less than twenty dollars—including popcorn.'"

Rees brings her own three teenagers on weekends to watch the shows and lean back in the . . . well, okay, the seats are a little stiff. But that's the fun of traveling back in time.

Rees says that the secret of her success is making herself into a "sponge."

"I'm not an arts council director because of my knowledge about the arts," says the paradoxically forceful yet self-effacing Rees. "I come at this job primarily from a commitment to the community."

D. *Do visual artists live in town? Is there an art gallery?*

Just one or two professional artists or sculptors living and working in town can exert a disproportionately strong influence on its cultural life, introducing talent, creative vision and that ineffable spark into a community.

Increasingly, visual artists *are* heading for the hills, seeking the same things the rest of us are after: slower-paced, less costly places to live and work. "Today, the artists you discover living in the country are in many instances astoundingly sophisticated masters of their chosen art forms," writes John Villani in his book *The 100 Best Small Art Towns in America.* "[L]iving a productive and artistic life in the mid-1990s means the artist gets to live wherever he or she damn well pleases. More and more, that means a rural community."

And though some artists may hold community at arm's length, others are eager to contribute in any way possible: by offering art classes, judging talent competitions, donating works to local auctions and fund-raisers and even capturing townspeople and scenes in their work—in so doing, preserving and honoring them. For example, Mount Airy, North Carolina, artist Tom Acosta was hired by the appearance commission to paint a 50-by-20-foot mural depicting Main Street in the 1890s on the wall of an old building abutting the municipal parking lot downtown. The work took him four months to complete; in the end, he found that he'd donated much of his time. But it was a contribution the West Virginia native (who'd moved with his wife to Mount Airy in 1985 expressly looking for a small-town base) was happy to make to his adopted hometown.

E. *What kind of music can you find?*

Rare is the small town that has its own symphony orchestra (though Tupelo, Mississippi, is a notable exception). But if you enjoy live music, ask if there's a chamber music group, a string quartet, a barbershop quartet or vocal groups. In some cases, a college, university or even the local high school may have excellent musical groups.

Depending on where you move, you may acquire a taste for certain kinds of folk music; if it's Appalachia, it'll be old-time and bluegrass music. If your tastes are more highbrow and you're a diehard opera or symphony buff, find out how close you are to a city that has one. If you're an hour or two away, you'll probably be able to go several times a year.

6. CLIMATE/SCENIC BEAUTY

A. *What is the average annual temperature and the range of temperatures?*

Only you can know what's the "right" temperature for you. Most chambers of commerce will be able to provide you with an average annual temperature chart breaking out the months with average daily highs and lows. Someone who likes four distinct seasons will be looking for average temperatures that vary significantly from winter to summer. If you prefer a milder year-round climate, make sure the chart does not show an enormous spread between the summer and winter months.

B. *How many sunny days and how many inches of rain does your community get per year?*

Once again, you should be able to get this information from the chamber of commerce or some other economic development entity. How you process it is up to you. You may abhor rainy weather, or perhaps you're among the rare few who enjoy a wet climate and frequent winter snows.

C. *What is the average relative humidity of the place?*

The degree of moisture in the air, or relative humidity, is a larger factor in human comfort than many of us realize. A high temperature with dry air can seem much cooler than the identical temperature with moist, humid air. Anyone suffering from such medical conditions as pulmonary disease or who is susceptible to bacterial skin infections, mold allergies or fungal infections, should avoid places with high relative humidity.

On the other hand, low relative humidity can be problematic as well. "When the relative humidity falls below 50 percent," writes David Savageau in *Retirement Places Rated,* "most persons experience dry nasal passages and perhaps a dry, tickling throat. In the dry areas of the Southwest, where the humidity can drop to 20 percent or less, many people experience nosebleeds, flaking skin and constant sore throats."

D. *What is the quality of scenic views from town?*

Just as the interior of our homes affects our moods and peace of mind, our physical surroundings—the terrain, geography and the views we see every day—exert an influence over us that is more powerful than we probably notice. To find out how you re-spond to a view, tour the town and look around 360 degrees. Is the scenery pleasing to you? Do you see panoramic views or is the town closed in? Are there mountains in the distance—an ocean, lake or desert? If you're a person who likes open spaces or varied views, take a good look—and snap a few pictures—to decide if the vista appeals to you and your family.

7. EARTH FRIENDLINESS

For many, a big attraction of small-town life is its greener pas-tures, cleaner air and water and wide open spaces. But be fore-warned: environmental problems are not only found in big cities; they also plague small towns. While some small towns are mod-els of environmental correctness, others are woefully retrograde when it comes to being earth-friendly. Following are questions to ask when evaluating a town's record on environmental poli-cies to let you determine just how earth-friendly Hooterville really is.

A. *Is there a curbside recycling program?*

Because curbside recycling programs are easier and less costly to set up in small towns than in big cities, experts say that smaller communities are more likely to have them. Norman Crampton, director of the Indiana Institute on Recycling in Terre Haute, says, "The larger towns or cities are lagging behind small towns by two or three years. Indianapolis, for example, doesn't have curbside recycling yet. Recycling began as a suburban phenome-non and spread rapidly into the hinterlands where it's really taken off."

In Indiana and elsewhere, he says, "the large majority of curb-side collection programs are in towns. The reason is scale." What's more, in small towns, citizens' groups lobbying for curbside recycling can see the process through to implementation much more easily than in big cities where such programs would have to go through extensive review and costly budgeting.

However, because some small towns are sparsely populated, curbside programs are too costly to operate. In their place, some communities set up recycling bins at landfills that collect aluminum cans, glass, newspapers and the like. Others have periodic "R days" (or recycling days) run by volunteers from civic clubs and the community at large.

B. *Is the garbage collected in an environmentally responsible way?*

If the town has adopted a pay-per-bag or -can program—thus giving people an incentive to reduce their amount of waste—this tells you that the community is practicing a pro-environmental policy. Such policies, which are catching on nationwide in communities small and large, encourage everything from "precycling" (whereby consumers shun overpackaged products, thus preventing those materials from ever entering the waste stream) to worm bins, backyard composting and recycling.

"People catch on quickly and understand that they can begin to control their garbage bills by pulling the recyclable items out of the garbage bag and putting them in the recycling bin," says Crampton.

C. *Is yard waste handled separately from other garbage?*

Ask if collections for leaves, lawn clippings and yard waste are made separately from general waste. Since yard waste can amount to anywhere between 20 and 30 percent of all disposed residential waste, when it's diverted from the waste stream, the savings in landfill space, in cost and to the environment are enormous. You'd like to see yard waste composted or, at the least, deposited in its own landfill. In some states, the law prohibits mixing yard waste with general waste in the landfills.

You might also ask if the municipality that collects yard waste and lets it turn to mulch then uses it on city grounds and schools and/or offers a giveaway program to the public.

D. *How would you rate air quality?*

"Look carefully at the kinds of industries in town," recommends Crampton. "Some stink—such as paper and poultry. Oil and gas refining can be great for the economy but terrible for the nose." (To say nothing of the lungs.)

Ask a county extension agent, town manager, or clerk if air-quality standards as issued from the Environmental Protection Agency are being met for the six pollutants considered most dangerous to human health: carbon monoxide, nitrogen dioxide, ozone, sulfur dioxide, lead and total suspended particles. If they are not, you may want to delve further to evaluate your health risks.

E. *What is the quality of the water?*

You'll first want to determine the source of the water and the supply. Is it groundwater, from a surface source, or some combination of the two? You'll be able to gather this information from the chamber of commerce or an industrial development commission. Ask a town employee or a county extension agent if there have been any actions against the town from the state or federal government concerning water quality. Ideally, you'd like to find a community in which there is an abundant supply of high-quality, unpolluted water.

F. *Does the town have landscaping ordinances on the books?*

You'd like to find a community in which landscaping ordinances require that "green spaces" be provided around new commercial and industrial developments. Typically in such ordinances, higher-density development is required to provide buffers for lower-density development. For instance, if a shopping center were built next to an office building, the center would be required to provide a "wall" of shrubs and/or trees between itself and the building. While this procedure is costly up front, in the long run the property's value will appreciate and the entire community will benefit. Such ordinances help prevent what former Mount Airy City Commissioner Mike King refers

to as the "creeping-asphalt" phenomenon, that is, paving everything in sight.

G. *Is locally grown fruit and produce available at a farmers' market
or in town?*

You'd like to be able to find locally grown fruit and vegetables
at farmers' markets and grocery stores. This helps to support the
local economy and provides you with fresh foods that have not
been shipped or stored for long periods of time.

H. *Are there any environmental organizations or clubs?*

Check the local newspaper's community calendar to see if environmental, ecological, conservation and/or sustained-living
clubs or groups exist and when they meet. Or ask someone at the
chamber of commerce or from a Welcome Wagon for a list of
community clubs.

Jeffrey Smedberg, recycling programs coordinator for Santa
Cruz County, California, says that eighteen such clubs are listed
in the Santa Cruz (population 49,711) phone book. In some
towns, such clubs may not come under the environmental banner. Instead they may be garden clubs and beautification commit-
tees.

WELLESLEY, MASSACHUSETTS:
TAKING OUT THE TRASH—WITH PANACHE

When it comes to taking out the trash, a reverse snobbery
rules in this ritzy town of 26,615. With no municipal
curbside garbage pickup, Wellesley residents cart their own
trash in the back of their Volvos and BMWs to their unusual
Recycling and Disposal Facility (RDF) on the town line.

The innovative efforts of these once-a-week garbage carriers have not gone unnoticed. In 1989, Wellesley won the recycling award from the Washington, D.C.-based Institute for
Local Self-Reliance for Best Overall Program for a Small

City. Visitors, including recent delegations from Russia and Japan, stream in from around the world to visit the fabled garbage facility.

Since 1976, when the town's incinerator closed for failing to meet federal air-emissions standards, Wellesleyites have been paying regular visits to the town "dump," which is open six days a week and is a magnet for cookie-selling Girl Scouts and glad-handing politicians. Here, at the highly social RDF, citizens drive on a one-way concourse through an impeccably landscaped, parklike, thirty-acre tract, pausing at one or more of the thirty-seven numbered stops to deposit carefully sorted recyclables. At each stop are different-sized trailers: brown glass goes into one bin, clear into another; old mattresses have their own bin, as do fireplace ashes; used clothing is dropped off at a huge Goodwill trailer.

At Take It or Leave It, a paved, open-air swap shop—probably the facility's most renowned feature—one person's trash is another's treasure. For instance, someone might leave a rusted lawn chair, then scavenge for a clay flowerpot. "I've seen rowboats, sailboats—just about everything but an airplane," says George Barry, RDF superintendent. "Anything people figure is reusable they drop off here."

For the town's many bookworms, an enclosed 15-by- 6-foot Book Exchange complements the swap shop. The beauty of it all for these frugal New Englanders is that not a penny ever changes hands, and they're doing their part to save the environment.

---

8. CRIME

A. *What is the level of violent crime per 100,000 residents?*

For this information, contact the town's police department and ask how many incidents of murder, rape, armed robbery and aggravated assault occurred in the last year (for which statistics were available) and the two years before that. To arrive at a number that can be compared to state and national averages, you'll have to multiply it so that it's represented in terms of violent crimes per 100,000 population. Typically, the crime rate will be lower in small towns than in big cities, but as with all measures, these numbers will vary from town to town. You'd like to see a stable—or even better—a declining rate of violent crime. According to Zero Population Growth's Urban Stress Test, "model communities report violent crime rates of fewer than 350 per 100,000 inhabitants and an increase of 3.5 percent or less."

B. *What is the level of property crime per 100,000 residents?*

Ask the local police department for the number of auto thefts, larcenies and burglaries over the last three years. Once again, calculate this figure so that it's expressed per 100,000 population. Again, you're looking for a stable or declining rate of property crime.

COMMITTING YOURSELF TO A NEW PLACE

Once you've answered all (or many) of the questions, made the rounds and met the people, toured the towns, poked into their past and peered into the crystal balls of their future, now comes the moment of truth—the moment of decision; now comes the time when you cross over from being an interviewer/tourist/voyeur to committing yourself to a new life in a new town.

By now, having completed this comprehensive survey, you'll have a good sense of which of the towns you've scouted fits your wants and needs. You'll have some idea of the strengths and weaknesses of a new community, and perhaps a notion of how you might be able to make a significant contribution.

If you still harbor some doubts, take it slowly. Come back during another season and see if your feelings for the place remain the same. Many a town that appeared idyllic in the summer months may look bleak and isolated in the chill of winter. Sleep on your decision for six months, or a year or more. Take this time to pull your finances together (you'll learn more about this in Chapter 4), solidify your thinking, planning and dreaming. Stay in touch with the people you've met, keep reading the local newspaper and following local events.

After all the rational analysis, when making a decision about a new town, ultimately, you have to let your feelings have the final say. "You have to fall in love with a place," says Norman Crampton, who moved with his family from Chicago to Greencastle, Indiana (population 8,984), in 1990. You'll know when you've fallen in love when "things feel good, and that has to do with people— the people you meet by chance and otherwise." For Crampton, the move to Greencastle satisfied a long-held dream of living the kind of life his wife had growing up in Kosciusko, Mississippi (population 6,986), surrounded by extended family. The move, he says, represented the ultimate "wish fulfillment."

It is a decision the family has never once regretted.

CHAPTER THREE

Recasting Your Career

Making a living in a small town is the foremost concern for the vast majority of people considering the move. Jobs are the biggest issue—rather than lifestyle—for those wanting to leave the city. People worry that they won't be able to find work and that, if they do, it won't pay enough to maintain the lifestyle to which they're accustomed.

The fact is that good livings *are* made in small towns by millions of Americans, many of them recent migrants from the big cities. Leading the charge are ambitious, career-oriented professionals "searching for a serious business environment where the daily tasks of living—work, getting to work and leisure—can be simple, easy and fun," writes David A. Heenan, author of *The New Corporate Frontier: The Big Move to Small Town U.S.A.* "They want it all: the stimulation of a first-class job with the ambience of a simpler lifestyle."

While job opportunities in the hinterlands may not be as plentiful as in the big cities and the paychecks are likely to be smaller, entrepreneurial opportunities (serving either a local, regional or national customer base) abound along with such transportable work options as telecommuting and independent contracting. What's more, when you tally in the lifestyle advantages of rural living (walking, biking or short commutes to work; eating lunch at home; knowing your co-workers and customers as neighbors and fellow community members; and allowing your work to be better integrated into your life), recasting your career in a small town may be just the ticket for you.

But don't expect to land an idyllic situation overnight and to negotiate the adjustments effortlessly. "It isn't what you see in the TV movies," says Milan Wall, co-director of the Heartland Center for Leadership Development, in Lincoln, Nebraska, where you "pick up and move to a ranch on Saturday, and on Sunday you're branding calves."

However, by approaching job-hunting, business creation or business relocation in a small town with a winning game plan and an upbeat attitude and playing by the rules governing small-town culture, most newcomers can establish a life for themselves that's *better* than in the city.

LOOKING FOR WORK

Looking Before You Move
If you've decided that you want to find a job, bear in mind that the job search is nothing more than a sales campaign. You're marketing yourself. Your future employer is your customer. How you go about finding work—whether you're aggressive or awkward, enthusiastic or irritable—demonstrates your ability to perform the job.

While still working as director of public information of the M.D. Anderson Cancer Center in Houston, Joan Baird Glover put her public relations and marketing skills to work in finding a job in her future hometown of 12,361. After doing five months of part-time spadework from Houston, she was on the brink of landing a plum position when she and her husband, Fritz Glover, arrived in Ellensburg, Washington, in August of 1988.

After checking in from the road with a potential employer at

Central Washington University, Joan Glover learned an interview was set up for the morning after her arrival from the grueling, 2,400-mile, weeklong trek. ("Trying to find my dress-for-success suit and pantyhose was quite a challenge," she recalls.) But Glover aced the interview, and swiftly things began falling into place. The following Monday, she was offered the newly created position of director of community relations for the university. She reported to work two weeks later.

How did Glover—coming in from the outside and not knowing a soul in town—manage to land a highly desirable position in what was then one of the top unemployment counties in the state?

As always, good timing was a factor, but a combination of a solid professional background, assertiveness, consistent follow-through and cultural sensitivity ultimately made the difference. But Glover also made all the right moves—moves that anyone putting down roots in a small town would be wise to emulate.

Career Self-Evaluation: Glover's first step was to evaluate her professional assets, to see what she could offer an employer and which skills were transferable. "If not the whole job, see what elements of your (current) job apply in different settings," she recommends. She then tried to determine which employers in town might need her and what she could offer them. With a background in public information and public affairs, she zeroed in on the university and the newspaper as potential employers.

Informational Interviews: Glover traveled to Ellensburg in April of 1988 and began asking questions of anyone and everyone she met. She set up informational interviews with, among others, the editor of the *Ellensburg Daily Record* and the vice president for university relations and development at Central Washington University, who ultimately hired her. "I was careful to make face-to-face contacts," she says. After obtaining correct spellings of names and titles ("so it looks like you know what you're doing from the beginning," she says), she wrote follow-up letters to these key contacts containing "information" about her career. "I didn't ask for a job," she says significantly.

Networking: Glover's networking paid unexpected dividends.

The newspaper editor whom she'd favorably impressed during an informational interview turned up on the interview panel for the university job, and she was able to call him by name. After returning to Houston, she stayed in touch with her contacts by mail and telephone, letting them know her plans as they took shape. "People talk about the importance of networking in the big city, but it's no less important in a small community," she says.

LONG-DISTANCE JOB-SEARCH TECHNIQUES

So you've settled on the town in which you want to settle down but the moving date is still six months off. How do you go about conducting a long-distance job search if you don't know a soul and aren't a self-starter?

You can start by taking the following steps that should help send you on your way to small-town career success.

Call or Visit Your College Alumni or Career-Services Office

If you're moving to a small town, you may gather job-hunting leads from the alumni or career-services office, which is often underutilized by college graduates, especially those who've been out of school for a while. Its resources may include some of the following: audiovisual materials, career-search books, counseling services, classes and referrals. Most often, you can use these at no charge. Even if you can't go in person, in many cases career-placement officers will give you time over the phone. At Northeastern University in Boston, for instance, long-distance alums are given a half hour of telephone guidance.

If you plan to move to a geographic region different from where your college or university is located, contact your alumni office and ask if the office has a reciprocal relationship with a college or university near where you'll be living. If it does, a career-placement officer will initiate an exchange of letters enabling you to use the career services at this other institution. Generally, reciprocal users can take advantage of most services, such as the all-important job bank and job listings. At Northeastern University, for instance, individual appointments and on-campus recruiting are the only services from which reciprocal users are barred.

Tap into Your College Alumni Network

The alumni network is "a wonderful resource—particularly for people looking to relocate," says Carol Lyons, dean of career services, Northeastern University, Boston. Alumni should drop by or call their alumni or career-services office to inquire how to use this service. Most (though not all) colleges and universities have developed networks through their alumni or career-service offices into which you can plug the town you've selected. Even if the contacts you find do not work in your field, if they live where you want to move, they can sometimes be of enormous help. They can provide you with information about the economy, housing, recreation and schools; they can offer the names of others in the area and, in some instances, may even know of some job leads. Invite your contacts to lunch—and even though *you're* the one looking for work, always pick up the check.

If no alums live in the town you've selected, look for some residing in the next nearest city. If they've lived in the area for a while, they may know your town and be willing to share names and numbers of their contacts there. If you were a member of a college fraternity or sorority, contact the central office to check out its nationwide alumni directory.

Key into a Nationwide Database

Through your career-services office, consider keying into such programs as Career Search or One Source, which are nationwide databases available on computer through CD-ROM. With one of these, you can conduct a geographic search that will turn up all potential employers in a specific field in a given area. Because these are costly programs to maintain, some career-services centers don't have them, while others charge alums (and sometimes even students) a fee for use.

However, if you know where you want to move and have little

time to do your own research, it may be worth it. For instance, if you'd like to find a job in banking, you could ask the database to show you all the banks within a certain radius of, say, Kingman, Arizona. The program will then spit out all the employers in that area, including names, addresses and telephone numbers. One Source, a corporate database, would supply sales information, as available, and sometimes include abstracts of journal articles about the firms.

Obtain the Local Yellow Pages

The most frequently overlooked resource in the out-of-town job hunt is the humble little Yellow Pages. You can get a telephone directory in town from the phone company or in many cases from the chamber of commerce. Or if you're calling from out of town, you can have one sent to you by the telephone company (sometimes for a fee).

"It's amazing to me how infrequently job hunters turn to the Yellow Pages," says Joann Kroll, director of career planning and placement, Bowling Green State University in Bowling Green, Ohio. It's information-packed; it's cheap; it's current. In it, company names, addresses and phone numbers are listed. In short, Kroll says, "It's a no-brainer."

Plan a Trip to Town

On the trip, you can scope out potential employers, writing them well in advance to schedule interviews and following up with telephone calls. Take a full week if possible, using vacation time if necessary. Nothing convinces an employer of your serious interest better than an in-person visit. If they know you'll only be in town for a limited period, they'll often be especially accommodating in granting you an interview.

Tell Your Personal Story

When setting up your trip to town, write letters to all the businesses that are prospective employers. While selling your professional credentials, always remember to tell your personal story. If you plan to move because you've fallen in love with the town, tell the human resources manager this in your cover letter. Small-towners are flattered when city folk are taken with their corner of the earth. Cite specifics, such as the impressive school system or the bountiful farmers market. If you're eyeing Toppenish, Washington, compliment its striking, ubiquitous murals. If you've always been an admirer of Haeger Pottery and a search for its factory led you to Macomb, Illinois, in the first place, tell that to a potential employer.

Even if your main motivation to leave the city is to escape some urban horror, say so. This will engage potential employers in your personal drama and reinforce their belief that small-town living is superior to its urban counterpart. Tell them that your twelve-year-old son recently witnessed a drive-by shooting and you're afraid he might be the next victim, or that property taxes have risen so high that you may be forced to move to a smaller home. (However, be sure to include positive reasons for the move as well.) Once you've interested someone in your personal story, you're halfway home.

Carry the Ball

After you've visited, send a thank-you note to every person you've met. Then stay in touch through notes or telephone calls. While there's an outside possibility that you'll be offered a job during your initial visit, don't count on it. More likely, the employer will want to size up your seriousness to see if you really will move. As in Joan Glover's case, he'll wait until you've arrived in town to make you an offer.

Subscribe to the Local Newspaper

Take out a six-month subscription to the newspaper of the town in which you've decided to locate. While help-wanted ads may not list every job—especially high-level positions—by scanning them, you'll familiarize yourself with the names of the major employers and community business leaders. It's also worthwhile to read the business news, including new business openings, plant closings and layoffs.

Visit the Library

Here you can check out such resource materials as the *Census of Retail Trade,* the *Census of Manufacturing* and *County Business Patterns.* All three books are published on a state-by-state basis by the Census Bureau and include county-level data. Another book, *Wage Rates in Selected Occupations,* also published at the state level, will help readers determine what people in their fields earn in a given county. And while you're at it, don't overlook the *U.S. Census Report,* which provides a wealth of information about everything from demographics to occupational breakdowns by profession by county.

Don't hesitate to ask for help. "Reference librarians are the best source of information I know," says Susan Vacca, associate director of Harvard University's Career Services Office. "They know what resources are available."

Brainstorm New Options

Making a career decision these days is not as momentous as it once was, in view of how often people change jobs and even careers. As you look at your future, broaden your range of options. Branch out. If your work has been as a home-rental agent, consider getting your real estate license. Or why not try selling cars? Or prefabricated homes?

The experts tell us that one in every five Americans now changes jobs every year, and one in ten changes careers yearly. "On average, a student leaving college today can be expected to have three, four or five careers and ten, eleven or twelve jobs during a work life that will last forty to fifty years," says David L. Birch, formerly a professor of urban studies at MIT, and now the president of Cognetics Inc., a Cambridge, Massachusetts, economic research firm. While we've all heard about the lack of security of today's work world, the upside is that you can explore new and different fields—in search of that perfect fit for you—without necessarily committing yourself for life.

Looking for Work After You've Moved

If you haven't had the chance to launch an extensive job campaign in advance of your move, don't despair. On scene, you'll be able to follow the same steps outlined above—in a more concentrated fashion since presumably you now have full time to devote to a job hunt. An advantage of this approach is that once you're living in town, you'll have a better feel for both the range of jobs available and the range of salary levels and may resist the temptation of accepting the first job that comes along. On site, you'll be able to expand your network more easily than from a distance.

SMALL-TOWN JOB-SEEKING STRATEGIES

Define Yourself More Broadly

In major metropolitan areas, a great many jobs are narrowly defined. In small towns, few are.

When you are seeking a job in a small town, you'll need to define yourself more broadly than when looking for work in the city. Job seekers "must think of themselves in broad terms rather than narrow," says Dr. Joel Worley, professor of management, division of business, Northwestern State University, Natchitoches, Louisiana. This self-definition should be reflected in your thinking about what kind of work you're seeking and should also show up on your résumé.

A long-term benefit of broadening not only your résumé but your career experience is that you'll be adding another string to your proverbial bow, enhancing your professional desirability and versatility. And career experts say that each individual's security in the future will depend—not on any single employer—but on her own efforts. Self-improvement by adding new and developing existing skills is perhaps the best means of building long-term professional security. William Bridges goes so far as to argue in his 1994 cover story in *Fortune* magazine that the job itself "is a social artifact. . . . Today's organization is rapidly being transformed from a structure being built out of jobs into a field of work needing to be done."

Develop New Skills

Skill flexibility—the idea that whenever possible you should broaden your repertoire of marketable skills—while hardly revolutionary has become even more important in this era of corporate downsizing. And it's the law of the land in a small town. A tile layer from the city might learn plumbing to keep himself busy during down times as well as to be able to offer customers the complete bathroom-remodeling package. A writer or editor, for example, might make herself more attractive to small-town employers by learning PageMaker and Quark Express to be able to design, lay out, and produce a company newsletter or advertising circular as well as write it.

If that same writer learned how to operate a camcorder, she could sell herself as a "multimedia person," says Peggy J. Schmidt, a Portola Valley, California, career expert and columnist for *The Boston Herald* and *The Atlanta Constitution.* "A company will look more favorably at a person who can not only do job X, but also job Y."

Create a Job

Defining how you can help a prospective employer, as Joan Glover did when she approached Central Washington University, is one of the most effective approaches to finding work. Skills she had acquired in previous positions matched unmet needs of the university. As director of community relations, her two major objectives were raising funds within the community and creating a parents' association. Once she demonstrated her track record in these areas, "they created the job," she says. "I was lucky. I presented the skills they wanted at the time."

Experts say that selling your capability for doing a job and then selling the job itself—especially in the more limited environment of a small town—is not an uncommon practice.

Look for local businesses with unmet needs, advises Dr. Joel Worley of Louisiana's Northwestern State University. "Go in and tell them: 'It looks to me like you need this and that. I can do it.'"

Prime candidates for this kind of self-marketing are growing businesses in which the principal players who have been doing everything themselves are overextended. Often they're so pressed, they don't even want to take the time to look for someone to help lighten the load. But if you can come in and make a case for your services, you're likely to get some work. Worley cites the case of a young woman who found herself a job by tackling two areas that were being neglected: bookkeeping and PR/advertising.

Piece Together an Income

Often people in small towns don't do just one thing, they do seven. These days, piecing together an income from multiple jobs "is not that unusual," says Karl Coster Jr., the mayor of Cheney, Kansas (population 1,719), who earns his income from three sources, aside from politics. A local man we know co-owns a small motel, a stained-glass-window business and a telephone-installation service. Another operates a VCR-repair shop out of his basement, drives a tractor-trailer and works with ham radios.

This is also our approach. We run a cherry, peach and apple orchard in Carroll County, Virginia; write books and articles; have established a small publishing company, Orchard Gap Press, which has published several books of regional interest; consult with businesses and individuals; teach at Surry Community College in Dobson, North Carolina; do special projects for the Surry Arts Council in our hometown of Mount Airy; and lecture about simple living and writing. Our orchard work is largely seasonal, so we're more likely to be peddling our prose from late fall to spring, and more likely to be pushing fruit from June through November. Wearing various hats, we serve local customers (writing classes and seminars); regional customers (our fruit, the motto of which is "the finest in fruit since 1908"); and national customers (our writing).

KARL COSTER JR.: MAYOR/FARMER/NFL CAMERAMAN

❦ ❦

If Karl Coster Jr., the mayor of Cheney, Kansas, tells you he's a jack of all trades, he's not exaggerating. Indeed, Coster cobbles together his income from four disparate sources, the least lucrative of which is his political office, which pays "about ninety dollars a month," he says.

His best-paying gig is as a cameraman for NFL Films, for which he travels from coast to coast, often shooting the Kansas City Chiefs as well as other teams. It is, he boasts, "the world's greatest part-time job." Together with his mother, he owns and operates a six-hundred-acre wheat and milo farm that's been in the family since 1891. He's a certified property valuation officer for the state of Kansas, for which he hears appeals from people contesting property-tax valuations. And, of course, he's mayor of the bustling burg of Cheney, twenty-five miles west of Wichita.

Though some might find wearing so many hats disorienting, most people would agree that the interplay of professional endeavors brings each one into sharper focus, while funneling in new ideas. "Agriculture satisfies my desire to be close to nature and to experience and participate in those things that are deeply rooted in my identity. It also provides a certain solitude," says Coster, forty-three. His contract photography work for NFL Films feeds his unabashed love of excitement and provides "an outlet for my creativity. You get a real rush when you see the same thing on TV that your mind saw when you were looking through the camera, knowing you're a part of the history of the NFL—a recorder of history." And working as mayor satisfies Coster's idealistic side, his desire to help people and to make Cheney a better place to live.

"I'm the kind of guy who's equally comfortable having a cup of coffee in blue jeans with the guys at the coffee shop and being at a black-tie party in Dallas," he says. "I just like people."

Getting Your Foot in the Door

One surefire method of getting a job in the company of your choice is to go to work there in any capacity, endear yourself to your boss and co-workers and demonstrate your abilities. If you've handled yourself well, when the position you want does open, you'll be in line to get it.

This was the strategy pursued by Carmen Misiaszek, a beeper-wearing nurse-manager at McLean Hospital just outside of Boston, who moved to Newport, Oregon, in 1993. That spring, when she and her husband, Myron, were visiting the town, she filled out an application at the forty-six-bed Pacific Communities Hospital. She was told that positions don't often open up. In July, she began calling the hospital to remind them of her interest. Over the phone, she was offered a job as a per-diem (full-time temporary) nurse on the medical surgical unit.

Though Myron Misiaszek was not ready to fold his lucrative floor-sanding business in Boston, the couple decided to sacrifice togetherness for the sake of long-term stability. "We made a decision at that point if Carmen didn't take this position, that they might take offense," he says. "So Carmen went off to get herself established."

Within six months on the job, Misiaszek was offered a staff position. Ironically, she had come to relish her newfound freedom ("I could set whatever schedule I wanted and only had to work eight hours a day!") and delayed accepting her dream job until August of 1994—just before her husband moved West to join her.

Consider Temping

Just as in the cities, temporary work is a big-time employer in small-town America. And temping offers you several significant advantages over regular employment. It's a good way to scope out a new place, to test out a variety of companies around town and to gain access to the "hidden job market," that is, jobs generally not listed in newspapers, which experts say account for three-quarters of all job openings. What's more, if you prove to be reliable and efficient, your good reputation will spread quickly throughout town.

If there's more than one temporary agency in town, visit them all to compare how the employment consultants treat you and what suggestions they make. Find out what areas (if any) they specialize in and with which companies they typically place workers. If your ultimate goal is full-time work, let them know it. (Temp agencies call these "temp-to-perm" jobs.) You may sign up with more than one agency before deciding which one you want to affiliate yourself with, but remember, just as they're being "auditioned," so are you.

"Someone wanting office work should walk in with a résumé and letters of reference—especially if they're from out of town—and be dressed appropriately," says Teresa D. Yeatts, owner of Surry Temporary Services Inc. in Mount Airy. Once workers are placed into a job, she says, she most appreciates "dependability" and dedication—especially if the worker treats the temporary assignment as if it were a full-time job by "giving 110 percent."

You can also become an "independent temp," meaning that you market yourself independently of an agency. To do this, you approach companies and let them know you're available as a temp worker, emphasizing your areas of specialization. While you can make more money independently, you do have to work hard to market yourself, negotiate your fee and collect your pay. If you're not a natural self-promoter, it might be easier to go with a temp agency, at least initially.

Seek Out Other Urban Expatriates

One effective strategy for finding work is to locate the sympathetic ears of fellow urban expatriates. Having been through this themselves, more than likely, they'll be eager to help you find your way in their town.

"Find someone who's in charge of hiring who was once a native urbanite like you," advises Lisa Angowski Rogak, publisher and editor of *Sticks,* a bimonthly newsletter about rural living published in Grafton, New Hampshire. Be sure to ask about their experience, being careful to do more listening than talking. But be forewarned: Occasionally you'll run into ex–city slickers whose attitude can be best summed up as, "Last one in closes the barn door." Ignore such people.

Attend Professional or Club Meetings

"If there are professional associations in town, attend their monthly meetings," says Morton J. Marcus, an economist with Indiana University School of Business. Call the chamber of commerce to find out whether professional associations hold regular meetings and whether or not they are open to the public. In most cases they will be. Attending them on a regular basis and in professional garb will help to get you acquainted with those working in your field in town. If you let it be known that you're job-hunting and they like you, you're likely to be the first to hear about vacancies.

If you're a member of a service organization like Rotary, Kiwanis or the Lions Club, find out when it meets and make it a point to attend.

Consider a Job in Town

While your long-term plan may be to go into business for yourself, as a newcomer you might consider taking a job in town to open some doors. Indeed, nothing will acquaint you with the workings of the community—its politics, players and resources—so quickly as a job. It's a great way of making contacts and scoping out the potential for your own business.

When Joan and Fritz Glover first moved to Ellensburg, Washington, from Houston in 1988, they had their hands full with their new apple orchard. And even though a paycheck wasn't necessary for their financial survival, Joan Glover sought out a job to fast-track her into community life. "That job was my way of getting to meet a number of interesting people who are my friends today," she says.

Likewise, when Wanda accepted the position as editor of a start-up weekly newspaper in Mount Airy in March of 1992, she accelerated her involvement with the town she's come to love. Although *The Surry Times* failed to find its legs financially and was forced to fold in less than a year, Wanda's time there was well spent establishing a network of relationships in town. As editor, she was invited to join the dynamic Mount Airy Rotary Club, which led to consulting work for the City of Mount Airy, writing the city's application for the 1994 All-America City award and board membership on the United Fund of Greater Mount Airy. Getting to know people on a professional basis—something that was harder working in isolation out of her home office at the orchard—has provided her with a deeper level of involvement with the community.

In fact, her attraction to the town has been so strong that in the fall of 1995, Wanda set up shop in a spacious office over Pages Bookstore on Main Street in Mount Airy that had been vacant for thirty-two years. The landlord, genial, hardworking Floyd E. "Flip" Rees, told her she could have it rent free for a year in exchange for the "sweat equity" involved in removing dead pigeon carcasses and over a quarter-century's accumulation of dust, painting and spackling the walls and buffing the solid oak floors.

REALITY CHECK: ISSUES TO GRAPPLE WITH— MONEY AND STATUS

Your move to a small town is likely to be accompanied by some changes in earnings and status.

Big Fish in a Small Pond

For many, a move from the city to a town represents an enhancement of status, as well as the ability to have a greater impact on one's new community—both professionally and from a community-service perspective. For example, where you were *one* of many professional writers in the city, you may now be the *only* one. Or where you were once a high-powered developer with numerous competitors, you may now command the field.

"The cliché of a big fish in a small pond is an accurate description," says Burke Robertson, a commercial real estate developer who moved with his wife and two school-age daughters to Mount Airy from Charlotte, North Carolina's largest city, in 1991. In 1992, he negotiated the deal for Wal-Mart to build a larger store up the road from its previous location and, the following year, renovated a shopping mall in downtown Mount Airy, which he named "Willow Centre" and into which he moved his own suite of offices.

"You could renovate a building in Charlotte and no one would care, but you do that in Mount Airy and it makes an impact on the community," he says. "That does feel good."

Robertson has quickly risen to leadership positions in a number of organizations ranging from the Greater Mount Airy Chamber of Commerce, to United Fund, to Vision Mount Airy, a public/private advisory committee that created a land-use plan for the city. After Mount Airy was named an All-America City by the National Civic League in 1994—one of just ten in the nation—he volunteered to be co-chairman of the marketing committee. In this capacity, Robertson and committee members designed, ordered and sold such items as golf and T-shirts, lapel pins, plastic cups and baseball hats, and produced and distributed window decals, envelope stickers and street banners downtown. In September of 1994, he accompanied the mayor and the chairman of the county commissioners to the Rose Garden where they accepted a commemorative plaque from President Clinton.

While Robertson had developed seven shopping centers in Charlotte and was active in civic and church affairs, arguably he made less of an impact there in ten years than he has in only four in Mount Airy.

Thank You, Officer, for the Speeding Ticket

When Kevin O'Grady, a twenty-year veteran detective and policeman with the Bronx, New York, Police Department, moved to Damascus, Virginia (population 1,100), in 1993 to assume the job as police chief in a four-person department, he felt as if he were stepping back in time. Instead of delivering bodies to the morgue, he was delivering milk and kerosene to citizens isolated during the blizzard of (March) '93 and conducting police business on his front porch.

"The crime rate in Damascus compared to the Bronx," says the fifty-two-year-old O'Grady, "it's incredible. Whenever you came into the precinct on a Saturday or Sunday morning, there was always a homicide waiting for you. Here you get the normal home break-ins and kids vandalizing property." In a scenario that resembles one of Sheriff Andy and Deputy Barney's escapades on *The Andy Griffith Show*, the most exciting case O'Grady has encountered since moving from New York turned out to be a nonevent. In his first six months on the job, he received an FBI tip that a robber was planning to strike the local bank. The bank was staked out, but the criminal never acted.

Since then, one of O'Grady's larger challenges has been persuading stubborn constituents to install locks on their doors and windows.

Though his salary is "one and a half times less" than it was in the Bronx, his status has skyrocketed. "In New York, if you had to stop a car, you'd brace yourself for a confrontation. People would say: 'No, I'm not speeding,' or 'I didn't run that stop sign.' Here, they admit it. And when you give them a summons, they say, 'Thank you, have a nice day!'"

The staff seems taken with the Yankee in their midst. When an inquiry was made about Chief O'Grady, the clerk answering his telephone gushed: "He's a handsome and charming Irishman and he's doing a great job for us in Damascus!"

But perhaps the biggest boost to O'Grady's ego comes from little things, like the way people in passing cars greet him in his patrol car. "They say hello to you by raising their forefinger off the steering wheel. In New York, if you're in a police car, you always get the middle finger."

You Can Expect to Make Less Money

In most cases, like O'Grady's, even if you take a comparable job in a small town, you can count on earning less money than you did in the city, and you'll need to adjust your expectations accordingly. (But remember, the cost of living—especially housing and property taxes—is also likely to be lower, and, presumably, getting out of the big-bucks rat race is one reason you wanted to move to a small town in the first place.)

Joan Glover's salary was snipped by one-third when she took the job at Central Washington University. She was making in the low forties at Houston's M.D. Anderson Cancer Center, but accepted $29,000 in Ellensburg. And the perks of power all but disappeared when she went from overseeing a staff of ten to having no subordinates and only occasional secretarial help at CWU. But because her quality of life increased, Glover had no trouble making the transition.

Downshifting

When you leave a lucrative and/or prestigious position in the city—one that may be difficult if not impossible to replace—you've got to face the fact that you're downshifting in professional status. Unless you're prepared for it, your ego may be in for a terrific bruising.

Thomas Naylor didn't have to agonize over resigning his position as a tenured professor of economics at Duke University in 1993 in order to move with his wife, Magdalena Naylor, a psychiatrist, and their son, Alexander, to Charlotte, Vermont (population 300), from Richmond, Virginia. Perks and position never meant much to Naylor.

In lieu of teaching at Duke, Naylor took temporary appointments at nearby Middlebury College and the University of Vermont—which pay just a fraction of his Duke salary—and now has more time to devote to writing and working in the community. (The stress of his teaching commitment at Duke had been compounded by his twice-weekly, five-hour, round-trip commute to Durham, North Carolina, from Richmond.) Indeed, the move has reduced the Naylors' total household income by two-thirds, and the perks have all but disappeared. At UVM, in particular, Naylor must park in the outer fringes of campus and walk a distance to his night classes compared to right-behind-the-building parking at Duke.

Many egos could not withstand the comedown. But Naylor says his identity "has always been connected to my work, not to being a Duke professor." The stipend for a recent class at UVM—a new preparation at that—was a mere $4,500, but it turned out to be the "fattest" paycheck he's ever received. The class, "The Search for Meaning in the Workplace," provided inspiration for his current book project by the same name, a follow-up to the recently published *The Search for Meaning* (Abingdon: 1994). Since moving, the fifty-eight-year-old Naylor has more time for things such as regular volunteering in his seven-year-old son's classroom, where he helps students with their spelling and copyedits their group classroom stories, and sitting as the only male on a parents' advisory board—activities that feed his interest in community life. Released from the velvet coffin of his secure, tenured job, he now claims a new lease on life.

"It's exhilarating, uplifting and freeing," he says. "The writing really flows—more so than before!"

But what about the loss of status?

"Oh, that!" He sniffs. "That's for the birds."

QUIZ: ARE YOU AN ENTREPRENEUR OR A COMPANY PLAYER?

Fill out this questionnaire and find out. Select one of the three answers that best describes you.

1. On a daily basis, do you crave office-place camaraderie or prefer your own company?
- Most of the time, I crave camaraderie _____ (1).
- Sometimes I crave camaraderie; sometimes I prefer to be alone _____ (2).
- I mostly prefer my own company _____ (3).

2. Do you prefer giving orders or taking orders?
- I prefer giving orders _____ (1).
- I like a mix of giving and taking orders _____ (2).
- I'd rather take orders _____ (3).

3. Would you rather work among co-workers or work alone without distractions?
- Most of the time, I'd rather work around people _____ (1).
- Sometimes I like to have others around, sometimes to be alone _____ (2).
- Mostly, I'd rather work undisturbed by the distraction of others _____ (3).

4. If a $5,000 windfall came your way, would you rather invest it in a potentially highly profitable venture involving risk or put it in the most secure possible place?
- Since I didn't have the money to begin with, I'd roll the dice and hope to make big bucks _____ (1).
- I'd take some risk for a higher return but would try not to jeopardize it _____ (2).
- I'd put it in the safest investment possible—probably an FDIC-insured bank account _____ (3).

5. If you disagree with someone, are you more likely to set him or her straight or to keep your differences to yourself?
- Most of the time, I speak my mind _____ (1).
- Sometimes I speak out; other times I keep my mouth shut _____ (2).
- Generally, I'd keep quiet so as to avoid disagreement _____ (3).

6. Are you comfortable selling yourself or does self-promotion give you the willies?
- I find it an exciting conquest to meet total strangers and sell them on me _____ (1).
- It depends on my mood. Sometimes I can sell myself; other times I could no more do it than sell copies of *Das Kapital* in Moscow _____ (2).
- I'm almost never comfortable selling myself _____ (3).

7. *Can you easily accept fluctuations in your income or do you need a regular paycheck to feel secure?*
   - I can handle lean financial times because I know that prosperity is right around the corner _____ (1).
   - I can stand some financial uncertainty—but not too much _____ (2).
   - My peace of mind depends upon a steady paycheck _____ (3).

8. *Do you enjoy creating things or would you rather appreciate others' creations?*
   - I have plenty of my own visions and enjoy implementing them _____ (1).
   - I enjoy establishing a balance between my own creativity and that of others _____ (2).
   - Others are more creative than I _____ (3).

9. *Can you detach yourself from professional rejection or do you take it personally?*
   - When rejected, I just shrug it off and move on _____ (1).
   - Depends on my mood. Sometimes it stings terribly ; other times it's not so bad _____ (2).
   - A personal rejection can eat at me for days _____ (3).

10. *Do you like being your own boss—or would you rather have someone else in that role?*
   - I find the idea of being my own boss exciting _____ (1).
   - Sometimes I like to be in control and other times let someone else call the shots _____ (2).
   - I'm more of a support person and would rather someone else run the show _____ (3).

To Score:

Score each response using the numbers in parentheses. Add up your total scores.

• If your score is *between 10 and 16*, you're an *entrepreneur* type, an independent risk-taker who likes making your own decisions. If you're not already working for yourself, you might want to make hanging your own shingle a professional goal.

• If your score is *between 17 and 22*, you're like most people—somewhere *in the middle.* You like a balance between giving and taking orders, between risk and security. You could go either way: Open your own business or work for someone else. In your lifetime, you very well may do some of both.

• If your score is *between 23 and 30*, you're a *company player.* You're loyal and committed but you prefer a safe, secure spot behind the scenes rather than out front. For you, the key is to find a good workplace where your contributions are appreciated and where you can grow with the company.

Copyright © 1995 by Wanda Urbanska and Joanne H. Pratt

QUIZ: DO YOU WANT TO WORK AT HOME?

Whether you're an entrepreneur type or a company player, for more and more people working at home is becoming an option. For many *entrepreneurs* home can be the best place from which to launch a business. If you're a *company player,* you might demonstrate to your employer that becoming a telecommuter is a better deal for you both.

Here's a quiz to determine whether or not you're suited to working at home.

1. Are you a self-starter?
Yes ___ (1) Sometimes ___ (2) No ___ (3).

2. Do you work well independently?
Yes ___ (1) Sometimes ___ (2) No ___ (3).

3. Can you set your own schedule, deliver assignments on time and turn out good quality work without someone breathing down your neck?
Yes ___ (1) Sometimes ___ (2) No ___ (3).

4. Are you able to easily perform tasks at home without being distracted by the refrigerator, the TV, phone calls, drop-in visitors, mail-order catalogs, etc.?
Yes ___ (1) Sometimes ___ (2) No ___ (3).

5. As a social creature, do you need much face-to-face contact with co-workers or customers?
No ___ (1) Sometimes ___ (2) Yes ___ (3).

To Score:
Score each response using the numbers in parentheses. Add up your total scores.

- If you score between *5* and *8*, you would work well at home, either in your own business or as a telecommuter.

- If you score between *9* and *11*, there are roughly equal advantages to working at home and at an office. You could go either way.

- If you score between *12* and *15*, you may be better suited to working out of an employer's office just now.

Copyright © 1995 by Wanda Urbanska and Joanne H. Pratt

BRINGING YOUR BUSINESS WITH YOU

"The Straight Line to Success"

Perhaps you're one of those fortunate souls with an up-and-running business and a loyal customer base and income flow that can be rolled up and moved as easily as an Oriental rug. If so, according to Milan Wall of the Heartland Center for Leadership Development, you're in a near-perfect situation for small-town relocation: "Ideally, you have some business service you can sell to already established customers. Then you start figuring out how to develop different markets after you get there. That's the straight line to success."

If you fit into this mold, you're a "lone eagle," the moniker given by Philip Burgess, of the Center for the New West, to someone with a transportable career and great flexibility regarding where he or she can live. As a result of advances in telecommunications and computer technologies, such people represent a growing segment of the labor market. Experts say that the numbers are increasing in small-town America and elsewhere. "There are 10 million potential lone eagles and their numbers grow with each corporate downsizing, each drive-by shooting," says Burgess.

One such lone eagle who's flown the coop of Manhattan's Upper West Side is Peter Davis, a writer and documentary filmmaker who together with his wife, Karen Zehring Davis, and their two children moved to Castine, Maine, in 1990. From his two-story workshop behind their home, Davis is currently finishing a book on extreme poverty in America.

"Living in Castine provides a cleaner, more pristine, less interrupted atmosphere," says the fifty-nine-year-old writer. "I like *me* better here. Some of the very things that used to stimulate me in New York when I was younger now make me anxious. At some point, the bustle of the city overtook those stimulating qualities and became a little mind-clogging."

Typical of lone eagles, Davis was already well established professionally before making the move. He had won an Oscar for directing the documentary *Hearts and Minds* about the Vietnam War, and more recently, co-produced a two-hour documentary on John F. Kennedy for CBS. The author of three books, he finds his career in full throttle; in fact, he has *more* city contacts than he needs. What Davis needs at this stage in his career is *less* of the rush of the marketplace and more solitude for production. "The city is where you communicate," he says. "The town is where you concentrate. You collect elsewhere and recollect here."

Lone eagles could be working in such fields as consulting, brokerage sales or advertising design. (Other "birds" identified by Burgess are "wise old owls" (retirees), "country hawks" (back-to-the-landers) and "golden eagles" (the independently wealthy.)

Lone eagles don't have to be high fliers to make the city-to-country transition work for them. They can be in support fields, such as data processing and secretarial services. When Lesley Loftus O'Grady moved from New York to Damascus, Virginia, in 1993, she brought her part-time typing and transcription work for large securities firms in New York City with her. It makes no difference to her employers whether their contract work is done in the Bronx or in Southwest Virginia—as long as the job is done quickly and accurately. "They Fed-Ex it down to me," she says. For this, she earns on average ten dollars to twelve dollars an hour (sometimes more, as she's paid by the page)—money that she funnels into her hobby of antiquing and picking up collectibles at flea markets.

Likewise, Wanda found that the payments she receives for writing articles for such publications as *The Washington Post, Los Angeles Times,* and *Shape* stretch further in the country than they ever did in the city. And because she'd already demonstrated her abilities to editors before relocating, her location was no strike against her. In many cases, New York and Los Angeles publications are only too eager to have representation in the hinterlands. And for freelancers, there's a double boon: if you're already established, they don't cut their rates because your cost of living is lower.

For migratory "birds," the expense of relocation (covered in Chapter 4) and new office setup will be the primary costs when moving to a small town.

LOWERING THE COST OF DOING BUSINESS

A major motivation for many entrepreneurs and small business owners to move to a small town is to lower the cost of doing business. In America's small towns, you can find cheaper labor, lower taxes, less expensive office or warehouse space and a lower cost of living for your employees and yourself.

Dave and Mary Jo Burnett moved from Long Island, New York, to Alliance, Nebraska, in 1989 and expanded Burnington's, Inc., their locomotive parts supply business, which sells primarily to customers overseas. "We bought a 4,000-square-foot building, an old Sears store, for $40,000," says Dave Burnett. "You couldn't look at a building like that—suitable for forklifts—in the city for less than half a million." The company is now grossing seven figures and last year its net income topped $100,000. Husband and wife run the business together with the help of one other full-time employee and two part-timers.

"Frontier locations offer significant savings in head-office costs," writes author David A. Heenan. "Within the same region, these expenses can be 20 to 50 percent lower than they are in the city or suburbs. Naturally, cost-conscious companies want to pinch every penny."

Former Washington, D.C., resident John Springthorpe entered into a business partnership with his brother, Bruce, and they now co-own SouthData, a coupon-book printing business for banks and others in Mount Airy. Springthorpe says a lower-wage, higher-caliber labor force is one reason for the success of their nine-year-old company. "We can find people here who don't mind putting in a day's work. We're not the best-paying people in town, but we're also not the worst." The commute time in Mount Airy is neglible, and SouthData offers employees "more flexibility" than they could find at other businesses—the ability to leave early if a child is sick, or take a lunch hour at an odd time to make a dental appointment. Many employees find this kind of flexibility worth slightly lower wages.

FROM PART-TIME INCOME TO FULL-TIME WORK

Frustrated that he didn't have enough time to do what he loved most—carve waterfowl—Chris Murray and his family made a bold move. In 1984, they left suburban Philadelphia where they owned and operated three wildlife gallery/art shops and moved to tiny coastal Castine, Maine, where he hung a shingle and began to carve decorative wooden birds full time.

The profitable shops sold wildlife art, carving tools, artists' supplies and what few duck decoys Murray had had time to carve. But the shops demanded eighty- to ninety-hour work-weeks from Murray and his wife, Lynn Johnson Murray. And as their retail trade increased, Murray's carving languished, and he had less and less time for his wife and their two sons, Keith and John. "We were spending no time together, going crazy," he says.

Although Murray knew he could make money from carving ornamental decoys, he didn't know if he'd be able to support his family over the long haul. "I'm not making as much money as before, but I don't owe anyone money," says Murray. "I own my own home. I make a good income."

His stress level has fallen and the blood-pressure problems that he'd developed in Philadelphia in retailing (and earlier, broker-ing cement) have disappeared.

"There's still a little stress, because I have deadlines and com-mitments, but I have to answer to myself," he says. "If I want to go to the variety store and get a soda, I put a note on the door: 'Back in fifteen minutes.'"

Murray's story exemplifies Milan Wall's prescription for lone-eagle success: Bring a core base of customers with you to your new locale, then build upon that base. Murray brought with him to Castine a year's worth of commissions along with a tidy nest egg from the sale of his three shops and home. But still, the move came with no guarantee of success.

Setting up shop first in a back porch of their early-1800s Federal-style house on Main Street and later in what had been a "dilapidated old garage" before it was remodeled, Murray threw himself into the business of carving anatomically correct ducks, swans and the like, for which collectors pay thousands. He now carves between thirty to thirty-five pieces a year—which range in price from $350 for a simple swan to $25,000 for a highly detailed, world-class waterfowl tableau—and has seen his business grow each year in profitability and recognition. "Since I've been able to devote 100 percent of my time to waterfowl carving, business has improved dramatically," he says.

For three years running, Murray has placed first in his class in the Ward World Championship Carving Competition held annually in Ocean City, Maryland. Perhaps his greatest professional triumph came in 1994 during the presentation of one of his prize-winning birds, a common merganser valued at $6,000, on behalf of the Maine Republican Party to former President George Bush at his summer home in Kennebunkport. The bird had won first place in the decorative floating division at the 1991 championships. When the bird call came from the Republicans, the merganser was on display in a glass case in Murray's shop. Initially reluctant to part with it, he quickly recognized that the public relations value alone made such a generous gift worthwhile.

"Just to get a shot of the president with my bird into my portfolio was worth it. And I got a nice write-off, too." Already one of Bush's Houston friends has dropped into the shop and taken note of the giant framed photograph of Murray, Bush and the bird.

Not that he needs more publicity. From his perch in Castine, Murray's reputation has grown worldwide. He sells pieces to collectors in New Zealand, Japan and France. He's also sold to such celebrities as Jack Nicklaus, Meg Tilly and the late Thomas Watson. Customers dock their yachts or sailboats at the harbor and take the short walk up Main Street to his shop.

The evolution of his work and his thinking (a former hunter, he's long since given up the sport) is intertwined with his move to

Maine. "Castine is a natural setting for what I do because it offers abundant resource material day in and day out. Most of the species I carve live here: songbirds, water birds and raptors. I walk the shoreline and get most of my ideas viewing birds in and around the town."

SUPPORT SERVICES FOR THE INFORMATION AGE

If you plan to go into business for yourself or become a telecommuter, you'll need to do some digging to make sure the support services provided to the town are up to snuff.

Jim Schriner, a partner with the Chicago-based PHH Fantus, one of the nation's premier corporate relocation specialists, says a key requirement for businesses considering setting up shop in the hinterlands is that a "communications infrastructure" be in place. "The U.S. has on the order of 1,400 independent phone companies, most of which provide local phone access, the critical link to the outside world," he says. Their offerings vary and, in some remote areas, telephone service is surprisingly outdated.

The following eight questions, provided by the Denver-based Center for the New West, should help you determine whether or not the town has the services to make it business-friendly. These questions should be asked of businesspeople in town, economic developers and (if you're considering a home-based business) prospective neighbors.

1. Is electric service reliable and consistent? Are there frequent power outages that could destroy computer files and equipment?

2. Is phone service reliable and advanced enough to handle fax and modem?

3. Does the community offer advanced telecommunica-

tions, including one-party, voice-grade, touch-tone, 9,600 baud with enhanced services such as voice messaging, call waiting and call forwarding?

4. Is there computer-based digital switching, wireless telephony, including digital cellular/mobile services?

5. Is there access to cable or satellite TV news?

6. Is there local access to Internet or other on-line services?

7. Is there access to overnight mail services?

8. Are you within a one-hour commute of a commercial airport?

CITY BUSINESS, RELOCATED
A Key to Success—Aggressive Marketing
Master clockmaker Joseph R. "Ray" Bates already had a successful, full-time business going in Boston when he and his wife, Beverly Bates, moved to bucolic Newfane, Vermont, (population 119) thirty years ago. They bought an enormous old house in town that in previous incarnations had been a mill and an inn. The building was large enough to serve as a staging ground for raising their three sons as well as to accommodate both of their businesses (Ray Bates set up his shop, The British Clockmaker, in the inn's former bar, and Beverly Bates later established her speech-pathology office at the other end of the house).

Because of the specialized nature of his work, Bates figured much of his clock-repair clientele would follow him from Boston. ("I'm one of the few craftsmen in the United States, trained in England, where I spent five years serving an apprenticeship in the design and manufacture of clocks," he says.) His calculation proved correct.

"It doesn't matter where I am," says the sixty-three-year-old clockmaker. "With Federal Express, UPS and faxes, I could be anywhere."

However, when he first moved to Newfane, Bates wanted to make certain that his business would fly and so was "pretty aggressive" about marketing. "I was aware of the fact that you can't plunk yourself down in town and say, 'Hey, I'm here; bring me your business.' We cast a wide net. I'd target an area and saturate it with ads in newspapers and magazines like *Yankee* and *Vermont Life.*" Even today, with more work than he can handle, he continues to underwrite radio ads on Vermont Public Radio.

"The public is very short in memory," says the native of Scotland, now a naturalized American. "You have to hit them over the head with a two-by-four to keep their attention. My thrust is education. I want to make the public aware of the quality of antique clocks: how fragile they are. You'd be amazed at how many people take a clock worth $100,000 to a guy that tinkers with clocks. Fifty percent of my work is undoing damage done by amateurs."

Although he's capable of building a clock from scratch—a feat he had to accomplish in order to attain Master Clockmaker status in Scotland—his "mission" as he sees it, is "to save as many of these antique clocks as I can, to bring them back to their original mechanical integrity, using all the same techniques and materials from their periods."

Although almost none of his business comes from the tiny town of Newfane, the town does provide an ideal base. Between living "over the shop" and having the friendly eyes of neighbors watching the place when Bates and his wife are gone, Bates has never had his valuable inventory burglarized.

Today, The British Clockmaker is so successful that even working fifty- to sixty-hour weeks with his eldest son, Philip (an apprentice and future partner), he still has a year's backlog of business. He turns business away. "I work solely on antiques," he says. "I don't touch anything that's mass-produced." Bates has worked on clocks in Old Sturbridge Village, Massachusetts, and

Mystic Seaport, Connecticut, and has a contract to keep running some one thousand grandfather clocks at Dartmouth College in neighboring New Hampshire.

Having established himself in such a highly specialized niche, he now attracts the public in droves. It's not uncommon for people to fly their clock mechanisms in from California; more frequently, customers make the four-hour drive from New York City and Montreal or the two-hour drive from Boston. And Bates makes house calls, going on average every six weeks to Boston and every three months to Montreal. But he draws the line at traveling into Manhattan. ("It's such an uncivilized place," he says.)

Though he won't divulge figures, The British Clockmaker says he is doing well. "We live very well. A lot of people envy us. Still, you have to work at it. You have to have a unique skill, a niche market. And you have to beat the bushes and keep your name in front of the public."

STARTING OVER WITH SOLID SKILLS

Like Bates, Myron Misiaszek brought with him a set of practical skills to his new hometown. But unlike the lucky lone eagles who can carry their "booty" (namely their meal-making clients) with them, the floor sander from Boston could hardly service old customers from his new base in Newport, Oregon. He had to make a fresh start with a local clientele.

Still, Misiaszek believes his big-city experience and efficiency will give him an edge in Newport's slower-paced work climate. "People here are not used to prompt service," he says. "The old adage is: In California they do things tomorrow; on the Oregon coast, they do things next week." This sluggish status quo provides Misiaszek's BCM Hardwood Floors with a competitive advantage, which he intends to exploit to launch his business. He vows to return every call that comes in the same day and to deliver his services on time.

With thirteen years of business experience under his . . . well . . . feet, Misiaszek's strategy is to work with homeowners rather than contractors and to get his name out by word of mouth. He expects BCM Hardwood Floors to become a well-established player in Lincoln County in a matter of months. "When I started this business, I used to worry about phone calls coming in. But no more. You do your best to acquire new business in terms of getting the word out. If we don't have enough business here, we can go to a larger (nearby) city like Corvalis or Salem and get business."

But really, he's not worried. "The market here for quality service is equal to or higher than the Boston market because of the newcomers coming in and lack of expertise," he says. "It will work out."

PROVING YOURSELF ALL OVER AGAIN

No matter how proficient you are—even if you were a big shot in your field in the city—don't assume that your reputation will carry you to success in your new town. In establishing yourself in a small town, you'll need to walk a fine line between tooting your horn and keeping quiet. If you come off as smug and superior, you'll be viewed with wariness, but if you keep mum about your past professional life, people may conclude you were a do-nothing or are running from defeat.

It's best to talk in general terms about your career, focusing on your goals in this new setting, using examples from past accomplishments to illustrate what you might be capable of doing in the future. Provide detail only if the listener is genuinely curious or interviewing you for a job. Always bear in mind that *you're* the new kid on the block. You have to prove yourself all over again.

Betsy Ogden was a dancer and choreographer in New York City for twenty-seven years before moving with her husband to Thorp, Washington (population 150), where they bought a spread that they turned into a commercial dude ranch. Trying to pick up extra income by teaching dance to children in nearby Ellensburg proved to be an eye-opener for Ogden, who'd danced in *Promises, Promises* on Broadway and "assistant choreographed" *The Act* for Liza Minnelli. The lesson: she had to start at square one.

"I taught for twenty years in New York City. Students used to come to me to study; they used to seek *me* out," she says. In Ellensburg, her dance classes were competing with volleyball and cheerleading. "Here, everyone's nine years old and white with blond hair," Ogden says. "I would show them a step and then they'd decide if they wanted to learn it or not. They didn't know—or care—who I was. You get put in your place real fast. You can't take anything for granted."

At first, she was chagrined by the lack of respect. But in the end, having no laurels on which to rest forced Ogden to approach dance in a whole new way. "I had to *make* them want to dance. I had to make it fun. Forget technique. I've learned to simplify and make dance less complex."

Now, she says proudly, her students regularly reach the pinnacle of performance success in Ellensburg. "They always win the fifty-dollar prize in the Kiwanis talent show."

BECOMING A BUSINESS PARTNER

You may find opportunities in your field in small towns that might be unavailable to you in a city; in some cases, you may even be able to advance *further* in a given profession—as Misiaszek believes he will—than you could in a city. Such was the case when Ann Moltu Ashman moved with her husband to Elkin, North Carolina, from Stamford, Connecticut, in 1983. (She'd previously lived in San Francisco and Washington, D.C.) She brought with her eight years of experience in the insurance industry. After having two children and taking three years off to care for them, she was ready to go back to work.

At the end of her maternal hiatus, Ashman found a golden opportunity: the chance to purchase an interest in a prosperous and well-run independent agency, Insurance Service Center Inc., of which she's now vice president and junior partner. With small independent agencies dwindling in the wake of industrywide consolidations, Ashman jumped at the chance.

"I guess I was just lucky," she says. "I feel like this sort of opportunity would not come my way were we living in the city."

It wasn't just luck. During Ashman's three years of child rearing she'd worked hard to achieve the rigorous CPCU (chartered property casualty underwriter) and CIC (certified insurance counselor) credentials, all the while developing a relationship with the company's owner, Ben Mastin.

"Such businesses are usually passed down from generation to generation," explains Ashman. "Because Ben didn't have an heir to take it over, it meant an opportunity for me." The two worked out a ten-year payment schedule that was both fair and reasonable, but stopped short of breaking the Ashmans' bank account. "From a financial standpoint, this is not something I could swing were I living elsewhere."

Since Ashman came aboard, the agency has continued to prosper. And her career has flourished both locally and statewide. Being invited to join the prestigious board of directors of the Carolina Association of Professional Insurance Agents was a "tremendous honor" she says, one that would never have come about in the city. She credits the honor to co-owning the company and earning credentials shared by less than "1 percent of licensed property and liability agents nationwide"—two milestones that the slower pace and decreased financial pressure of small-town life enabled her to achieve.

WORKING AT HOME
"Open-Collar Workers" and the Savings of Home Offices

If you're bringing your business with you to a small town—or starting up a new venture—you're likely to set up shop initially in your new home. This could be a temporary arrangement while you're getting the lay of the land and deciding where to rent or lease office space. Or it could evolve into a long-term arrangement.

Starting a business from home enables you to keep start-up costs low, helping to put you on the road to profitability more quickly. According to Paul and Sarah Edwards, authors of *Working From Home,* setting up a home office can save you on average from $7,000 to $20,000 a year on office rental. What's more, they write, it enables you to test out new business ideas and keep more of what you earn.

Should you decide to work at home, you're part of a growing group of Americans whom the Edwardses call "open-collar workers." While a generation ago, a stigma was attached to working at home, which people viewed as a euphemism for being unemployable, today it has achieved widespread respectability.

"There's an increasing trend toward working at home, or 'away from the office' is a better way to put it," says Abhijeet Rane, a senior analyst for LINK, a New York City research and consulting firm of the electronic information services industry. The Bureau of Labor Statistics reports that home workers now comprise 31 percent of the U.S. workforce above the age of eighteen. A LINK survey put the number of work-at-home households in 1994 in the United States at 36 million—a 6.5 percent increase over the year before. The company divides home workers into four distinct groups: primary self-employed workers, part-time self-employed workers, after-hours corporate workers, and telecommuters. Nearly 30 percent of all home workers are primary self-employed workers.

Telecommuting

If you're already a self-employed or company-employed telecommuter, you have perhaps the easiest means of relocating. You can simply fold your tent and tote your business to any new locale. (Or you may be employed by a company that will allow you to move to the location of your choice.) If all the chips fall into place, the consequences will be few.

Rane says that certain occupations are tailor-made for telecommuting. "Any job that involves a large proportion of information gathering, information dissemination and information management is well-suited for a location other than an office. If you have the right access equipment, you can do your job anywhere: at home, at a beach or on a mountainside."

For book producer and employment expert Peggy Schmidt, the move in 1992 from the Upper West Side of Manhattan first to Atherton and later Portola Valley, California, was professionally uneventful. "When you're at your computer all day, it doesn't matter where you are. I've been telecommuting for seven years. I started by telecommunicating my column on careers to *The New York Times*. Now it's a way of life."

As a book producer who packages, sells and delivers camera-ready manuscripts to publishers, Schmidt stays in contact with lots of writers, whose locations are irrelevant. "I don't care where anyone is. Washington, New York, wherever." Schmidt makes only one demand of them: that they sign on to one of the on-line services so that they can send her files electronically. A few of her writers, she admits, have had to be "dragged kicking and screaming onto the information highway." However, once the ride begins, they're invariably grateful for the tug.

TOP TEN TELECOMMUTING PROFESSIONS
FOR SMALL TOWNS

The Center for the New West compiled the following list of professions that are most easily transferable to small towns. These telecommuting lone eagles can serve nationwide or worldwide markets.

1. Accountants

2. Lawyers

3. Stockbrokers

4. Marketing/public relations consultants

5. Business management consultants

6. Environmental consultants

7. Political consultants

8. Freelance writers

9. Researchers/information specialists using electronic data bases

10. Software developers

From Home Business to Specialty Antique Shop

Many people use their homes as new-business incubators, hatching future firms in warm and fuzzy environments before moving to larger quarters. In 1988, when Michael Belanger left Manhattan with his partner, Gary DiMauro, for tiny Tivoli, New York (population 1,039), in Dutchess County along the Hudson River, he started his antique business in his . . . well . . . church. (Actually, his 5,000-square-foot home had *been* an Episcopal church and boys' school up until 1969. The two men bought the two-acre property with its Civil War monument on the front lawn for $192,000 and have spent countless hours and dollars in the intervening years upgrading it.)

Even though he started small, Belanger did not start from scratch. "I'd been doing interior-design work in the city to supplement my acting," he says. "It involves a lot of shopping. I would travel a lot in the country and became familiar with the sources. I began to develop an appreciation for and knowledge of the antiques business. Interior-design work and selling antiques are a perfect blend of occupations. When I'm out buying for clients, I can buy for the shop as well. The two complement each other."

Both men set up businesses in their historic home, formerly Trinity Church and School. Belanger dealt antiques from a downstairs room, and DiMauro sold real estate from the priests' robing room above.

"Selling out of the house allowed me to establish a reputation, a following, and learn the business. It gave me leeway before opening the shop and let me build up capital." It also enabled him to develop a look—a specialty—which every dealer likes to have. His "look" is the American Empire and Gothic Revival furniture that is well suited to his own interior.

An added benefit that their Italianate brick 1854 house—located just off Broadway in downtown Tivoli—brought to Belanger's business in its start-up phase were tourists who would wander by and, assuming it to be a public building, come in. The downside to working out of their home was that things could "get a little hectic," admits Belanger. "You want to come home and have privacy. But you never know when there'll be a knock on the door."

Last year, Belanger and DiMauro both outgrew their home quarters and rented side-by-side storefronts just around the corner from their home. Belanger named his company J. S. Clark & Co. for the first rector of the church, who also ran the boys' school and was Tivoli's first mayor. "People constantly ask for Mr. Clark," he laughs. "We have to tell them, we're the 'and company.'"

"We're living in this nineteenth-century village, with a nineteenth-century lifestyle," he says. "We just walk around the corner to work."

TWELVE TIPS FOR DOING BUSINESS OUT OF YOUR HOME
1. Never Remind a Client That You're Working at Home.
Home-office users need to do everything possible to make their home-offices "invisible" to the client, advises Joanne H. Pratt, a Dallas-based telecommuting consultant and author of *Myths and Realities of Working at Home: Characteristics of Homebased Business Owners and Telecommuters.* Never mention that your toilet has overflowed; your child has a nosebleed; or that you didn't catch the phone on the first ring because you were just stepping out of the shower. "Be sure there are no noises of children and animals in the background," Pratt says.

By the same token, never gloat about what a wonderful life you have. "No one has to know that as I'm sitting here talking with her on the phone, I'm watching a family of quail walking by outside my window," says Peggy Schmidt, who works out of her home office in Portola Valley, California.

Personal references are likely to either annoy clients (you're not focusing on them) or inspire envy (how come *I* can't be at home during the day?) Unless a client specifically asks what it's like to work out of your home, don't volunteer anything. If he does inquire, give a succinct, upbeat report: "It's great working at home where you don't have to send out for coffee!"

2. Watch What You Call Your Office.

Always refer to your office as simply your office or your home of-fice. Never say that you're "working at home," advises Pratt. "'At home' has a residential ring to it. It sounds to others like you're sitting around the den with a yellow pad on your knee. How you think of yourself communicates to the world."

Women especially must safeguard against the impression that they're just hobbyists or really housewives trying to pick up a few extra bucks.

3. Develop a Winning Telephone Manner.

When you are conducting business on the phone (and who doesn't these days?), a winning phone manner is vital to your success. Be sure to use a positive, confident (but not pushy) tone when calling; plan in advance not only what you're going to say but how you're going to say it.

"There's a whole strategy and psychology about when in the day to begin your phone calls, when to stop making them," says public relations consultant Bonni Kogen-Brodnick, who works out of a home office in rural Pound Ridge, New York (population 4,664). Kogen-Brodnick routinely pitches stories to print and television media. "There's a certain hour of the day—after four P.M.—when you'd never pitch a story to a print editor. They've been hearing them all day. You might as well wait till the next morning."

Likewise, Kogen-Brodnick cautions against starting too early.

"Never start at nine A.M. Nine-thirty is early. Ten is off and running."

When you're making cold calls, listen for the kind of person you've reached—whether he seems pressed for time or eager for company. "I listen to whether I should talk fast or slow," says Kogen-Brodnick. There are some people who you can anticipate will be busy. "If I'm calling *Good Morning America,* I've got to remember that they're under enormous pressure. They don't want to schmooze. You have to get to the point in thirty seconds or less." For others, establishing a friendly rapport—which might involve fifteen minutes of shooting the breeze—could help clinch the deal.

Such sensitive telephone skills apply not only to those dealing with the media, but to anyone selling to any client, customer or boss.

4. Minimize Talk About Yourself.
You may be an incredible ham or a gifted athlete or you may be blessed with the world's most amazing family. But when servicing a client, don't waste his or her time bragging about yourself. "If I were in a client's position, I wouldn't want to hear about my personal life, either," says one home-based consultant who bills clients $85 an hour. Keep your theme on business unless, of course, the client chooses to stray. In that case, let him or her define the length, tone and subject of the digression.

5. Be Sure to Have Adequate Telephone Equipment.
Nothing signals an amateur operation so quickly as an inadequate telephone system. If you don't wish—or can't afford—to add a second business line to your home office, Joanne H. Pratt recommends training the family to answer the phone like an answering service. For example: "Hello, this is 555-4837." If the call is for you and you're not in, have your spouse or teenager take it professionally, inquiring when the best time is for you to return the call. (Be sure to leave message pads and pens at every phone.

If your teenagers need an incentive, you can reward them by paying them anywhere from a quarter to a dollar for every message taken completely.)

6. Invest in Premium, Top-Quality Stationery.

This presents the image of professionalism to your client, which is *especially* important if you're working from home. Kogen-Brodnick typically spends between $500 and $600 for an order of 1,000 sheets of heavy-stock letterhead and 1,000 envelopes. Her "signature" typeface—a Gothic typeface in eggplant ink on cream paper—has followed her from numerous addresses right through to her last move in 1991 to Pound Ridge. She also has a stamp made up in the same lettering to use on oversize parcels and manilla envelopes. "Everything's got to look professional," she says.

Pricey?

Not when you put it in perspective. "When I'm working here, my stationery is my outfit, my presentation," says Kogen-Brodnick. "I no longer invest in clothing or shoes like I did when I was in the city. What I would've spent on an Armani suit, for example, is spent instead on letterhead and envelopes."

7. Keep Your Home and Office Separate.

Ideally, you should have a separate room, wing, floor or cottage for your business. But if you're just getting started or are tight on space and have to use one room for both living and working, be sure to put up a partition, screen or bookshelf that clearly defines the boundaries between home and "office."

"Having separate work space is paramount to sanity," says one home worker, speaking for many. "If you can't get away from the office, it'll overtake life."

That is precisely the trap that we fell into when Frank set up his home-office desk in the bedroom and Wanda put hers in the living room of our small apartment in West Los Angeles. We could never escape our work, which quite literally overtook our lives. We never made the connection between our ceaseless desire to go away weekends and the encroachment of our home-offices into our home life. In hindsight, we might have been better off converting the bedroom into a home office and used the living room as a kind of studio apartment with a sofabed, TV and dining area. This would have allowed us the opportunity to shut out our work at the end of the day.

Chris Murray, the wildfowl carver in Castine, Maine, has the ideal setup. His workshop is a freestanding building just a few steps from the house. In it, Murray has not only all the tools of his trade, but "all the amenities" including a TV and VCR on which to watch (or at least listen to) movies while he's carving and a cot on which to nap during down times. Even though his real bed is just a backyard's length away, he says he prefers taking daytime naps in his studio. "You have to maintain a separation between work and home for concentration," he says.

8. Make Sure the Infrastructure of Your Office is Sound.
Arrange adequate storage space for files—those that exist now and in anticipation of the future. Buy file cabinets and shelving with generous room for expansion. Designate a special area for supplies. A writer, for instance, will need to keep ample supplies of legal pads, pens, highlighters and stationery. Another area should be set aside for the bookkeeping of your business, such as your business checkbook, tax receipts and accounts payable and receivable.

9. Create a Comfortable—and Professional—Office Space.
Invest in furniture that reinforces your sense of professional self and into which you'd feel comfortable inviting clients. Select furnishings that can be rearranged to accommodate different situations and arrangements, such as a modular couch, but be sure that what you select speaks to your spirit.

Kogen-Brodnick says her home office is furnished much like the office of her first job, about which she feels sentimental. "My office here reminds me of my office at *Glamour*—all white Formica."

Wanda is more of a pack rat and has arranged the top shelf over her copier with a mélange of stuffed animals, the mask of El Diablo that her father brought back from Central America in the 1960s and a jellybean-filled champagne bottle on which a friend painted "Congratulations Wanda!" when her first book was published in 1986.

Invest in *ergonomic chairs* that will increase your productivity, especially if you're working at a computer all day.

The beauty of creating your own space is that you can tailor it to meet your needs—within the limits of your budget. Consider what's most important to you. For Wanda, an office without windows would be a depressing holding tank, whereas to others, the passing scene is mere distraction. Newsletter publisher Lisa Angowski Rogak selected a windowless cubicle in the middle of her Grafton, New Hampshire, home over a side bedroom at the end of the house. "I figured here I wouldn't be distracted by looking out the window." An added wintertime benefit, she admits, is, "I'm warmer."

10. Bring Technology into Your Home Office.

In most cases, it's a necessity to outfit your home office with up-to-date technological equipment. Indeed, LINK Resources' Abhijeet Rane says that the use of such technology—including personal computers, laptop computers, fax machines, modems, on-line computer services and mobile products such as mobile phones—is exploding.

According to LINK's 1993 survey of telecommuters, 55 percent of those surveyed owned their own personal computers; 21 percent owned cellular phones and 14 percent owned personal fax machines. In our case, we are well supplied with a copier, three computers, a fax machine and a modem on our Macintosh.

11. Set Work Hours and Stick to Them Religiously.

Work for yourself as you would if you were punching a time-clock. Bonni Kogen-Brodnick is always at her desk by 9:15 sharp to collect her thoughts before starting to make pitch calls at 10

A.M. In our case, when we're wearing our writing hats, we've set business hours between 8 A.M. and 6 P.M. and have put our family and friends on notice that at these hours we're not to be interrupted.

"When I'm on assignment, it's full-tilt boogie at my desk," says Kogen-Brodnick. She rarely even stops for lunch, often going at it on the phone or into her computer for six or seven hours straight. When she's in her home office, Kogen-Brodnick describes her work mode as one of "monofocus."

12. Check the Local Zoning Codes.

That way you will be sure you can legally do business out of your home. Simply visit or call the town hall and request a copy of the local zoning ordinances. If home offices are legally allowed, your operation is likely to have such restrictions imposed as limiting outside signage and lighting as well as the number of parking spaces. If there are no restrictions on the books, you may be required to get special permission from the planning office or zoning board to keep it legal. If so, you may have to make the case before the planning board that your home business won't disturb the residential character of your neighborhood.

STARTING SOMETHING NEW

While the safest bet after relocating to a small town is to look for work and accept a position with a steady paycheck, this is rarely the most adventurous route. It *is* possible for a newcomer to start something from scratch in a small town, though experts advise caution—especially if your customer base is to be local. Milan Wall of the Heartland Center for Leadership Development warns against what he calls "multiple innovations." Better, he says, to bring a preexisting business with you to a new town, or to try out a new business in familiar territory.

However, given all the contingencies of life, that isn't always possible. And if you're looking for a *total* life change (location and job), you may want to take the plunge with a new business right from the get-go.

Frank Crail, co-owner of a small computer consulting firm in San Diego, did precisely that. In 1981, he plunged into a new business in a new town, founding the Rocky Mountain Chocolate Factory in Durango, Colorado (population 12,439). The company has now entered small-start-up business lore. In 1995, *Money* magazine named it the No. 1 chocolate in the country based on a taste test, and *Success* magazine ranked the company No. 7 on its list of 100 best franchises in America.

Perhaps what's most remarkable about the success of Rocky Mountain Chocolate Factory is how casually Crail, now the CEO, entered into it. When he moved to Durango, he knew only two things—that he wanted to raise his family in a small town and that he thought it "would be fun to run a retail business." He didn't have a clue about what business to start.

Once in town, he checked around for suggestions. "The answer came back that they needed a car wash, but I'm not the car-wash type," he says. A T-shirt salesman suggested that Durango needed a candy shop, and Crail figured that between the summer tourists and the peak demand for chocolate from Christmas through Easter, he'd be able to "make a go of it." He went back to Southern California to quiz candy merchants and arrange for a $50,000 bank loan. "It was all (done) by the seat of the pants," he says.

Today, the company employs 200, has projected 1995 sales of $20 million and produces 1.6 million pounds of chocolate annually for its 152 stores nationwide and in Canada. In 1995, "we'll put up fifty new stores," says Crail, now fifty-three.

How did he get from point A to point B?

By hanging in there and hanging tough through hard times. "The business almost went broke a couple of times," he says. Though he did not receive help from local economic developers and financial institutions when he was trying to grow his business (or when it was on the verge of collapse), Crail holds no

grudges. "No one's going to come to your rescue. Whether growing a business or raising a family, *you* have got to make it happen
yourself," he says. Though he's been courted by other communities in recent years, he remains committed to Durango.

"I have the best of both worlds running a 20 million-dollar
company in a small town. It's nice to be in a place where you
know most of the people and like the majority of them. We're
treated very well in town. The company gets a lot of respect. People are happy and proud that there's a business in Durango that's
gotten national attention and is not just tourist-oriented."

If you'd like to take the tack of starting something from
scratch, like Crail, you'd better get used to the idea of taking
risks. Unless you start extremely small, there's a good chance
you'll find your business to be undercapitalized. Because conventional financing for most new, home-based businesses is virtually
nonexistent, you're likely to go into debt to get yours going, and
you may have to wait for years in order to start seeing much clear
income. When you're starting out, most likely you'll be working
on several fronts: to build a customer base and your own expertise, while pumping whatever profits you do generate back into
the business.

Starting a new business can be as all-consuming and frustrat-
ing (and satisfying) as tending a newborn: you'd never guess by
its size how hungry it could be or how much nourishment—and
attention—it needs in order to grow.

Still, if you're dreaming of becoming an entrepreneur, you're
unlikely to be daunted by these negatives. Your dreams of inde-
pendence, control and being your own boss and your belief in
your business idea will cause you to forge ahead. And you'll by no
means be alone. Indeed, experts say that today growth-oriented
small businesses provide the leading source of job creation in the
U.S.

Author David A. Heenan cites such corporate Cinderella stories born in the heartland as Wal-Mart Stores Inc., J. M. Smucker
Co. and L. L. Bean Inc. to make the point that an obscure location need not have a "negative impact on earnings." "(M)any of

this country's most famous corporate names built their reputations in 'the sticks.'"

NEW BUSINESS STRATEGIES
Finding a Niche

Newcomers who make it are adept at going into a new town or community, looking around for a while, spotting an unmet need and finding a way to fill it. "If you want to use one word, it's finding a 'niche' that's not being filled," says Dr. Kenneth Stone, professor of economics at Iowa State University in Ames, an expert on the impact that Wal-Mart stores have on small-town retailing and author of *Competing with the Retail Giants.*

Niche businesses are often singular in character, catering to specific customer bases—local, regional, national or even international. Many are highly specialized. The nineteen rural niche Nebraska businesses spotlighted in *What's Behind Small Business Success: Lessons From Rural Communities,* a book produced by the Heartland Center, range from a company out of Friend (population 1,111) that makes custom-sized sheet sets, comforters and mattress pads for truck cab sleepers, to one in Broken Bow (population 3,778) that sells a variety of steel goods from hand tools to tire changers via mail order. The "outstanding yet typical" examples demonstrate the authors' assertion that "almost any type of enterprise can be developed in almost any rural American community."

Davis & Daughter: Building a Home-Grown Niche Business— from Scratch

In her Manhattan incarnation, Karen Zehring Davis was a highly successful, highly stressed businesswoman. She and her former husband owned the exclusive Café des Artistes restaurant; later, she owned and published *Corporate Finance,* a magazine about corporate deal-making. She had been overworked in the city, and when she and her family moved to Castine, Maine, in 1990, her plan was to take a breather from the world of commerce and stay home and . . . bake cookies.

In 1992, after she had been baking cookies for two years, the proverbial lightbulb went off in her head. After she had taught a class for children in entrepreneurship, she and her then eleven-year-old son, Jesse, and some of his friends decided to start a baking company in town. Almost overnight, Davis Baking Company was born—a small, seasonal, run-out-of-the-kitchen business, which quickly found its legs.

The following summer, when Jesse was going off to nearby Camp Robin Hood, Davis partnered with Jesse's younger sister, Tonia, then eleven, and looked toward expansion. Why not start a mail-order business selling care packs of chocolate-chip cookies to the parents of Jesse's fellow campers? Using her direct-mail background, Davis put together an appealing promotional package including a letter, price list and brochure to send to all camp parents, whose names and addresses had been graciously provided by the camp.

When she received the camp mailing list, Davis was amazed by the clientele. "I was looking through this list of two hundred or so families," she says. "And I thought, 'Oh my God.' It contained people like the Rockefellers. If I didn't recognize the names, I recognized the addresses and zip codes. Thirty percent of them were international. I started to worry that maybe it wasn't the right scene for Jesse. But from a business point of view, I thought, 'Wow!' "

The partners timed the mailing so that it would arrive in people's boxes the Monday after camp started. The response exceeded all expectations. "From ten in the morning till seven at night, when I turned off the phone, we had $1,500 in orders," she says. "By the end of the first week, we had about $4,600 in orders."

In classic mail-order fashion, Davis had put out the mailing before stocking the inventory. And having to deliver the merchandise caught her flat-footed. "It was just overwhelming," she says. Having no equipment aside from a thirty-inch Dacor oven and a K-45 KitchenAid mixer, she and Tonia worked day and night baking cookies, brownies and pies. Packing and mailing came next. "It was like the Outward Bound of business," she says. "I never worked so hard in my life."

Karen Davis provided what she called unpaid "slave labor" for one summer for each child. But that was the limit. "I let them know they would have to do it on their own, or we would have to come up with some more equitable arrangement—because that is real life, you know."

Tonia cleared $2,400 that year and donated 10 percent of it— per her mother's stipulation—to foster children in Somalia and Nepal.

The following year, 1994, mother and daughter renamed the business Davis & Daughter to reflect their new partnership and signal the change in product line from just cookies to what they call "camper carepaks," which include specialized packages for sailing, tennis or riding camps. They bought a convection oven and hired a part-time baker with New York culinary-school training. The mailing list was expanded to encompass camps all over New England as well as the list from an exclusive Manhattan toy store. Eight thousand dollars' worth of inventory for the gift packs was piled into the dining room. ("We almost had to dig a moat around it," Davis says.)

But before the season had gotten under way, Tonia, having already proved her mettle as an entrepreneur the previous summer, decided to bail out and devote full time to being a teenager. Her mother carried on solo, serving a clientele that included women who were stressed the way she used to be. "If they're rude and impatient, and they think that they're talking to some nobody," she says, her voice trailing off, "I understand because I used to be overworked and stressed. It rolls right off my back. After we've talked and they've learned that I can relate, the customers are so grateful to have somebody who's there because they can't be. They all want to be Pillsbury moms, but can't. I can!" By the end of the year, Davis & Daughter had netted around $4,000.

But having hatched the business and warmed the nest for three summers, Davis was ready to hand it back to her son. At the ripe old age of fifteen, Jesse took over the operation in the summer of 1995 and moved the business out of the home. "It was time to separate it from Mom," Davis says. "He can phone me if there's a problem, but it's good that I won't always be right there. That's the real world. It's sink or swim for him now."

SERVICE-INDUSTRY OPPORTUNITIES

The experts agree that the best opportunity for people wanting to start new businesses in small towns—or big cities, for that matter—is in the burgeoning *services industry.* "Services are growing like crazy," says Iowa State's Kenneth Stone. Families, individuals and companies all want to contract with others to alleviate some of their work burden.

"Those of us in multiple-income families, with both spouses working outside the home and teens working too, don't have time to do anything. I used to do my own lawn and car maintenance. Now I don't have time," says Stone. "The fastest-growing business in the state of Iowa is building maintenance. With the downsizing of industry, companies have found that it's less expensive to contract with an outside firm than to have janitors on the payroll." Other service occupations include such things as accounting, writing, landscaping, advertising, catering, babysitting, elder care, pet-sitting, laundry and dry-cleaning services.

Pied Piper Pony Rides: A Service Industry Even a Cowpoke Would Love

Lauren Hubsher's love of animals launched her on a hayride that ended up with a successful service business: giving pony rides and providing a movable barnyard-animal petting zoo for children's birthday parties. Hubsher, a thirty-eight-year-old former advertising account supervisor who worked for eleven years in Manhattan and later in Connecticut, established a business called Pied Piper Pony Rides in 1991. Several years earlier, she and her husband, Jeffrey Hubsher, had purchased a three-acre farm on the outskirts of Ridgefield, Connecticut, to keep her horse, Harper, while she continued to work in advertising in nearby Stamford. At the first birthday party of her daughter, Sierra, in

1991, an idea struck Hubsher as she led delighted young guests on pony rides around a barn road. She came up with the idea of expanding her hit party into a business and, on the spot, sketched out a logo of silhouettes that evoked "a playful, whimsical feeling" of skipping kids, a pony, a dog and a balloon.

That first year, the business grossed $19,000. By 1994, revenues had shot up to $100,000, while her menagerie had expanded to include fifteen horses and ponies; pygmy goats; sheep; lambs; rabbits; chickens; roosters; Daisy Mae, the potbellied pig and four horse trailers.

Having a veterinarian for a husband gives her a competitive edge, Hubsher says. "When I'm giving my spiel to clients or potential clients, they're happy as can be knowing that they'll be sure to get a clean, healthy animal. I'm not going to show up with a mangy goat and a sickly pony."

Pied Piper's mainstay is the birthday party, but the business also stages parties for companies, church fairs and neighborhood associations. Hubsher charges $150 for the pony's first hour (and $100 for each additional hour) and has managed to attract such upscale clients as the Greenwich Country Club and Keith Richards and Patti Hansen, who recently hired her to do a birthday party for their child.

Though Hubsher's net profits have yet to approach her ad-agency salary of $45,000, going to work is now a treat rather than a chore. "I love animals and making a living of sorts from my farm, where I can wear workboots and jeans and a flannel shirt."

Her memories of her advertising days creating ad campaigns for cosmetics and fragrance accounts for such clients as Cover Girl and Ralph Lauren now focus on the "hours and hours in meetings over minutiae that don't matter in the big picture," she says. "You'd put all this energy and angst into this stuff to get another SKU (shelf keeping unit). You wanted more on the shelf than your competition. I had to ask myself: Does the world need another men's cologne?" Only in retrospect does her Christmastime firing seem to be a blessing in disguise.

Not only does Hubsher get to work with her beloved animals,

but she's in charge. "No one tells me to do something that doesn't make sense," she says.

ADVICE FROM THE HORSES' MOUTHS

From those who've actually been there and done that—successfully—here's the lowdown on what to keep in mind when considering starting a new business in a small town:

🐴 *Give it everything you've got,* says Betsy Ogden, who opened Circle H Holiday Ranch in Thorp, Washington, in 1988. "Be prepared to use every skill you can come up with," says Ogden. "You live by your wits, but it's worthwhile." While living through the unprofitable years to build her business, she's utilized every skill she has and has even added some new ones. Ogden acts as a receptionist, taking reservations, seating guests, scheduling trail rides, tallying bills; and she even learned to cook. ("I know enough to save my ass if the cook doesn't show up," she says.) To supplement the ranch income, she teaches dance in nearby Ellensburg and sells antiques.

🐴 *Stick it out for the long haul,* says Ogden. "Be prepared to take losses for a long time before you see the light at the end of the tunnel." But enjoy the adventure of the ride while you're on it. "My son and I eat a lot of Campbell's soup in the winter," she says. "In the summer, we have a cook." It took six years before the ranch started to achieve even marginal profitability. The ranch is now "barely maybe" profitable, she says. "I don't think it'll ever be lucrative, but I've found a way of life that I like."

🐴 *Don't assume that because something isn't done that it can't be done,* says Ben Feder, who bought a dairy farm in Clinton Corners, New York (population 1,200), in 1969, and then decided he'd rather produce wine than milk. "There was no law that allowed small producers to produce wine," he says. So Feder, a former book jacket designer in Manhattan, prevailed upon then Governor Hugh Carey in 1977 to institute a New York version of a California law, the Small Farm Winery Act, that allowed small farms to grow grapes, make and sell alcohol. The law goes so far as to allow Sunday wine sales.

Clinton Vineyards has become a success. *The New York Times* pronounced its Seyval Blanc and Johannisberg Riesling "the best white wine produced in the Eastern U.S.," and the label received a boost from left field during the 1992 Democratic Presidential Convention in New York when it was picked up as a designated wine "at every single hotel where delegates for Bill Clinton were staying," Feder says. Clinton Vineyards now makes two thouand cases per year, and on a good year the firm can enjoy a net profit of up to $80,000.

🅢 *Don't presume that what you want to do is new.* Just because there was no resale shop in your hometown when you were growing up, don't assume there isn't one there today. By the same token, don't assume that because there isn't one today, there wasn't one that opened and closed after ten months.

Find out who's already in town and how much of a market exists for your business. "You have to ask yourself: 'Am I going to share in a growing market and hence be welcome?'" says Morton J. Marcus, an economist with Indiana University School of Business. "Or am I going to move into a small market and try to take business away from someone who's already there and hence be unwelcome?"

🅢 *Invite people to lunch.* Walk into your future competitor's office, introduce yourself and invite him or her to lunch. Morton J. Marcus suggests saying to that person, "I'd like to invite you to lunch and talk about business in town, to see if there's the need for another print shop here." Some might be suspicious and close-mouthed, but you'll be surprised how many will open up and give you lots of information. If you go on and open a business, this will be the first step in establishing your collegial relationship.

🅢 *"Follow your passion,"* says Betsy Ogden, who'd always dreamed about starting a dude ranch in which she could show off her passion for the entertainment business. "Show biz is what I know, so I tried to make this place a fantasy." Guests check in wearing cowboy hats and boots and are shown to cabins named Roy Rogers and Dale Evans. To enhance the effect, Ogden keeps the Roy Rogers movies rolling in the lodge.

"In the old days, they called them 'dude ranches,'" she explains. "Dudes were people from the city who wanted to experience the Old West and learn how to ride horses. Now the proper term is 'guest ranch.'" It's a point of pride that she uses neither, preferring instead the term "holiday ranch" because she wants guests to feel as if they're on vacation.

❊ *Wait and watch before you leap.* "When I moved here, I said: 'I will not do anything for a year, commercial real estate wise,'" says Mount Airy developer Burke Robertson. "I tried to sell other people's property but I would not develop anything for a year. I spent the first year trying to understand the market, to get to know the people."

❊ *Locate your business downtown.* Small-town downtowns—especially those with character and well-preserved older buildings—are the hot spots of the future. "Every town has a 'cultural landscape' that consists of your values, the style and pace of life in your town, and some of the old buildings you may live or work in," writes Jack McCall in *The Small Town Survival Guide: Help for Changing the Economic Future of Your Town* (Morrow, 1993). Jump aboard.

"You go to Crabtree Valley Mall in Raleigh, Southpark Mall in Charlotte, Hanes Mall in Winston-Salem, and there are the exact same tenants," says Burke Robertson. "That's what makes downtown Mount Airy unique. For the past twenty-five years, malls and Wal-Marts were unique. Now the downtowns are unique. We have a tendency to go in cycles in everything."

❊ *Be prepared for close local scrutiny.* When your business goes through its inevitable false starts and setbacks, let the gossip roll right off your skin. While most will be supportive, some people may enjoy watching you twist in the wind.

"When you're growing your company in a small town, if things go bad for the company, everyone knows it," says Frank Crail. "When things went bad for us, people would say, 'These guys are going under.' Or, 'They don't know what they're doing.' In a small town, it's more personal than in a big city. In a city, you don't have the high visibility and, frankly, no one cares."

⊞ *Don't wait for them to fire you.* If you aren't a good fit for your job, spare yourself the humiliation and pain of being fired. Make a proactive move and quit. Then launch the next chapter of your life.

"If you have this driving feeling, you've got to do something different—you may lose the lifestyle, you may not be able to buy the fancy clothes, or as many dinners out—but it's worth it if you're saving your sanity," says Lauren Hubsher.

OPPORTUNITIES AND GROWTH FIELDS

Tourism and tourist-related businesses: Small towns are increasingly viewed by the public as attractive weekend and vacation destinations for rejuvenating doses of simpler living and slow-paced rest and relaxation. As a result, business leaders have begun to focus development on tourism. Many small towns have identified their assets. As a newcomer, you can bring fresh ideas and help market them. Consider opening a bed and breakfast, a restaurant, a tour-guide business, an antique store or gift shop specializing in items of local interest and/or manufacture. If the numbers of tourists justify it, consider introducing a business that's big in the city, such as an espresso bar or a soda shop serving a premium ice cream, such as Ben & Jerry's.

Value-added and specialty agricultural items: In sheer numbers, agricultural jobs in rural areas (as elsewhere in the country) now account for a smaller piece of the total employment pie than in years past, according to Dr. Larry Leistritz, professor of agricultural economics, North Dakota State University, Fargo.

But if your heart is set on farming, there's growth in niche and value-added products. Marilyn and Tom Ross termed such people "countrypreneurs" in their book *Country Bound!* Look for exotic, off-beat products for which there's a shortage in your new town. For example, if your town and its retail sales area has a growing population of immigrants from Middle Eastern, Caribbean, Asian or African countries, you might consider raising goats. Goat meat, a dietary staple in these areas, is unavailable in many American communities and can command a premium price. Goat's milk is also in high demand for its easy digestibility (compared to cow's milk) and buffering qualities, making it attractive to ulcer sufferers and better for babies. Organic products, including meats and sausages, vegetables and fruits, wines, juices and specialty products like olives, shiitake mushrooms and herbal teas are likewise good to consider producing or selling.

Financial services: As tax laws become more complicated and the population-rich Baby Boomers approach retirement age, more and more people are turning to accountants, financial advisers and brokers to handle their money. If there's a shortage of individuals with this expertise in a small town, it could offer an attractive opportunity for you. To get an idea of how well off residents of the town are, look up in U.S. Census Bureau materials the median household income and get the total bank deposits from local banks and divide by population for a per-capita figure.

Auto repair: If you're a gifted automobile mechanic, you're probably well aware that there's an enormous demand for your services almost everywhere. If dealerships handle most of the repair work in town, you may be able eventually to set up your own garage and undercut their prices. (Consider working in a local shop first for at least six months to learn the ropes and supply channels of the community.) If you have a specialty, such as mufflers or air-conditioning, consider establishing a shop.

Holistic medicine/therapeutic massage: Be sure that your town has population sufficient to support such alternative services, which are popular among progressive, college-educated people. Check with national associations for information about the necessary credentials to set up shop. They should also be able to provide you with a list of practitioners in small towns elsewhere, whom you can contact to ask questions about marketing to a small-town clientele. If you're the first or only to set up shop in a town that can support you, you may be able to establish a virtual monopoly and even be able to pick and choose among customers who may travel longish distances for your services.

Temporary help agency: A small independent temporary agency is an extremely attractive business prospect for towns in which local businesses use agencies in the next biggest town or city. One way to evaluate whether a town is ripe for this service is to look at the numbers of businesses and industries employing clerical workers and industrial workers in jobs such as shipping and construction. If the numbers are significant, a town as small as 4,000 may be able to support a temporary agency. (By contrast, a bedroom community of 8,000 with scant business activity would be a poor prospect.) Also, look for a higher-than-average unemployment rate so that you'll be able to pull from an adequate labor pool. Also, keep in mind that you'll be drawing workers from a twenty-mile radius.

Though it's desirable to learn the ropes by working at a temporary agency before starting your business, it's not necessary. Business start-up guides, such as the one published by *Entrepreneur* magazine, will give you the lowdown.

Mail-order business: For anyone locating in a small town, the mail-order business is a good option because your overhead—labor and space—is likely to be significantly lower than it would be in the city. With mail order, it doesn't matter to the customer where you're located. Product, delivery time and customer service are all that count.

Writing services: Here's an often unfilled niche in small towns because many people with writing ambitions and skills depart for the big cities at the first opportunity. Many businesspeople have their secretaries write business reports, product information and important correspondence when they should be done by a professional. What's more, handling regional and national media requires expertise; even local newspaper editors and radio deejays respect and respond more favorably to professional rather than amateurish solicitations.

Computer consulting: Computer consulting is a terrific field for anyone who knows computers well enough to make house and office calls, do needs assessments, install software and equipment and provide training. Many customers—especially the computer illiterate—don't have the time or inclination to read manuals but like to learn by doing, and they like to learn by doing *with a consultant present* as a safety net. There's potential here to market yourself to the school systems as well.

Computer repair: This is a potential gold mine for anyone knowledgeable about computers—especially in towns that are some distance from cities that provide such services. An enterprising computer repairperson could offer service contracts providing on-site visits or at-shop repair and loaners. You'd be well advised to get acquainted with the computer salespeople at local stores (such as the nearby Radio Shack) who can refer you, as well as with the computer instructors at the local community college. One reality of computer repair in a small town is that you'll be expected to know computers of every stripe: from IBM to Apple to their many clones. Consider combining computer consulting and repair.

Dance/exercise instructor/personal trainer: Individuals with the expertise to design and monitor workouts and weight-lifting protocols are in a position to clean up in a small town where there's little or no competition. Likewise, anyone who can teach dance or exercise is likely to mark off territory for him- or herself. Often you can market your services to a fitness center, large business or industry, town government or the local school system.

Repairperson: As the conservationist nineties unfold and consumers become increasingly frugal and environmentally oriented, they'll be looking to service everything from toasters and microwaves to vacuum cleaners. They want to buy less, buy quality and keep what they have in good repair. As with the computer repairperson, the more versatility you can offer, the better. If you can repair a variety of small appliances, you'll be better off than if you only do lawnmowers. Like the rest of us, small-towners will pay for convenience.

Iowa State's Kenneth Stone envisions a repair service with home pickup as a perfect business for the 1990s and beyond. "In the military, if you had anything wrong in your house, you'd put a sign on your window telling them, and they'd come by, pick it up and fix it. What a great service that would be in the civilian world. I'd be willing to pay for that. It could be done fairly easily. If an appliance repairperson didn't know how to fix a particular item, he or she could broker it out to a specialist."

BUSINESS, SMALL-TOWN STYLE

Adjusting to the potentially alien culture of a small-town business environment may be the most dramatic change you'll end up making. Assuming that your business is based on the local economy or that your job is in town, this section will give you ideas about how to make the transition from big-city to small-town work ethic while avoiding making major gaffes.

"The Farnham Syndrome"

Probably the most common mistake—and worst damage you can inflict on your career—made by former urbanites coming into a small-town work environment is best described by Charles W. "Chuck" Stroup, director of economic development for the state of North Dakota. He calls it the "Farnham Syndrome" and recalls with a chuckle a man by that name who was the first city planner of Hazen, North Dakota (population 2,818), in the early 1970s. The "Farnham Syndrome" is Stroup's paradigm for how *not* to behave when entering a rural community.

"Farnham presumed that because he had a master's degree in planning he knew what the town's wants and needs were going to be," says Stroup. Yet for all his education, Farnham failed in the most critical first step—*creating a favorable environment* in which to work. Says Stroup, himself a Hazen native whose work takes him to small towns all over North Dakota (the *entire* state is composed of small towns, with the one exception being Fargo, population 74,111): "In order to succeed at the task you're assigned to, it's critically important that you earn the trust and confidence of the people you work for. Farnham told the city council: 'I'm telling you what has to be done.'" Instead, he should have been finding out from them what needed to be done. Stroup says that as a newcomer you need to allow a *minimum of six months* to "acquaint yourself" with the individuals you need to influence in order to achieve your objectives.

"You may be smarter than everyone else, but you don't go around telling people that," he says. What's more, keep in mind that how you sell yourself in a rural community is markedly different from how you sell yourself in the corporate world. In rural communities, he says, people have lived for generations "knowing that it's the *relationships with each other that form the foundation* of dealing with community. Building trust leads to trusting relationships in a rural community—not impressing someone with your dazzling thinking. The 'Farnham Syndrome' happens so often to people who come in from the outside."

So how do former city dwellers avoid falling into the "Farnham Syndrome"?

Joan Glover went to great lengths to put her co-workers and colleagues at Central Washington University in Ellensburg at ease. In fact, you may have to bend over backward not to intimidate others who've perhaps not ventured far from home if you come into a situation with a glittering résumé or credentials—especially when you're new on the job. Glover's approach was soliciting the input of co-workers.

"Be sensitive to the fact that those people know the territory far better than you do," she says. "You, as an outsider, may have better skills in some areas, but the most irritating thing that a new person can do is presume he or she comes with answers and solutions without first listening. The smartest thing you can do is make it clear that you can learn from them. You must gain their trust."

"You Have to Be a Person First"

While having a high opinion of yourself—and the easy articulation of that opinion—may be a necessary survival tool in the city, it can prove lethal when broadcast in a small town.

A recent article in the *ABA Journal* about the life and times of a small-town lawyer living in Princeton, Illinois (population 7,197), maintains that any hint of arrogance can be "deadly" for an attorney's practice. One lawyer put it this way: "You can't be a good small-town lawyer and think that just because you wear a jacket and tie, you're something special. You have to convey an attitude that says, 'I've got to wear this uniform because it's what's expected of me.' *You have to be a person first,* one who just happens to be practicing law."

Indeed, a key component of the small-town work ethic involves *people firstism.* Many who flee big-city careers do so in a conscious attempt to seek a more humane face to the business environment.

"In Washington [D.C.], I got tired of people not caring about people," says Patricia Kicak, vice president for communications and development, Habitat for Humanity in Americus, Georgia (population 16,512). "It was whom you worked for that counted. I can remember standing at a cocktail party talking to people while they looked over my head to see if someone better had come in."

In her Washington incarnation, Kicak was no slouch. She worked for the American Red Cross for eight years, first as the director of corporate marketing and later as director of media and external affairs. Her decision to accept the position at Habitat came partially from a personal resolution to seek out a small-town work environment in which "you're working so you can live—not living to work."

Though Kicak was brought to Habitat to introduce more "efficiency" to the operation, to update, reorganize and internationalize it, in overseeing her staff of one hundred, she plans to maintain the centrality of workers' personal lives in the workplace. "I don't want to bring so much of that [efficiency] here that someone is afraid to say: 'I'll have to leave early. My wife and I are working the concession stand at the high school game. Is that OK?'"

More Relaxed Dealings

Not only do people generally cut one another more slack in small towns but they tend to be more forgiving, allowing greater room for discussion and polite disagreement, according to Kicak.

"In Washington, people were always concerned with the bottom line," she says. "In general, in the city, business is personal— if someone doesn't agree with you professionally, it ends up becoming a personal affront. Here, it's much more relaxed. You may disagree with someone professionally, but that doesn't mean you don't like each other. People are courteous regardless."

Just about everyone who's made the transition from big city to small town cites being a "people person" as a requisite for business success. "The good merchants always keep the wants and needs of the customer uppermost in their minds and will go the extra mile for them on such things as returns," says Iowa State's small-town retailing expert Ken Stone.

Not only merchants, but professionals of every stripe must tailor their services to people in the small town to a larger extent than in the city. Precisely because the business is so personal, many former urbanites maintain that they do a *better* job than before. Virginia Emerson Hopkins believes she "may be more effective" practicing law in Anniston, Alabama (population 26,623), than she was in Washington, D.C., simply because she's now able to develop a "more complete relationship" with her clients.

In Washington, Hopkins was a partner in a major law firm with offices in four cities. She typically dealt with clients over the phone. Sometimes she'd have an initial meeting with the chief legal officer for the division with which she was dealing but doubts she would have recognized even long-standing clients if she'd passed them on the street. Often her clients were out-of-state. By contrast, in Anniston, if she doesn't already *know* the party seeking help when he comes in (and his spouse, children and what church they attend), she gets to know him during a face-to-face meeting.

Because of this personal contact, "I may be able to more quickly help a client arrive at a solution," she says. "It's not that I'm trying harder, it's just that I have more information. You get to know a lot about somebody if you see them interact with their spouse. You get a feeling if they want to take a conservative position. You get a feel for their tolerance for risk and publicity." Looking a client in the eye enables Hopkins to "tell if I'm going too fast (or too slowly) in explaining things. Do I need to go back over it? Are they thinking about something else? Have I gone off on a tangent? Those kinds of things you don't get over a phone very well."

This more holistic approach to servicing law clients mirrors a larger reality of small-town life. Just as business is not simply cut-and-dried when you have a personal or ongoing relationship with a client or customer, by the same token a person is more than just his or her job. In a small town, you're judged on your character, and on whether or not you're a community player. In a sense, your work is *less* important in a small town than in the big city, where it can be all-consuming.

"Being a lawyer is *part* of who I am—not all of who I am," says Hopkins. "When I was in Washington, I was defined by being a lawyer; now that I'm in a small town, I'm defined more broadly. My life is more integrated in Anniston."

Certainly Hopkins's work schedule in Anniston is more flexible than it was in Washington. She now works between thirty-five and forty-five hours per week, down from the sixty-hour weeks she used to put in. And running counter to the majority of American workers, for whom, according to Dr. Juliet B. Schor, author of *The Overworked American: The Unexpected Decline of Leisure* (Basic Books: 1992), "travel time to and from work began rising after 1975, for an overall increase of about three days (23 hours) a year," Hopkins's commute has been cut from forty-five minutes each way to five minutes. Likewise, her fee has dropped from $147 to $100 an hour.

Turning Down the Intensity

But turning down the juices isn't always easy for the dedicated workaholic. Indeed, it's a major challenge for many who were previously on the fast track to turn down the intensity with which they formerly pursued their jobs and adopt a more leisurely pace. For Joan Glover, the biggest adjustment came quite literally in accepting her more limited work hours. In Houston, ten- and twelve-hour days were the norm; in Ellensburg, at Central Washington University, everyone watched the clock. "You worked eight to five," she says. "Everyone across the board at the university went to lunch between twelve and one. It was amazing to me—after being used to a service environment— to see the workload handled in a very precise number of hours."

Glover admits something of a struggle in making the adjustment. "For me, part of the challenge was getting my psyche to relax a bit: to go from seventy-eight rpms to thirty-three," she says. "It was something I had to teach myself. It was not only an acceptable style, but that was the way people worked. That was the *culture*." She knew she'd successfully made the transition when it became "unusual" for her to stay late or come in early.

But some say that it's not that you work *less* in a small town, but that the approach to time is different, that the small-town style is less harried, more measured.

"There's a little more laid-back approach in Mount Airy," says real estate developer Burke Robertson. "But I'm not working any less than I was in Charlotte. And I'm not working any more."

The main difference is one of style. In the city, a laid-back attitude can signal a slow-lane career. But in the small town, Robertson says, "Most people don't *appear* to be rushed to do anything. But I don't think that impedes things getting done."

Transplants from the big city insist that this slower, less stressful pace makes for a healthier working environment. "People in Washington were under a great deal of stress to win," says Virginia Hopkins. "There was much more of a zero-sum mentality. In Anniston, you find much more a win-win mentality."

Of course, working in a small town is not without its demands and obligations—especially if you're the only one or one of few of your kind in town. Professional pressure on small-town generalists to keep up with new developments in multiple fields can make it harder than ever to be a regular Joe, to make the ball games, the bean suppers and high school plays. Often demands can stretch you thin. And once you become a community "yea-sayer," people will come back to you again and again with more requests and demands.

The upside is that you're much more easily able to have an impact in a small town than in the city and to advance your personal or professional agenda. It amazes many newcomers how quickly they can effect change.

Janet D. Schwab, a forty-one-year-old nurse/midwife who in 1994 left her job at Brooklyn Hospital Center to become the first nurse/midwife at the conservative Mount Kisco Medical Group in Mount Kisco, New York (population 9,108), has already had an impact on hospital policy. She was invited to join a group rewriting practice guidelines for the hospital's obstetricians to lower their high rate of cesarean sections. Schwab did her homework and proposed eliminating "big baby at term" as a justification for induction.

"I did a literature review, with a lot of recent research," she says. "When they did controlled studies—some with induced babies and some not—they found that induction raised the C-section rate." The five doctors at the meeting were "surprised but accepting" of Schwab's information. As a result, big babies at term were removed from the guidelines for induction at the Mount Kisco Medical Center.

At the giant Brooklyn Hospital Center, where Schwab's patient population was low-income, inner-city women needing prenatal care, such a policy change would doubtless have been much longer in the coming and much more highly deliberated. At Mount Kisco, she was able to effect change in the course of one meeting. She says: "I'm proud of that."

SIX WAYS TO DEVELOP A WINNING SMALL-TOWN STYLE

1. The Best Business Isn't Always Business

You talk about things that interest others in a small town, says Habitat for Humanity's Patricia Kicak, and they aren't always business. "Usually, it's hearth and home. You stop and say hello and talk about trees and shrubs." Or children or family. Or the weather. Avoid politics unless you know someone well or have established a jocular relationship with that person. Small talk comes first, business later.

Just as you take your time with people in person, likewise you do so when talking with small-towners on the telephone. Never answer the phone by saying: "What's up?" And never cut into someone's monologue by snapping: "Get to the point." If you're making a call, be sure at minimum to inquire how the person is, or make some comment about the weather before getting down to brass tacks.

2. Honesty Is the Best Policy

Do what you say and make no promises that you don't intend to honor. Though you may come out in the short term by slick or self-serving dealing, such maneuvers will invariably come back to haunt you in a small town.

Because you know your business associates, you're more likely to be able to count on their word. "When you strike a [verbal] deal, you've still got to get it backed up in writing, but when someone in town says, 'I'll do that,' you're more likely to be able to depend on it," says commercial developer Burke Robertson. "You don't have to worry as much."

A code of honor exists in some small towns that practitioners of certain professions rely on. "People do things on verbal agreements," says attorney Virginia Hopkins. "In Washington, it was unusual to do things on verbal agreement. It's pleasant to know if you can reach agreement on a point with an opposing council they're not going to spin you, or deny it happened, or change what it meant. It's not 100 percent fail-safe, but you know real soon who won't treat you right."

Such collegiality among professional peers is, of course, not found in every town, but it is *possible* in a small town. "Calhoun County has a reputation for having one of the more congenial bars around, and I'm not talking about going out for drinks," Hopkins says. "People trust each other. There's a higher level of trust." As a result, there's less red tape.

"The easiest way for me to see the difference between the city and a small town businesswise is in the legal profession," notes Robertson. "It's in the number of words and the number of pages. A document in Charlotte that's thirty pages will be ten pages in Mount Airy. From my personal perspective, one's just as good as the other."

3. Become a Community Player

Stay aloof from community life at your own peril. An unwritten pact you make with a small town when you move there is to give of yourself to the community. It's like joining a family. Be willing to share your gifts and talents with that community. Not that you have to do *everything*, but decide in which ways you'd like to help. Then pitch in.

Of course, no one will force you to do volunteer work, to donate to fund-raising projects or raise funds. But if you shun participation in all things, you not only lose the pleasure of being part of the community, but you may hurt yourself professionally. People may be less likely to patronize your business.

4. Never Act as Though You're Just Passing Through

Little will gall small-towners as much as someone from the big city who acts as though life in the hinterlands is no more than a sentence to some hardship post.

This mistake was made by several people we've encountered locally, including one young reporter who made it clear that he had "bigger fish to fry." In fact, he did leave the town for another slightly larger one, but he took with him not a single friend and no reservoir of goodwill.

Realize that some small-town folk—especially those who wanted to try their wings in the big city and never had the moxie to do so—will be especially sensitive to this attitude. No matter how you landed here, make the most out of it by keeping the right attitude.

5. Sign Up for Seminars

If you're at the top of your game professionally and wanting for professional peers, compensate by traveling a lot, signing up for as many national and international meetings as your bank account and calendar will allow, subscribing and keeping up with trade journals and generally staying abreast of the changes in your profession.

For all the life- and work-style advantages of Americus, Georgia, Patricia Kicak misses being able "to run out at lunchtime and go to an American Marketing Association lunch and hear a speaker" as she did in Washington. She misses being able to call corporate sponsors and invite them to lunch *tomorrow*. In Americus, she says, she has to "call them up and make a special deal, plan it in advance."

She compensates for these deficits by keeping up with her reading, staying in touch with professional peers on the telephone, traveling extensively and encouraging her staff at Habitat for Humanity to follow suit.

6. Extend the Helping Hand

It wasn't his impressive résumé or record, or the fact that he had New York City experience that endeared Police Chief Kevin O'Grady to his new constituents—the people of Damascus, Virginia. Only after he donned his parka, put chains on his tires and plowed out into the blizzard of '93 to deliver milk and kerosene to stranded citizens did people open their arms and their hearts to him. This happened exactly two months after he assumed his post.

"People said they would never forget it," says O'Grady. And they haven't.

7. Adopt the Dress Code of the Natives

Usually a move to a small town will signify a shift in sartorial style; you'll either begin to dress up or dress down.

Although this will vary according to region of the country (the Southeast and East Coast tend to be dressier, while the Western states and New England are more casual), it also depends on the individual corporate culture and professional etiquette.

"I don't have to wear stockings every day," declares Habitat for Humanity's Patricia Kicak. "Today I'm wearing topsiders and a T-shirt." In general, she says, "I'm probably dressier than most. In the winter, I still wear suits. But in the summer I can get by with a pair of tan slacks and several colors of linen blazers and a pair of flat woven shoes."

Likewise, Joan Glover's new work environment at Central Washington University in Ellensburg was more casual than her Houston workplace. At first, she admits, "I overdressed. I was one of the few people who wore the dress-for-success suit. Most women did not. They wore skirts and blouses and dresses, much more laid-back than in Houston. . . . I continued to dress up for a while; that was the image I had of going to work. It was not so much a mistake as a matter of style. My co-workers would laugh about the fact that my feet hurt at the end of the day. I was still wearing high heels. They were wearing Birkenstocks. Now I wear lower heels and my dress-for-success suits are in the closet. I hold on to them because I think, 'Who knows? I may use them someday.'"

THE MERRITT HOUSE BED AND BREAKFAST: "OUR DREAM AND FANTASY"

When Pat and Rich Mangels opened their bed and breakfast in the historic Merritt House on Main Street in Mount Airy, North Carolina, in 1993, they were fulfilling a dream that was born around the time they married thirty years earlier.

The fiftysomething pair, who had worked for the Broward County School System (she as a secretary and he in maintenance) near Fort Lauderdale, Florida, had spent years plotting the move. "Rich and I are literally living our dream and our fantasy," declares Pat Mangels. "We thought we'd find a clapboard farmhouse, but this is much grander than anything we'd imagined. My nephews in California call this house 'the mansion.'"

Opening a bed and breakfast in a small town is one of the most cherished fantasies of those dreaming of escaping hectic urban lives—perhaps because for many "B&Bing" is a favored form of weekend recreation. "The bed and breakfast establishment has become almost an integral part of the charming town," writes Larry Brown, author of *America's Most Charming Towns & Villages* (Open Road, 1994). But running a bed and breakfast is never as easy as it appears. In reality, it's hard, often grueling, work.

As with other successful transplants from big cities to small towns, the Mangelses did most everything right. They carefully researched their business and its potential market before taking the plunge. And once they selected their property and moved, they threw themselves into community life. Pat Mangels joined the chamber of commerce, the downtown business association, the Rotary Club and the garden club. They offered to host numerous civic functions—everything from an "after-hours" mixer for the chamber to Mrs. Wiley's Tea for the Surry Arts Council every September at Mount Airy's annual Mayberry Days festival. This level of civic involvement contributed to the successful launch of their business.

What follows are some insights on starting a B&B. Read along and see if you're a match for this business.

Do Extensive Research
This is the fun part! Once the Mangelses made the decision that they wanted to own a B&B, they spent five years taking weekend "mini-vacations" at bed and breakfasts throughout the Southeast. They kept a detailed log of their experiences. "We read and asked a lot of questions at the places we'd stay," Pat Mangels says.

Target Your Locale
The Mangelses zeroed in on three states: Georgia, North Carolina and Virginia. From a cousin living in the nearby town of King, North Carolina, Pat Mangels learned about Andy Griffith's hometown of Mount Airy and "became convinced" that it needed a B&B. The Mangelses decided that they could "build upon" three things: the town's scenic location just fourteen miles south of the famous Blue Ridge Parkway in nearby Virginia; its serving as a base for a large textile industry; and the fact that it is an expanding tourist mecca for Griffith fans and others.

Look for Historic Property
A historic house or property that has a story to tell will enhance the appeal of your B&B. The Mangelses' historic W. E. Merritt House—which is under protective covenant by the Historic Preservation Foundation of North Carolina—has proved to be an endless source of curiosity to visitors, who read the countless framed articles on the walls and even seem excited to read a college thesis on the house's long-time resident, Elizabeth "E. B." Merritt, written by her great-niece. E. B.'s father, W. E. Merritt, who built the house in 1901, was a pillar of the community. He helped to found Mount Airy Furniture, Merritt Hardware, the Renfro Corp. (a hosiery mill), and a brickyard.

"We give tours not only to our guests but also to people who stop at the visitors' center across the street," she says.

If You Know What You Want, Act Decisively
Once the Mangelses learned through their realtor that the home was available, Pat Mangels sent her cousin to scope it out. The cousin spent four hours there, then called and said, "'You'd better come.' We threw a bag into the car and drove all night from Florida. I went to my cousin's house, freshened up and ate breakfast. We drove to Mount Airy, sat across the

street from the house and said : 'That's our house.' " The couple made an offer that day.

Be Realistic About Hours and Workload
Though the thought of having guests and feeding them breakfast may seem like living on Easy Street, consider this : Since you're charging good money, you can't skip your housework that day or postpone repairs, such as that dripping faucet or the wallpaper that needs regluing. You have to do laundry every day, cook, clean, market, answer the phone, dress professionally and act that way from 7 A.M. till 11 P.M. Likewise, you can't serve the yeast bread that failed to rise— even if you'd make your own family eat it.

"Working a bed and breakfast can *consume* you," says Pat Mangels. "Some days, it's eighteen hours or more a day. You don't have what most people consider 'a normal life.' You always have to be there."

You Have to Be a "People Person"
"You have to love people," says Pat Mangels. Or at least one person of the couple has to be a bona fide extrovert in order for it to work. "My gimmick is me."

Price Reasonably
Base your price not on how much you've invested in the home but rather on what the market will bear. Pat Mangels checked B&B rates in the neighboring communities of Winston-Salem and Pilot Mountain, North Carolina, and Carroll County, Virginia, and arrived at the current rates : $40 for a room with a shared bath, and $75 for a room with private bath.

Lavish Guests with Service
"You have to do something that makes you stand out," declares Pat Mangels. When she knows in advance it's a special

occasion such as a birthday or anniversary, Mangels will leave guests a bottle of wine and some cheese in their rooms. Specialty soaps and shampoos are stocked in all the rooms. "You have to go beyond just having a room for someone," she says. "When our guests come through that door, they're given everything to make them feel comfortable and special, like they're queen and king for a day; yet we don't hover over them."

Prepare Gourmet Menus

Pat Mangels makes it a point to fix gourmet breakfasts—things people would not fix at home for themselves. "Everything we make is from scratch. Nothing comes out of a box or mix. I make homemade breads, muffins, quiches, crepes, scones and stuffed French toast with praline sauce. We have fresh fruit and juices and flavored coffees and teas."

Furnish the Rooms to Fit the House

"Almost all our rooms have antiques in them, most of which we bought locally," she says.

Give rooms themes and even names. One of theirs is called Richard's Room, which is furnished with fireman memorabilia in honor of Rich Mangels's late father and grandfather, both New York City firemen. Remember, lots of guests want to see the other rooms, so be sure they're made up and ready for viewing—even if they're not booked that night.

Put in a Gift Shop

Be sure to stock it with local wares and tasteful tourist items. You can add such a location to a nook, cranny or side room in the house. In the Mangelses' case, they located it in an old ice house outside.

If you're interested in starting a bed and breakfast, consider subscribing to one or more of the following magazines or newsletters.

Country Inns/Bed & Breakfast Magazine
P.O. Box 457
Mount Morris, Illinois 61054
(800) 877-5491—for subscriptions
(201) 762-7090—editorial offices
(Six issues for $17.95 a year)

Inn Marketing
P.O. Box 1789
Kankakee, Illinois 60901
(815) 939-3509 or (800) 787-2762
(Ten newsletters for $47 a year)

Innkeeping Newsletter, published by PAII, Professional
Association of Innkeepers International
P.O. Box 90710
Santa Barbara, California 93190
(805) 569-1853
(Twelve newsletters for $65 a year)

Prospective B&B hosts may write away for free literature at
the following:
The American Bed & Breakfast Association (AB&BA)
P.O. Box 1387
Midlothian, Virginia 23113
(804) 379-2222

CHAPTER FOUR

Evaluating the Costs

Maybe it's the vision of all that affordable living space—space you've never had in the city—of a colonial house with dark green shutters and plenty of room for envious guests. Or maybe it's the picture of a white picket fence, of geraniums in hanging pots on the wide front porch, of swinging in a hammock on a lazy summer evening on a quiet and shady street. Or maybe it's the thought of that half-acre or acre lot, of the backyard orchard you've always wanted to plant, of the stone pathways weaving their way through your very own herb and vegetable garden. Or perhaps you're happy with the amount of living space you have but would like to spend less for it and put your money to other uses.

Mere pipe dreams? By no means. The fact is, you *can* get there from here. No matter how out of reach the house and grounds of your dreams may be in the city, they *are* affordable in many small towns and in the surrounding countryside.

Indeed, housing in most cases will represent your greatest savings when you move from a major metropolitan area to a small town. And property taxes—a second major expense in the urban homeowner's budget—are significantly lower in most small towns. Combined with the prospect of realizing as much as double your value for housing dollars, the chance to trade city life for that of a small town can be very compelling.

Consider the experience of Art and Dee Dee Fistel Rosenberg. In 1987, the Rosenbergs bought an 1,150-square-foot house in San Diego, with no yard, for $104,000. From 1987 through 1992, they paid an average of $2,000 a year in property taxes. In 1993, after selling that house at the top of the market for $155,000, the Rosenbergs moved from San Diego to Galax, Virginia), where they bought a house in excellent condition with 3,000 square feet, a two-car garage and a half-acre lot (with four apple trees) for $79,000. The house, located in an attractive neighborhood, is four blocks from the Galax Post Office, where Art Rosenberg walks five mornings a week to his job as postmaster and from which he returns to have lunch with his wife and two small boys. For their Galax house—almost three times the size of the house they had in San Diego—and lot, the Rosenbergs pay $550 a year in property taxes.

For Dave and Mary Jo Burnett, too, it is a tale of two cities. In 1989, the Burnetts sold their house in Nassau County, Long Island—"the New York City suburbs," as they put it—for $140,000 and moved with their three sons to Alliance, Nebraska, Mary Jo Burnett's hometown. On Long Island, living in a 1,500-square-foot house, the Burnetts were paying $5,000 a year in property taxes. In Alliance, where they started what has become a $2.2 million-a-year railroad parts company with the money from the sale of their Long Island house, they bought a Victorian house for $60,000. The house has 3,000 square feet. The property taxes? Seven hundred a year.

Of course not all small towns offer these kinds of bargain-basement prices. In small-resort or college towns, for example, where demand is high, housing costs and property taxes may be more in line with major metropolitan areas. And not everything else costs significantly less in small towns. The Rosenbergs discovered that supermarket prices in Galax are only *slightly* lower, on balance, than those in San Diego, confirming our own experience and that of many others that you are not likely to see substantial reduction in your grocery bills by moving to a small town.

But when all the cost-of-living indexes are factored in, most people find that it is decidedly cheaper to live in a small town than in the city. Studies comparing the cost of living in major cities like New York, Los Angeles and Chicago, to a variety of small towns in the Rocky Mountain states and Midwest reveal the cost of living, for the same lifestyle, to be 15 to 30 percent cheaper in small towns.

Whether individual costs are lower, higher, or about the same, if you're on the fence about moving and are concerned about whether you can afford it, examining the price tag of small-town living could be the decisive factor in prompting you to take action. Alternatively, if you've decided to make the move, knowing what you can expect to pay for the things you need and want is crucial as you take stock of your financial resources and draw up your budget.

As you contemplate a move—before or after your decision—this chapter will help you by showing you how to evaluate the costs of your new life. Embracing both the short and the long term, we'll walk you through the major cost categories of living in a small town. (To examine the costs and strategies related to the actual move itself, see the following chapter, "Making the Move.") These categories include:

- Buying a house
- Building a house
- Renting
- Transportation
- Taxes
- Homeowner's insurance
- Utilities

- Food

- Clothing

- Furniture

- Health care

- Education

- Child care

This chapter will help give you the information you need to make sound choices with your money—information that will help you not just to survive financially in your new hometown, but to *thrive*.

TAKING YOUR FINANCIAL X RAY

Do you know your current financial picture? What are your total assets? Your total liabilities? What is your net worth?

First things first. Before you can budget the move, you need to do a personal financial statement, a kind of financial X ray. It's always surprising to us how many of our acquaintances have only a very rough idea of their financial status at any given time. Odds are, it's been a while since you, too, have updated the information necessary to make accurate projections toward your goals—indeed, the results may surprise you!

Before you do anything else, fill out the following worksheet:

First, calculate your assets. If need be, estimate the value of your personal property.

ASSETS

Cash on hand	$_____
Checking account(s)	$_____
Savings account(s)	$_____
Certificates of deposit	$_____

U.S. Government securities $_____

Other securities (stocks, bonds, etc.) $_____

Mutual funds $_____

Cash value of life insurance policy(ies) $_____

Trust funds $_____

Loans to others $_____

Real estate owned (estimated value) $_____

Mortgages owned $_____

Other $_____

PERSONAL PROPERTY

Automobiles $_____

Furniture $_____

Jewelry $_____

Other $_____

TOTAL ASSETS $_____

Now for the painful part! Sorry, we have to do this one, too. Calculate your liabilities.

LIABILITIES

Bank notes $_____

Line of credit $_____

Other loans $_____

Credit card charges $_____

Mortgages payable $_____

Taxes payable $_____

Other debts $_____

TOTAL LIABILITIES   *$*_____

To determine your net worth, subtract your total liabilities from your total assets:

NET WORTH $ _____

Now you have a clearer picture of the state of your finances. You know how much is liquid—how much money is available to you immediately—and how much would be available down the road if you needed to liquidate other assets. You also know how much you are in arrears. Balancing assets with liabilities, you can begin to see the tantalizing possibilities of applying some of your current financial resources to your new life in a small town.

But in addition to your balance sheet, other financial factors enter into figuring the cost of your small-town dream. Perhaps you are drawing a pension or receiving Social Security benefits. Very likely you are earning a weekly or monthly paycheck. At the same time, you have monthly expenses, a monthly *nut* to cover. Looking down the road—for three months, six months, perhaps a year—how much money can you reasonably expect to save, money you might need to get established in your small town?

Keep these factors in mind, as well as your overall current financial picture, as we examine the costs of small-town living.

COSTS OF SMALL-TOWN LIVING

Buying a House
If you did a "reconnaissance mission" to your preferred small town or towns, as we recommended in Chapter Two, you stopped by the local chamber of commerce. If not, the local chamber is a good place to start in getting an idea of housing prices in your price range. Many chambers of commerce have packets for newcomers that include the names of realtors and real estate information—perhaps even a kind of "combination plate," or mixed listings real estate guide. If yours does not, ask the chamber for the names and phone numbers of at least three realtors. Realtors will be more than happy to send you their latest circulars.

A second wealth of information is the local newspaper. If

you've chosen a small town, we recommend that you subscribe to its paper well in advance of your move. Consult the real estate listings for the latest descriptions and prices of houses.

The *National Business Employment Weekly,* published by *The Wall Street Journal,* sells relocation guides for $3.95 by mail and $5.95 by fax for over fifty major metropolitan areas. They include names and phone numbers for real estate companies and give such information as the average price of an existing home. If the small town you're considering is located near one of these major cities, you can order a guide at (800) 730-1111. Any realtor could refer you to sister companies in nearby towns (if her company doesn't have an office there).

Other resources are relocation and real estate management service firms which generally provide advice free of charge about both cities and small towns to prospective clients. Call PHH Fantus Relocation Services at (203) 837 3500.

Unfortunately, the down payment on the price of the house itself will not be your only front-end expense. Before the transaction becomes final, you'll have to pay closing costs. Among other things, these may include the cost of a survey; an inspection fee; an appraiser's fee; an attorney's fee; a loan-origination fee, to cover loan processing costs; a loan discount fee, or "points," often 1 percent of the loan; title insurance; the first mortgage insurance premium; the first homeowner's insurance premium; a closing fee, paid to the closing agent; a title search fee; and a fee for recording the new deed and mortgage.

Just how much you'll pay for each of these closing costs—and whether you'll pay for only some or all of them—will depend on the price of the house, the lender's requirements and the customs of the community. To get a ballpark idea of what your closing costs might be, contact a realtor. Another good source of information is a loan officer at a bank familiar with home loans in the area. If you so desire, ask the realtor and the banker for the names and phone numbers of an appraiser, an attorney and a surveyor with whom they frequently work, and talk dollars and cents with those people, too.

If you're a first-time home buyer, remember that you'll need to purchase many of the ordinary accoutrements of home ownership when you move—curtains, a lawnmower, a water hose, trash cans—the list goes on. Factor in those costs as well.

Particularly with older houses—of which there tend to be a plethora in small towns—there's also a good chance you'll be doing renovations. With our house—built in 1939—after three years of setting money aside, and after getting extensive estimates, in 1989 we spent $10,000 expanding and renovating our kitchen, knocking out a wall, installing new cabinets, counters and a sink, hanging new valences and refinishing the floor. Perhaps you won't wait as long as we did. But unless you want to short-circuit your budget, you'll need to know the costs ahead of time by getting estimates and researching the prices of needed materials.

Building a House

Perhaps, like many Americans, your dream has always been to follow your bliss and build a house from scratch. Or maybe no house in your otherwise delightful small town meets your specifications. What will it cost you to build one?

Clearly the price tag will vary widely, contingent on the price of the lot, the style and size of the house, the nature and cost of materials and whether or not you do some (or all) of the work yourself. It will also hinge on a number of other factors. Do you want to work with an architect? A custom-built company? Do you want to do your own subcontracting or use a general contractor?

Knowing the answers to these questions will help you pinpoint how you'll be spending your money. When you move to the area—or perhaps even before, if you have the patience and stamina for long-distance communication—get estimates from the professionals with whom you may be working.

It's also true that construction costs vary from state to state, even from region to region within a state. Before you move, the simplest way to obtain a rough estimate of the cost of building a home is by calling a home builder and/or a building supply store in your small town. Follow the lead of Jim and Fran Van Zandt, who moved from Montvale, New Jersey, a New York suburb, to Santa Rosa Beach, Florida. Ask a home builder or building supply store expert to estimate how much home construction in that area costs per square feet. The Van Zandts learned that in Santa Rosa Beach (population 950), in 1989, it cost $50 per square foot to build a house. By later multiplying the number of square feet in his house plan—2,400—by 50, the Van Zandts then had a rough idea of how much money they would be shelling out for house construction. (Answer: $120,000.)

The cost of a small-town lot can be surprisingly high. Bob Bone, a California realtor specializing in small-town real estate, and author of *Discover the Good Life in Rural America: The City Slicker's Guide to Buying Country Real Estate Without Losing Your Shirt,* observes that, on average when building a house, a lot "will account for about one-quarter of the price of your house." Of course if your heart is set on purchasing a 100-acre farm on the outskirts of town, then building your dream house on the crest of the highest pasture, the percentage cost of the "lot" will run much higher. For the lowdown on lot and rural acreage prices, realtors and their circulars remain the best source.

Building your own house in rural areas often has what Jim Van Zandt aptly calls "hidden property development costs"—expenses that city folks aren't conditioned to expect. After renting a house for nine months in Santa Rosa Beach while they looked around, the Van Zandts bought two acres of undeveloped waterfront property on which they planned to build their house. In unincorporated Santa Rosa Beach, to the costs of the property and of building the house they added the costs of drilling a well—around $4,000—and installing a septic system—around $3,000. Another common development cost is that of building or upgrading a driveway or, in rural areas, a road.

Renting
Perhaps you prefer the mobility and relatively carefree mode of renting to the responsibilities and heavier financial load of home ownership. Perhaps homeownership—for now, at least—is sim-

ply beyond your budget. Or perhaps—like both the Rosenbergs and the Van Zandts—you want to rent until you've had ample time to survey the local housing market.

Because his job as the new postmaster in Galax, Virginia, was starting before his house in San Diego had been sold, Art Rosenberg rented an apartment in Galax while his wife, Dee Dee Rosenberg, stayed behind to help sell the house.

How did Art Rosenberg find an apartment? His second day in town, while having lunch at the Wagon Wheel, a local eatery, Rosenberg spotted an apartment listing posted on the cash register. He dialed the number, spoke with a Mrs. Phipps, an elderly widow, and the next day was ensconced in a lovely upstairs apartment in Mrs. Phipps's house, paying $200 a month. No deposit was required. "Just pay me the first month's rent," the landlady told him.

When Dee Dee Rosenberg arrived after the San Diego house was sold, the couple and their young son, Aaron, lived in the apartment for four months until the Rosenbergs bought their house. The family and Mrs. Phipps became close friends. Three days after the couple's second child, Adam, was born in November 1994, Mrs. Phipps appeared at the Rosenbergs' door, carrying a nightgown she had made for the new baby.

To be sure, the more typical story of finding an apartment in a small town is not quite as idyllic as the Rosenbergs'. Rental property in some smaller communities can be hard to find—not to mention spacious two-hundred-dollar apartments, no deposits and utterly gracious landlords.

But in getting a decent estimate of rental costs, in addition to checking with realtors and in newspaper listings, it pays to keep your eyes and ears open, like Art Rosenberg. If you're a prospective renter, any visit to your preferred small town should include not just the usual channels, but also the streets or surrounding countryside where property is being rented as well as places like restaurants and community centers where it is being advertised. Like Rosenberg, don't hesitate to dial the number and ask, or to knock on the door of a house with a For Rent sign.

In addition to the first month's rent, most landlords will require a deposit of the last month's rent as well. Be sure to factor that into your budget.

Transportation

Experts say that transportation costs—the cost of gasoline, car maintenance, registration and insurance, and public transportation—are second only to home mortgages in the average American consumer's budget. For our purposes, however, this statistic is somewhat skewed by the preponderance of urban consumers, many of whom rely, at least in part, on public transportation. It's a rare small town that offers public transportation, so cost estimates need to be based primarily on automotive expenses.

For many urbanites, the overall cost of transportation goes *up* when moving to a small town with the need to buy additional vehicles. When Norm Crampton and his family lived in Chicago, they got by on one automobile plus public transportation. When they moved to Greencastle, Indiana, they had to buy a second car so that he and his wife could each commute to work; when their son, Frederick, turned sixteen, they bought a third vehicle for him—a used pickup truck.

Provided the number of vehicles in your garage remains the same, however (and your commute to work is not vastly increased), you're likely to spend fewer dollars on transportation in a small town. Depending on the region of the country, you'll save little, if anything, on the price of gasoline. But odds are you'll be driving substantially fewer miles, saying goodbye to that grueling urban commute and saving both in fuel consumption and in wear and tear on your car.

When you do service your car in a small town, you'll usually pay as much for parts as in the city, but somewhat less for labor, particularly if you can establish a relationship with a qualified independent mechanic instead of paying the inflated labor charges at dealerships. So here, too, the small town can save you money.

To find out just how much you can save, call the chamber of commerce and ask for the names of several reputable garages.

Give them a call, tell them you're planning to move to the area, and ask them what their rates are per hour or per service. Then call a dealer for comparison. With our two Toyotas, we calculate we've cut the cost of labor for repairs and service by 40 percent by going with an independent mechanic. And while you're on the phone, ask what current gasoline prices are in town.

Any insurance agent who sells auto insurance can give you quotes over the phone for premiums tailored to your needs. The overall cost of auto insurance varies from state to state, depending in large part on state laws. Some states, for example, require no-fault and uninsured/underinsured motorist coverage that will add to the bill. But chances are you'll be seeing a substantial overall savings, thanks to lower small-town premiums based on lower accident and theft rates. In Santa Rosa Beach, Florida, the Van Zandts pay 35 percent less for car insurance than they did in their Manhattan suburb. Our savings in Carroll County, Virginia, are even more pronounced: a whopping 45 percent less than what we shelled out in the City of Angels.

Any out-of-state relocation requires the less than exhilarating tasks of registering your car and obtaining a new driver's license. In-state moves to another county or municipality will often require new local (not state) license tags. To find out how much the fees will set you back, call the Department of Motor Vehicles in the state to which you plan to move. (Don't despair! Despite Jay Leno's *Tonight Show* DMV jokes, we've found our DMV to be prompt and efficient.) For an in-state move to another county or municipality, call the office of the commissioner of revenue.

Taxes

Alas, death and taxes are the only sure things in small towns, too. But what kind of taxes? That will depend not only on the town but also on the state. Moving to Alaska, Oregon, New Hampshire, Montana or Delaware? Lucky you—you'll pay no sales tax at all. Moving to Idaho or Missouri? As in seventeen other states, you'll pay sales tax on food. Moving to Wyoming or Colorado?

You'll pay the lowest sales tax in the country—3 percent. Or maybe California or New York? You'll pay the highest—8.25 percent. Ouch! The national average is 5 percent.

Then there's state personal income tax. Seven states, ranging from Alaska to Florida, have no state income tax whatsoever. (Sorry, folks: Forget about moving to Cicely, Alaska, that quirky little town in the TV show *Northern Exposure*. It's strictly fictitious. But take heart: The outdoor scenes are filmed in, well, outdoorsy Roslyn, Washington, a beautiful town that we visited in late 1994—and Washington has no state income tax!) And tax rates and the ways in which they are applied vary dramatically. In Arizona, it's 7 percent for income over $150,000; in Utah, 7.3 percent for income over $3,750. In Alabama, it's 2 percent for income under $500; in New Jersey, 2 percent for income under $20,000. Go figure.

And what about property taxes? If you're over sixty-five and you move to Alaska, you won't pay them. *Nada.* But how many of us are over sixty-five with plans to move to Alaska? Maybe a few hardy souls. More likely we'll move to Arizona or West Virginia, two of six states where property taxes are determined at less than half the average national rate of 1.25 percent of the market value of the property.

So what will your tax bite look like? To find out, phone the town hall and ask for referrals to the government entities with taxing authority for the state, county, and town. Often one informed person—a town finance officer, for example—can give you all the information you need. Find out the state income and sales tax rates (if any), and whether there is a county sales tax. Find out what the rates are on personal property, and ask if there's an intangibles tax on the value of your stocks and bonds. Ask, too, whether there are special tax districts—e.g., a water district or hospital tax—and determine how those taxes might be applied to you.

For information on property taxes, the single best source is the town assessor's office (or county assessor's office, if you expect to live outside town). To get a rough idea of what you'll be paying, get a figure of valuation per $100 and multiply this times the anticipated price of your home (and land).

Homeowner's Insurance

To complement the aforementioned car insurance, your small-town odyssey will likely include a visit to a local insurance agent's office to discuss homeowner's insurance (including personal property coverage). Even if you decide to rent rather than own a home, you're well advised to take out residential insurance to cover personal property and liability. What change can you expect in your homeowner's insurance budget?

Most people moving to a small town can expect a positive change. For comparable property, homeowner's insurance—which includes property and liability coverage—tends to be less expensive in small towns than in urban areas. Small-town property is less likely to be burglarized, vandalized or suffer fire damage.

But premiums aren't always cheaper. Insurance companies set their prices according to territorial ratings of a wide variety of risk factors. These factors, write Ralph Nader and Wesley J. Smith in *Winning the Insurance Game,* range from how many fires occurred in the area over a given period of time to how likely wind damage is in the area. If your small town happens to be in a hurricane belt or flood zone, or if it's perched on the San Andreas Fault, don't bet the farm on a lower homeowner's premium.

Another important risk factor is the proximity of a fire station and fire hydrant. Even in a small town, proximity to fire protection can vary significantly. And in some areas, homeowner's premiums can be higher because only volunteer fire departments are available, often at considerable distance from a home. In unincorporated Santa Rosa Beach, Florida, The Van Zandts have no fire hydrants and no professional fire department. "Percentage-wise, our homeowner's insurance is actually higher here than it was in New Jersey," says Jim Van Zandt. "I attribute that primarily to the fact that we don't have very good fire protection."

Once you know what sort of small-town property you'll likely own, it's not too early to contact several insurance agents for ball-park estimates. (Most agents will be reluctant to do complete workups until you own the property.) An agent who wants to sell you a policy down the road should be able to ballpark the cost of your premium based on comparable properties in town. Tell her you won't hold her to any figure, you're just trying to assess the overall cost of your new life.

Utilities

Will you be paying more or less for utilities—electricity, piped-in natural gas, water, telephone—in a small town?

Good question. For electricity, your fate in part rests on cli-matic conditions from which, and to which, you are moving. If, like the Rosenbergs, you're leaving a temperate coastal city like San Diego, in which minimal amounts of both heat and air-conditioning are required, you might wind up paying more for electricity in a small town with a less temperate climate. For that matter, do you expect to be using electric heat? We do in part of our home—and our substantial winter electricity bills, more than three times what they are in warm months, reflect that usage.

Climate and your heating and air-conditioning choices are not the only factors. "Aside from how old the power plant is . . . the biggest factors that play a part in charges to consumers are who owns the company, and how the electricity is generated," write David Savageau and Richard Boyer in *Places Rated Almanac*. The authors report that "in general, publicly owned (municipal) elec-tric power companies charge much lower rates than their larger, privately owned counterparts. Moreover, utilities that operate nuclear power plants tend to charge the consumer much higher rates than others."

Another factor in both electricity and natural gas prices is the customer density of the area served—a factor that can work to the disadvantage of more remote small towns. And, as do elec-tricity prices in relation to coal, natural gas prices tend to rise in proportion to the distance from the source of oil.

For information about rates and how they are based, ask the

chamber of commerce (or virtually anyone else you talk to) what electric power and natural gas companies serve your small town. Then call the local offices of those companies and ask for the customer service department. If the person you talk to pleads ignorance or gives you the brush-off, ask to speak to the manager.

Compared with our former city of Los Angeles, a water-guzzling monster hundreds of miles from its multiple sources, water rates in most small towns seem amazingly cheap. But perhaps you're moving from a city with relatively low rates, or to a small town (perhaps in the desert Southwest) with expensive water access. To find out what sort of rates you can expect and on what basis they are charged, the best source is usually a spokesperson in the town's water billing and collection department. Ask the chamber for that number. If your town doesn't have that department per se, ask the chamber who has the information you're looking for—perhaps the town's public works department.

It's a nice fantasy to imagine, for a moment, that because leisurely conversation is so highly prized as part of the slower pace of small towns, telephone service comes dirt cheap. As we were saying—a nice fantasy. In reality, count on paying roughly the same monthly service charges for phone use and local calls as you've been paying elsewhere. And the long-distance rates, of course, will be the same. If you want specific information about a phone company's charges in your new town, call the customer service number and speak, if possible, to the manager.

For all utilities, don't forget the hookup, or connecting, costs. For electricity, gas, water and phone, costs can range from $20 to $50 each.

Food
Like to eat out? In most small towns the price is right. Don't expect many five-star restaurants in your new small town, though. And don't expect the kind of gastronomical variety to which you've grown accustomed in your urban incarnation. But do expect to save money. Small-town restaurant prices—with the

exception of chain restaurants and fast-food eateries like McDonald's—often run anywhere from 10 to 25 percent cheaper than urban restaurants of comparable quality. Except in resort towns, where tourists support (and expect) urban-scale prices, this is true even for the increasingly common upscale small-town restaurants. If you have a restaurant budget and don't mind limited variety, small-town dining will stretch your dollars.

When columnist Rheta Grimsley Johnson, now with the *Atlanta Journal-Constitution,* moved to Iuka, Mississippi (population 3,122), in 1987, she fell in love—not only with the town that would serve as the dateline for her syndicated columns (then for *The Commercial Appeal* of Memphis)—but also with a place called Norma's.

"Its real name is the Country Cupboard but everyone calls it Norma's," says Johnson, who ate lunch there every day for the princely sum of three dollars. "You could go there and literally eat till you had to roll out the door. The point is you can't cook that cheap. You'd be stupid *not* to eat there. You could eat any way you wanted—meat, stuffing, macaroni and cheese or fresh veggies. Norma Vandiver was conscious of people with cholesterol problems. She mothered you."

For most people, however, the money spent on eating out amounts to just a fraction of their total food budget. Groceries—or food at home, in the parlance of home economists—account for 16 percent of the average American consumer's expenses. But don't bank on appreciable savings in the small-town supermarket. According to David Savageau and Richard Boyer in *Places Rated Almanac,* "The costs don't vary widely in the United States except in New York where not a leaf of cabbage reaches the supermarket except by truck, or in Anchorage or Honolulu where a great many packaged goods arrive by ship."

Savageau and Boyer's assertion confirms what we have discovered in a number of small towns in our region: on the whole, grocery prices in Virginia and North Carolina simply aren't lower enough than they were in Los Angeles to write home about. True, some items are cheaper in most of the supermarket chains—chicken, eggs, milk, to name a few. But most of the other brand-name items are just as expensive, and a few products—usually shipped from afar—are more expensive. All in all, call this cost category a draw.

It's worth noting, however, that towns that are either extremely small or are in a remote location are likely to have *higher* prices, overall, than urban areas. On camping and research trips in many of the western states, for example, it's been our experience that towns too small for chain supermarkets and/or towns isolated by mountains or deserts tend to have startlingly high grocery prices. Frank remembers a recent backpacking expedition into the exquisite Wind River mountains in Wyoming, in which grocery-store prices in remote Pinedale, Wyoming—by no stretch of the imagination a resort town—momentarily took the wind from his vacation sails. A twelve-ounce jar of Jif peanut butter sold for an outrageous $3.59 and a nine-ounce box of Sun-Maid raisins went for $2.89. Naturally, towns of this sort also tend to be among the most picturesque in America. But move to them with open eyes, and an open checkbook.

Remember that often in exchange for the higher prices, you'll get the kind of old-fashioned counter service your grandmothers took for granted. "It always amazed me that people complained about the high cost of the one grocery store in Iuka that had a virtual monopoly," says Rheta Grimsley Johnson, who in 1994 moved to the larger small town of Carrollton, Georgia (population 16,029). "In Iuka, they'd drive twenty-five miles one way to Corinth where prices were a little cheaper. But I couldn't get over the convenience. You could ask the meat man to cut your meat a certain way. You'd ask him once, and he'd remember how you liked it. Or, if you were having a dinner party, he'd ask how many you would be serving. If you told him who you were having, he'd know who they were and how they liked their meat cut—things you can't pay for in the city."

And what about your small town? If you're on a tight budget—particularly if you have a lot of mouths to feed—and you're on the fence about moving, be bold. Call or write the managers of the supermarkets in your potential small town and ask the prices for a list of fifty of your necessary food items. An unorthodox request, to be sure, but well worth it, because grocery prices do add up over time and become one of the most significant factors in your budget. And if you don't like the prices, think about gardening. It's a time-honored small-town way to cut the cost of food. And many would argue that it's good for your health, in more ways than one.

Clothing

How much money will you be shelling out for clothes? This question is relevant because there's a good chance you'll be moving from one kind of climate to another. Prior to his move to Galax, Virginia, from San Diego, the Rosenbergs' young son, Aaron, had never seen snow before. Galax, a Blue Ridge Mountain town where snow and bone-chilling winds in winter are as common as fiddle tunes in August, required that the Rosenbergs outfit Aaron with a winter wardrobe he'd never needed before.

It works the other way too, of course. Like the snowbirds who flock to the Sun Belt, are you moving from cold winters to a town where balmy breezes blow year round? Then save some shekels for a wide variety of warm-weather clothes, a variety unimaginable in the frozen North.

As much as climate, the culture into which you are moving will govern clothing costs and styles. Laurie Moorefield Forbes, after living for two decades in New England, noted that when she moved back to the small-town South her look became more "feminine." And feminine, including jewelry, scarves, stockings and shoes, can be pricey.

"I notice that people in small towns—the ones who work in offices downtown—dress better than in larger places," says Rheta Grimsley Johnson, who grew up in Montgomery, Alabama. When she lived in Iuka, Johnson bought most of the additions to her wardrobe at the Iuka House of Fashion, a small store on the main street of town that she preferred to a large, impersonal mall store. "I like having *less* of a choice," she says. "I liked it when people asked me where I got something, to say, 'Iuka House of Fashion!'"

The fact that small towns everywhere are just a stone's throw from the great outdoors often dictates a less buttoned-down look for men. In certain professions this doesn't mean that you can mothball your business suit or coat and tie during the work week. Not only bankers, but attorneys, executives, some merchants and many salesmen must still dress to the eights, if not the nines. But it does mean that the casual, rugged look is in for men as soon as the work day is done—on the street or out on the land, at social occasions, even at many public functions. Savvy businessmen, though, understand that on or off the job they are projecting an image to customers and clients. Rugged is cool; sloppy or threadbare are not. As a result, and contrary to what you might think, don't expect the male clothing budget to plummet in small towns.

And don't expect prices to be cheaper for either gender. Although outlet stores (usually located adjacent to major interstate highways) can be found scattered in urban and rural areas around the country, discount houses are rare in small towns—particularly for upscale apparel. Chain-store prices aren't lower, overall, than those of their urban kindred. And except in their periodic sales, independent small-town clothiers are hard-pressed to offer prices competitive with urban stores. The good ones make up in personal attention and service what they lack in price.

Furniture

Suppose you're moving from a small apartment in the city to a three-bedroom house in a small town. Unless you plan to live a spartan life in your new digs, you'll be buying some furniture to fill the added space. And even if you're trading one house for another, perhaps you'll sell some of your furniture before moving and will need to replace it. How much will the (monetary) damages be?

That first year in town, furniture could comprise an alarmingly large fraction of your budget. When we moved into our house, we economized by buying used furniture—chairs for the living room and a La-Z-Boy for the kitchen, side tables for the bedroom and office chairs and desks for our two offices. And this in a region of the country where great quantities of furniture are made (and sold new, at cheaper prices, than in most other regions of the country). We were strapped for cash and did not want to borrow. So we made do—and still make do, to a lesser extent—with quality used furniture. We add quality pieces bought in High Point as the budget allows.

Not everyone will want to go the used route. Unfortunately, unless you move to our neck of the woods, you're not likely to find quality *new* furniture at lower prices than in most urban areas. But buying new furniture in a small town is cheaper than buying it in the city and moving it. (See Chapter Five, "Making the Move.") Still, if you're buying a lot—and particularly if you're buying high-end—count on five figures to furnish a three-bedroom house.

Health Care

Here's a smorgasbord category: health insurance, hospitalization costs, doctor and dentist's bills, drugs—it's enough to make you lose sleep at night, as indeed many Americans have over the past few years. Will small-town health-care costs help cure insomnia?

Probably not. The short answer is, if small towns offered major relief for health-care worries, undoubtedly word would have spread and there would have been a mass exodus by now. Fortunately, that invasion—which would have been fatal to the quality of life in small towns—has not occurred.

And the long answer? Well, along with the bad news there *is* one unique positive factor. No, the cost of your current health insurance premiums will not go down just because you've moved to a demonstrably healthier environment—less air pollution, fewer stressors, that salubrious community spirit. At best, your premiums are likely to remain the same for a while, until the next inevitable rate increase is decreed by your company. But, the fact that you are likely to lead a healthier life in a small town means that you are increasing your chances of staying out of trouble, which, in turn, increases your chances for paying less health insurance over time than in the city.

Indeed, if you are applying for health insurance, your lifestyle is one of the criteria insurance companies will use to price your premium. It helps, for example, to be a nonsmoker and a moderate drinker (or teetotaler). What also works to your advantage are youth or middle age; being male (women require more frequent medical attention than men); a history of good health and an occupation that insurance companies deem relatively low risk for incurring injury or illness. While you have no control over the middle three of these five factors, if you're applying for health insurance and changing occupations in your small town, you might just catch a modest financial break.

Assuming you have health insurance, and that your deductible is not inordinately high, a large percentage of hospitalization costs in your small town will be paid by your insurance company. That's a good thing, too, because the cost of room and board in a hospital—along with the costs of hospital medical services—will not usually be markedly cheaper in a small town than in a city. In some regions of the country (ours being one), the costs of room and board and certain services are a bit lower, thanks to the preponderance of nonunion labor and lower labor costs, as well as the potential for greater efficiency in relatively small units.

Do doctors and dentists charge less in small towns than in big cities? In our experience, no. Every small town has its own economic fingerprint that will, to some extent, dictate medical and dental fees. But any small town worth living in—that is to say, any *thriving* small town—will have its contingent of doctors and dentists who charge nothing less than what the market will bear. Exceptions abound, of course, and it's not uncommon to see flourishing friendships between doctors and patients in which free medical advice is dispensed as readily as gossip.

Occasionally, as in the thriving Yakima Valley town of Toppenish, Washington, which Frank visited in late 1994, small towns have farmworkers' or other niche clinics where affordable medical and dental care are available. The Toppenish rate is based on a sliding scale—that is, on the patient's ability to pay. Similar public-spirited clinics exist in other lucky pockets as well.

In Mount Airy, the Surry Medical Ministries clinic provides free, nonemergency medical care and medicine to the working poor one night a week. However, sliding-fee and free clinics tend to be the exception rather than the rule; if you intend to make use of these, you'll need to investigate their availability *before* you move. (For more detail, see Chapter Two, "Scouting a New Location.")

And finally, there are drugs. No, not the kind for which you get busted, but rather, the kind that bust your billfold. The sad fact is prescription drugs (we learned the hard way) don't come at bargain prices anywhere, certainly no cheaper in the three small towns where we've purchased them—at Wal-Mart as well as at pharmacies—than in cities. The moral of this tale? Buy generic, whenever you can. And do all you can to promote good health.

Education

Do you have school-age children? If so, here's a category that can offer much-needed relief. If your kids have been in private schools in the city, you're going to be saving serious bucks by moving to a small town and enrolling them in public schools. While living in Richmond, Thomas and Magdalena Naylor sent their young son, Alexander, to a private school. Like many Americans, the Naylors believed that public schools in their city were neither safe nor challenging for their child. Since moving to Charlotte, Vermont, Alexander has been attending a public elementary school that has been rewarding in two significant ways. First, says Thomas Naylor, a former Duke economics professor who volunteers one hour a week in his son's classroom, "The school is at the very core of the community. And Alexander is thriving." Alexander's new public school, Naylor insists, is actually an improvement on the pricey private school in Richmond. Second, the Naylors are saving over $5,000 a year in tuition. Not to mention the time and gas money burned up in shuttling Alexander to and fro.

Suppose your kids are transferring from public schools in the city to public schools in a small town. Here the financial gain is harder to measure. But in most cases, it's there. If your children have been driving to a school in the city—or you've been driving them—you'll likely save on transportation costs. Peer pressure to wear the latest fashions exists everywhere, but it's not as acute in small towns, a factor that could save you money on what in the city can be alarmingly expensive clothing bills. Whether it's driving to a soccer practice or paying for dance lessons, involving your children in extracurricular activities will not be as expensive in a small town, either.

And what about your own education? If you're the sort of person who believes that education never ends, but there's not a lot of time or extra cash in your budget for going back to school, moving to a small town with a community college, or having one nearby, can be a boon. At Surry Community College, in Surry County, North Carolina, we've taken a beginner's course in auto mechanics for $35 and, for free, a course in operating a small business. Each spring we teach evening writing classes in the continuing education program at the college in which adult students pay just over one dollar an hour—$35 for thirty-three hours of classes. As time permits, we plan to take advantage of more of the bargain-basement offerings at the college.

Child Care

If you have children requiring child care while you work, you'll be pleased by the likely savings offered by small-town child-care centers. Nationwide, the cost of small-town child care for children age two and up ranges from $50 to $75 a week per child. (The cost is slightly higher for infants.) Such prices are a bargain compared with child-care outlays in the cities, which range from $90 to $130 a week (somewhat more in major cities like New York and Los Angeles). Thus, if you moved from Philadelphia— where child care ranges from $100 to $125 a week—to Choctaw, Oklahoma, where child care runs about $60 a week, you'd be saving anywhere from $40 to $65 a week, or as much as $260 a month and $3,120 a year, per child.

Observes Monroe Watkins, who, with his wife, Carolyn Watkins, is co-director of Bright Beginnings Pre-School Center in Mount Airy, North Carolina: "People who've moved here from, say, Charlotte, can't believe how low our prices are." But Watkins, who along with wife, holds a Ph.D. in education from the University of Pennsylvania, maintains that the quality of child care in small towns is likely to be at least as good as—and maybe better than—child care in cities. "Child care in small towns and rural areas has really come into its own in the past few years," he says. "The standards and regulations are very rigorous now. And you have the fact that in a small town, where everybody knows everybody and all the parents ask questions and keep an eye on what you're doing, there's a lot of pressure on child-care centers to be high performers, to provide a stimulating learning environment for the children. You're likely to get more for your money in a small town, plus the fact that it's a much safer climate than in most cities."

With Mount Airy attracting an increasing number of urban refugees, Watkins says that he is getting calls almost every day from around the country. The callers? Parents who are contemplating a move, or who have already decided to move, asking for information about Bright Beginnings. To find out what child care will cost in your small town, do what those callers are doing—shop around. Call the child-care centers and ask for their rates and if there's a waiting list.

SMALL-TOWN FINANCIAL STRATEGIES

The Fishbowl Culture of Money

Being smart with your money is a small-town tradition. In many small towns, where people tend to be fiscally conservative, being smart may mean, among other things, being *tight* with your money. In our experience, the small-towners who prosper know how to save a nickel, knowing that, over time, those nickels add up. By big-city standards, this small-town conservatism may seem antiquated. But don't judge the elephant by its trunk. Don't for one moment think that financially successful small-towners balk at investing in the stock markets, or that they shake their heads at every relatively risky business opportunity that comes along. As much as anyone else, small-towners enjoy being savvy, enjoy the glow of success and the respect of the community that comes with being an astute investor. If you, too, derive pleasure from money smarts, you will not be a stranger in a strange land.

As an immigrant to a small town, however, your every financial idiosyncrasy will be of more than passing interest to the natives. No matter how uncomfortable it may make you feel, your behavior with money will be noticed—and assessed—inside the fishbowl. As the old saying goes, you can run but you can't hide. Whether you make a fortune in a small town or lose your shirt; or whether, more likely, you fall somewhere in between, how you are doing is fair game. Never forget that your fortunes have entertainment value, and small-town folks will enjoy the show— without having to pay a penny. And whether or not you think you can conceal your assets and liabilities, small-town folks will have their ways of knowing. Or at least of forming their opinions based on educated guesses and the rumblings of the age-old rumor mill.

In this context of the loss of the anonymity you may have had in the city, every major financial decision you make has community-wide repercussions. Build your dream house and not only will you be pumping dollars into the local economy, but you will also become a lead actor in community theater, with the entire small town your audience. Invest serious bucks in a real estate deal and you are suddenly a heavy hitter, a person who forever afterward will be regarded as a source of cash for innumerable charities and fund drives. For us—and for most small-towners we know—being center stage as an actor in the drama of money provides powerful motivation to play your role with skill. You are an unknown quantity, and all eyes are on you—and your skills—as you make your entrance.

Being Savvy

Unless you're set for life, as you plan for the move and after you arrive, your primary question will be: How am I going to make this work financially?

There are as many scenarios for success as there are people moving to small towns, and that's a lot of ways to skin the proverbial cat. But in addition to what we've mentioned in the cost categories above, here are Ten Commandments to save you money and grief, gleaned from our experience and that of others who've made the leap. Unlike the Ten Commandments that Moses brought down from Mount Sinai, these are not written in stone, nor do they have moral and ethical connotations. But they might just keep you from letting loose a small-town primal scream.

1. Make a Budget

Once you've completed your personal financial statement (see above), you'll want to devise a budget. Budgets can be drawn up in many shapes and sizes, but there are four essentials to any good budget.

A. Set financial goals. In moving to a small town, what are your priorities that require money? Getting out of debt? Home ownership? Buying land? Starting a business? Saving or investing money for retirement? Knowing your goals is the starting point of any budget. When we first arrived in Virginia from Los Angeles, we made it our primary goal to erase our debts—the mortgages on our house and land, our credit-card debts, our business debt. All other financial considerations derived from that goal.

B. Track current expenses and cut down on expenditures that reduce your ability to achieve your goals. One simple way to track expenses is to create a monthly chart in which you write down all expenses in each cost category. This allows you to see exactly where your money is going—not an easy thing to do these days unless you do it systematically, much as an accountant would. Once you see where your money is going, you have gained a large measure of control and can prioritize and trim expenditures.

C. Project your small-town sources of income and monthly living expenses, or overhead. Clearly these projections are not written on stone tablets—they'll need to be refined as time goes on—but they'll give you ballpark figures to work with. How much income do you expect to earn from your new job, your new business, your investments, etc.? For your living expenses, use the information you've gathered in researching the cost of living in your small town.

D. Budget in a cushion of money for unexpected expenses and allowing for the imprecision of your projections.

In addition, you'll need money to pay for the move itself. (See Chapter Five, "Making the Move.")

Together with your knowledge of your assets and liabilities, doing a budget will give you a clearer picture of what's affordable now once you make the move, and what you'll need to earn to achieve your additional goals.

2. Save Money Now

If you're living in the city and earning a good salary, *save, save, save* before you make the move. Don't spend that extra money now—spend it in your small town to help you achieve your goals. At least at the beginning, it's unlikely you'll be earning a comparable wage once you move—so make it work to your future advantage.

3. If You Have It, Don't Flaunt It

Even if you think that letting people know you have money will help make you more money, don't flaunt it, particularly before people get to know you. Small towns are not Beverly Hills. Don't wear your money on your sleeve and come into town already cast in the role of a Donald Trump wannabe. If you do, you're asking for trouble—including, potentially, financial trouble.

4. Whenever Possible, Rent Before You Buy

When New York City police officer Kevin O'Grady accepted the job of chief of police in Damascus, Virginia, he and his wife, Leslie O'Grady, rented a house for a year. "I wanted to feel it out first," he says. "I wanted to see if people would accept us, and how we liked it."

After a year, the O'Gradys bought an old, three-bedroom Victorian house in town, with solid oak floors and chestnut walls, a house they are now refurbishing. "We love it here," O'Grady says. "But I think we did the right thing to rent first."

We agree. Though, in our case, we had an old family house to move into—with a mortgage attached. We had lived for five months in a second old family house, prior to the final move from Los Angeles, testing to see how we liked life in the region. We heartily recommend that most people rent first, if only for six months to a year, to make sure that this is the place for you. Buying a house and then having to put it on the market soon after you've bought it is a tremendous waste of time, energy and money. Of course, there are people—like the Burnetts, who moved to Alliance, Nebraska—who know their own minds and buy the house of their dreams without delay. But if you have any doubt at all, why take a chance?

5. Talk with Your Accountant or Financial Adviser About the Capital-Gains Tax

If you're selling property in the city and buying property in your small town for less ("buying down," as it's called), you may be subject to the capital-gains tax. If you have a $300,000 property in Chicago, for example, and can find the equivalent (or better) property for $135,000 in Fayetteville, Arkansas, you're looking at a capital-gains tax (unless you're fifty-five or over and can take the one-time, tax-free capital appreciation on your home).

The IRS considers a number of factors in levying the capital-gains tax—the amount of the mortgage on the property you're selling, the amount of money you may pay to improve the house before the sale, the real estate agent's fee, the closing costs, the purchase price of your new home, how soon you live in your new home—and, with so much money at stake, you'll want a professional in your corner before making a decision.

Contrary to conventional wisdom, it's not always wise to buy property of equal value simply to avoid the dreaded capital gains. After careful consideration, both the Rosenbergs in Galax, Virginia, and the Van Zandts in Santa Rosa Beach, Florida, decided to take the capital-gains hit when they "bought down" rather than face the kind of mortgage payment pressure they'd experienced in San Diego and northern New Jersey, respectively. And, if the house of your dreams happens to be considerably less expensive than the house you just sold in Houston, why buy the house (if you can find one) that doesn't excite you at all but is selling at an advantageous price for capital gains?

6. Ride a Bicycle or Walk to Work and to Do Errands

Here's a golden small-town opportunity if there ever was one! What few people can do in the city almost anyone in good health can do in a small town. Riding a bike or walking will not only save you money, it will also provide much of your daily quota of exercise—and thus, like an apple a day, "keep the doctor away."

7. Buy Secondhand Clothes and Furniture

We've been amazed at the bargains we've found in quality clothing and furniture at shops selling used merchandise, and have achieved significant savings. For children's clothes and toys, thrift shops can be a godsend.

8. Pay Off Your Mortgage as Soon as Possible

We recommend making this a top priority. By increasing the amount of your mortgage payments as much as 5 to 10 percent on a thirty-year mortgage, you may save tens of thousands of dollars in interest. Making payments over as long a period as thirty years can mean that you'll be paying up to three times the purchase price of your house. Why do it? As Frank's mother used to say, "You're just working for the bank."

9. Buy a Woodstove

In parts of the country where there's an ample supply of firewood and no restrictions against burning it, using a woodstove for heat is a sure way of saving on utility costs. And there's nothing more romantic than sitting by a woodstove on a winter evening. Not long after we moved to Virginia, we bought a Vermont Castings stove with a window for viewing the fire, and it's been one of the best investments we've made—not only monetarily, but in providing an inspired setting for conversation and good books. You can also save money by cutting your own wood.

10. Eat More Meals at Home

Eating out can be fun, but it's amazing how costly it can be over a period of time. And the reality is, most small towns don't offer great restaurants, or certainly not the variety of terrific restaurants to be found in the city. So here's the perfect opportunity to discover the pleasures of home cooking, as we have. For couples, cooking your own meals together can be a surprisingly creative and romantic experience. And it's a great family experience.

Now that you have an idea of how much life is likely to cost you once you set up housekeeping in a small town, you're ready to begin planning your move.

CHAPTER FIVE

Making the Move

No matter how much better life will be once you arrive, hauling body and soul (and 137 possession-filled cardboard boxes) to the small town of your dreams is invariably a test of your mettle. Not only is the process of moving physically taxing, it's also emotionally draining. Experts rate moving as one of the most stressful experiences in life—right up there with death and divorce.

If only moving were simple. If only, like the tortoise, we could carry all our worldly possessions on our back and advance from point A to point B at our own pace. Not only does moving shatter rootedness and routine, it's also fraught with thorny questions and uncertainties. What should I take with me, and what should I leave behind? How much is it going to cost me? Will I be ripped off by a moving company? Will my most treasured possessions make it to my new home in one piece?

Fortunately, moving also has a tremendous upside. It provides us with the opportunity to start life anew, to break old patterns and replace them with new ones. Approached with proper planning and a can-do spirit, moving can even provide the outward map for an exhilarating inner journey. Indeed, those who master the art of the move will feel affirmed and ready to take on the challenge of life in a small town.

This chapter will help you make all the right moves. Providing you with essential information to make the move from a big city to a small town, we'll describe numerous options and offer a step-by-step guide to making the critical decisions that are right for you—given your budget, your schedule and your family situation. We'll outline a proven, flexible timetable for getting the job done, including a schedule of activities that can be modified to meet your particular circumstances. Drawing on the advice of relocation experts and tapping into our own experience and that of others who've successfully left big cities and moved to small towns, we will show you how to:

- Pick the right moving date

- Take an inventory of your possessions

- Decide how to move

- Work with moving companies

- Do the moving yourself

- Cut down on moving expenses

- Tie up the loose ends involved in leaving your city life

- Do your own packing

- Hold a successful yard sale

- Say goodbye to family and friends as painlessly as possible

- Cope with the stress of moving

- Find storage facilities

- Settle in at your new home

Of equal importance, this chapter will show you how to determine every significant expense of your move. Throughout, we'll offer tips for saving time and money. Though it's not always possible to save both at once, this chapter will help you weigh the tradeoffs. Ultimately, we will help you establish the priorities that will determine smart choices.

DECIDING WHEN TO MOVE

If, in the course of selecting your small town, you accepted a job that starts on a specific date, you may have already made the decision of when to move. Or, if your company is relocating to a small town, you may have had the moving date picked for you.

In most scenarios, however, the timing of the move is strictly your call. In deciding when to move, you'll need to consider a variety of factors and make your decision based on financial considerations, family and job circumstances, and your tolerance for uncertainty.

Off-Season Rates

If, like Ebenezer Scrooge, you like to "make a penny scream," the cheapest time to move is during the December holiday season. With moving companies, rates during this "dead" period can be discounted by as much as 45 to 50 percent of what you would pay during the peak moving period of May through October.

"Without a doubt, the best time to move is in November and December," says Courtland Weber, president of C&M Transfer, an Arleta, California, moving company. "There are plenty of trucks available, and you get top-notch service for the lowest price."

If your schedule is flexible but you don't like the idea of disrupting the holidays, the next cheapest option is to move during the January-through-April off-season, according to moving industry professionals. During these months, the fewest number of the 50 million Americans who move annually are using rental trucks and van-line services, and lower rates can either be negotiated or are already in force. "Our rates fluctuate according to the time of year, and this is a good time price-wise to rent," says Janet Cooper, a spokesperson for U-Haul. But if you do move during the off-season, be sure to have a rental property lined up or a home purchased before you go, as vacancies are often hard to find during these months.

Time of the Month

Especially during the peak moving months, it's usually better to move in the middle rather than at the end or the beginning of the month, when moving companies are busiest. This way you'll have a better chance of moving closer to your preferred date. And, though moving companies will never admit it, you're likely to get better service.

School-Age Children

If you have children in school, you'll want to think long and hard before moving during the school year. According to Suzanne F. Scott, a clinical psychologist and educational consultant in Philadelphia who counsels families that are relocating, the palpable stress for children of transferring to a new school is doubly compounded when they are uprooted *during* the school year.

In order to move during the summer months when children are not in school, some parents go to extraordinary lengths. Rather than move from Oakland, California, to just outside Dobson, North Carolina (population 1,222), as soon as they sold their house in November 1993, Peter and Bonnie Templeton rented a house for seven months while their three school-age sons finished their school year. This objective was so important to the Templetons that they were willing to move *twice* in less than a year.

"During that whole year, we had been weighing the pros and cons of whether to take the kids out of school or wait till summer," says Bonnie Templeton. "I talked to a lot of people, and we just decided it was better to make the transition during the summer when they'd have the chance to make new friends before school started. Our kids were the driving factor in our decision to wait till then."

If you do move during the summer months, and if you plan to use a moving company, be sure to make reservations at least a month in advance of the move. During the peak summer months, moving companies will be hard-pressed to accommodate your schedule on short notice.

For those parents who must move during the school year, Suzanne Scott recommends a trip to the small town—with your school-age kids—to meet teachers and classmates. "Let the child find out in advance what the new school is like," Scott says. "Bring the child to the new school to get her acclimated. If at all possible, encourage her to make a friend or friends at the school and then have her stay in touch with those children before the move." Such friendships, Scott suggests, help bridge the child to his or her new life, making the transition less traumatic.

One way in which Jeffrey and Ellen Hillis Tate helped their elementary-school-age children establish friendships was by setting up pen pals in advance of their midyear move. (Indeed, the Tates believe that it's actually *better* to move children during the school year so they won't have to spend a summer without friends.) When they moved their children from Houston to Rogers, Arkansas, in January 1993, "We contacted the principal of the school and asked whether a pen-pal situation might be set up," says Jeffrey L. Tate, a psychiatrist. The principal responded enthusiastically and, before long, Andrew, a sixth-grader, and Elizabeth, a fourth-grader, were exchanging letters and photographs with not just one pen pal but several in their respective classes. "When they went into class on the first day, they weren't strangers; the class was eagerly anticipating their arrival." By the time they got there, the two "new kids" were mini-celebrities, objects of curiosity rather than alien creatures.

Climate and Weather Conditions
Particularly if you're doing part or all of the moving yourself, you may want to avoid the extremes of heat, humidity, and cold

found in some regions of the country during certain months. For anyone with serious health problems, such as a heart condition or high blood pressure, avoiding the dangerous combination of exertion and extreme temperatures is a must. But for even the healthiest persons, moving to a small town in Louisiana and unloading a rental truck in the middle of July is likely to be an infernal experience not quickly forgotten. And a January move to one of the many picturesque small towns in Maine could be endorsed only by the most myopic chamber of commerce.

If you're driving, another factor to consider is the weather conditions along your route. When we set out from our former home in Los Angeles en route to our new home in Virginia in early April 1986, towing a U-Haul trailer behind our Toyota truck and a U-Haul car-top carrier on our VW Rabbit, we chose I-10, a more southerly route, rather than the more direct I-40, where the risk of late-season inclement weather was greater.

Unlike those of Myron Misiaszek, our nerves were never tested by the elements. Though Misiaszek's destination—the coastal town of Newport, Oregon—enjoys a mild winter climate, his February journey and northerly route from Boston became a latter-day version of the pioneer experience of the Oregon Trail.

With his wife anxiously awaiting his arrival in Newport, Misiaszek and several friends started loading two Ryder trucks in a Boston snowstorm, then finished the job the next day on a sunny but bitterly cold afternoon. Several days later, he and a hardy friend set out for Oregon, steering the two 24-foot-long Ryder trucks, each weighing over 24,000 pounds.

They crossed the wintry mid-Atlantic and midwestern states without incident. But when the twosome, traveling in tandem on I-80, reached Wyoming, they ran into snow, sleet and freezing rain. For two days they holed up in a motel, then ventured on into Idaho—only to run into hazardous conditions again.

"The whole thing was scary," Misiaszek recalls. "I was concerned about the safety of the trucks on the road. When you hit ice on the road, all of a sudden you've got no brakes. Two different nights after we stopped driving, we ice-skated to our motel rooms. We were holding on to our Labrador retrievers as if they were sled dogs. It's sobering. Here you are hauling all this stuff cross-country, and all you keep seeing is this image of the truck sliding off the road and winding up in some canyon somewhere."

Weary from their journey, Myron and his friend rolled into Newport under balmy skies with temperatures in the fifties. "It was probably a difference of forty degrees from what we'd experienced much of the trip," he says.

The previous year, Carmen Misiaszek had taken much the same route, preceding her husband to take a nursing job in Newport. She and a friend took a more leisurely approach by driving her Saab in September 1993. "It was a pleasant trip," she recalls. "Beautiful." Because of the dry, warm weather they encountered throughout most of the trip, Carmen and her friend were able to enjoy detours to such scenic wonders as Mount Rainier in Washington. For Carmen, it was the ideal season in which to enjoy America and arrive in Newport with her sanity intact.

If he had it to do again, Myron Misiaszek admits, he would wait until late spring or early summer to make the move. "If I'm trying to move precious cargo cross-country again, another Outward Bound course is the last thing I need!"

WHEN YOU DON'T ALL MOVE AT THE SAME TIME

As the Misiaszeks demonstrated, family members often move at different times. Carmen preceded her husband to start work as a nurse at Pacific Communities Hospital in Newport. Myron stayed on in Boston to fulfill his commitments to clients of his floor-finishing business.

Similarly, Art Rosenberg moved to Galax, Virginia, from San Diego two months ahead of his wife, Dee Dee Fistel Rosenberg, and their young son, Aaron, to assume his position as postmaster of the Galax Post Office. Dee Dee Rosenberg remained in San Diego to sell the couple's house while taking care of Aaron.

These are but two of many scenarios in which family members should or must make the move at different times. Under certain conditions, it may be advisable for one partner to move ahead of the other to look for a job or place to live, while the other continues to earn money in the city. At other times, it may be necessary for one partner to stay behind until a child finishes his school year, or for a partner to move with school-age children to the small town to get them started in school, while the other partner stays behind to tie up loose ends. Though moving at different times involves additional family hardships, most notably the separation of loved ones, you may want to consider it if the positives outweigh the negatives.

MAKING THE SEPARATION WORK
FOR YOU: THE MISIASZEKS

❦ ❦

The old saying "Absence makes the heart grow fonder" lost none of its force during the time that Carmen Misiaszek lived in Newport, Oregon, and her husband, Myron Misiaszek, remained at their old Boston home. Like Shakespeare's lovebirds Romeo and Juliet, the couple yearned for their permanent reunion, a yearning exacerbated by Myron's one visit to Newport.

"The actual physical separating was too painful," Carmen remembers.

"Having to go back East was so difficult," adds Myron. "And it takes an awful lot of energy to go back and forth. You enter into a time warp. You have to readjust to a whole different culture."

STAYING IN TOUCH

As a result, the couple chose not to repeat that two-week visit, and chose instead to communicate via an 800 number that Myron used for his floor-refinishing business. Saving on their phone bill with the 800 number, they talked from thirty to forty-five minutes every night, sometimes more.

"If we weren't feeling right," Carmen says, "we might talk ten, twelve times a day. Just little check-in calls."

For Carmen, however, the "good feeling of knowing Myron was on the other side of the phone—there if I needed him," was balanced by new discoveries about herself. Without her old regimen and husband, she felt a greater sense of freedom than ever before in her life.

THE OPPORTUNITY OF A LIFETIME

Prior to their separation, she says, "Myron had had the opportunity to be apart from his family and be independent more than I had," she says. "It was wonderful to learn that I could survive. I felt like I could manage things on my own if I had to. I managed the move. I settled into the job. If someone asked me out to lunch, I didn't have to worry about 'What's Myron doing?' The separation forced me to be active. It was fun meeting new people. The whole experience was good for me."

Ironically, some of Carmen's hospital co-workers assumed that because of the prolonged separation, the Misiaszeks' marriage was splitting up. "Many people at work said to me, 'I can't believe you're leaving him alone. He'll get lonely. He'll find someone else.' In fact," she says, "Myron and I trust each other implicitly. And the separation actually made our relationship stronger."

DECIDING HOW TO MOVE

Now that you've weighed the factors involved in timing your move, you're ready to think about just how you're going to swing it. How, in short, are you going to get from Point A to Point B?

In their brochures, moving companies and rental companies make moving look like a piece of cake. The moving companies depict sweat-free employees with plastered smiles and neatly pressed uniforms doing all the work for you. The do-it-yourself brochures portray people supposedly like you having the time of their lives packing boxes and loading trucks. No one looks tired. No one looks grungy.

Both sets of images are misleading. But so, too, are most of the horror stories about moving you're likely to hear from friends and strangers. Bad things do happen in the course of moving. But most horror stories that revolve around the experience of moving stem from ignorance, poor planning and a failure to ask the right questions.

Talk to people who have moved; lessons learned from their experiences could be valuable. And don't lock yourself in at the outset to one way of doing things, or think that you need to do things exactly the same way you did the last time you moved. Very likely your situation has changed. Approach this move with an open mind, talk with your partner regularly, and don't rush decision making. Almost every mover you talk to is going to want your business, and many of them will assume that you know little or nothing about the costs and procedures of moving. But you're the boss. Don't make any commitments until you're ready.

GETTING STARTED: THE FULL-TIME JOB OF MOVING

When moving a family with a large number of possessions, try, if at all possible, to free up one partner to devote full time to the move two months before the date.

Does this sound like an extreme measure? Perhaps, until it becomes clear just how time-consuming every stage of moving can be. And how many details there are to take care of.

But, you might ask, won't you lose income you could be earning from the job you leave two months before the move?

Yes and no. Yes, it's true, you won't be earning that income. No, because there's a very good chance that by having the extra time to devote to the move, you'll save substantial amounts of money by doing the packing yourself and/or finding the best deal, either with a moving company or a rental company. In fact, depending on how lucrative your job is, chances are pretty good that you'll save as much money as you would earn by staying on the job—and you'll get the job done right.

But even if you come out a bit short financially, you'll save body and soul. The experience of moving will be less exhausting and stressful if you plan ahead than if you wait till the last minute or try to cram the enormous job of moving into those odd hours when you're not at your regular job.

By giving yourself a cushion, you'll arrive at your new hometown ready to go, rather than needing two weeks or a month to recuperate. By taking care of yourself on the front end of the move, you'll be more productive on the back end. In the long run, that productivity might even translate into a net financial gain.

If, however, you're not able to take off two months, set aside substantial chunks of time during your weekends to accomplish your tasks. If you have a family, assign tasks to each family member. Set aside more time—perhaps as much as four months—to really get the move going.

Taking Inventory

It's two months before your projected move, and you're ready to take the plunge. Taking inventory can be overwhelming, but from a psychological as well as practical standpoint, it's the perfect place to start. Taking inventory is relatively easy, at least physically, and once you get started you'll feel instantly better. Taking inventory makes the idea of moving a concrete reality. And though you may get a bit dusty mucking around in the basement, up in the attic or out in the garage, the job can be an eye-opener.

Chances are, you've forgotten about half of what's lurking down in that basement. Taking stock of your possessions will reveal exactly what you have. It will also give you a chance to start making early decisions about what to take to your new home, what not to take and how to dispose of what's left behind. Now is a golden opportunity to recycle or discard obsolete items or anything that no longer functions properly. Because heavy and/or bulky items are going to cost more to move, this is also the time to assess what condition they're in and decide whether you want to sell them or donate them to the Goodwill.

Taking inventory will also give you an early indication of what your stuff is worth. For those items you'll want to transport, knowing the value of your cargo will be a necessity when it comes time to take out moving insurance. For those items you'll want to leave behind, you'll have a rough idea of how much money their sale could bring in, a figure that can be factored in to cash-flow projections.

Determining Cubic Feet

This is the most efficient time to estimate the number of cubic feet your possessions take up. When you rent a truck and/or trailer, you'll need to have a rough idea of the total cubic feet of the load to know what size equipment to rent. (If you plan to go with a van line, they'll make their own estimate of cubic feet.)

To determine the cubic feet of an item, multiply its length times its width times its depth. For example, a table 2 feet long by 3 feet wide by 2 feet deep would measure 12 cubic feet.

HOW TO TAKE INVENTORY

To start the job, you'll need a pencil, inventory sheets, and a measuring tape or yardstick. Some of the moving companies offer inventory sheets, but designing your own is simple. You'll want to make sheets for each room of your house or apartment, as well as the garage and porch.

Let's say you're starting with your kitchen. First, title a blank sheet of paper "Kitchen." Then make seven columns across the page, the first one narrow, the second one broad, the third through seventh columns half as wide as the second. Then grid the sheet by drawing equidistant lines across the columns.

Next, title each column. The first column is "Number"; the second, "Item"; the third, "Year Purchased"; the fourth, "Original Price"; the fifth, "Current Value"; the sixth, "Cubic Feet"; the seventh, "Ship?" (See sample kitchen inventory form on page 214.)

KITCHEN

NUMBER	ITEM	YEAR PURCHASED	ORIGINAL PRICE	CURRENT VALUE	CUBIC FEET	SHIP?

Now you can begin taking inventory. If you don't remember the year of purchase or original cost, make your best guess. And try at least to ballpark the current value. Remember that this inventory is all-inclusive—not just furniture or major appliances. It will include everything from your electric can opener to your Tupperware. When you're finished, add up all the "Current Value" columns to arrive at a rough estimate of the value of your possessions.

For the "Ship?" column, answer yes or no. Your answers don't have to be definitive, but jotting something down will force you to examine each item carefully for its utility as well as for its keepsake value. Though familiar objects can be comforting amid the uncertainties of relocation, think long and hard about the value of each item. "This isn't the time to be sentimental," writes Nan DeVincentis Hayes in *Move It!: A Guide to Relocating Family, Pets and Plants.* Instead, it's a rare opportunity to free yourself of clutter, to make a fresh start toward more streamlined living. Keep in mind that if you do take the item, you're investing moving dollars in it as an object that you value. That investment will make it even harder to let go of the item in your new home. Move it now and chances are you'll keep it the rest of your life.

So it pays to be ruthless. As you take inventory, continue to ask yourself, "What can I get rid of?" If you have any doubt about the item or haven't used it in a year, get rid of it. As you're taking the inventory and plan to discard an item, go ahead and place it in a box marked for discard. Later you can decide whether you'd like to sell the item at a yard or tag sale or give it to charity.

Ten Jobs to Get Started On

> **"We cannot do everything at once but we can do something at once."**
>
> —CALVIN COOLIDGE

As soon as you've finished the inventory, you'll need to start tying up the multiple loose ends woven through your urban life. You'll want to make your own list, depending on many individual variables, but here are a dozen jobs for starters, some of which you can tackle immediately and others that can be done as time allows:

1. Round up personal records. Almost a career in itself! Gather all those dental, medical, academic and veterinarian records you, your family and your pets will need in your small town.

2. Get W-2 forms from previous employers or arrange for them to be mailed to your new address.

3. Transfer memberships in professional and social organizations. For those memberships that aren't transferable, sell them or resign.

4. Notify any lending agency of your move. Like it or not, lenders will want to know where to find you!

5. Tag items you want to sell or donate to charity. Start recycling and discarding other items that you don't plan to take with you. For items you want to sell, get the word out through word of mouth, signs, and advertising. Collect receipts for donated items for tax deductions.

6. Set up a record-keeping system for moving expenses. Many of the lesser expenses as well as the major ones, such as the costs of meals and lodging during the trip itself, are tax deductible. Get a three-ring notebook with divider pouches that can hold receipts, and keep it one place, such as on top of the refrigerator.

7. If you're selling your house or condo, start spiffing it up. Repairs and upgrades, such as installing new carpets, may be necessary or advisable. Consider hiring a professional cleaner. A thoroughly clean house is a must for making the sale you want.

8. Take stock of your frozen, canned, and boxed foods, and start using them up or giving them away.

9. Start collecting boxes, containers and packing materials. Pick up boxes at every opportunity: grocery store, liquor stores, anywhere you can find them.

10. The earlier you can start packing the better. Having a longer period to pack allows you to be more careful, more efficient, and more patient. Relocation experts say that you actually get more done if you pack two hours every day over five days rather than start Monday morning and work for ten hours straight. (See sections following, "Finding Boxes and Packing Materials" and "Packing.")

OPTIONS FOR MOVING

It's useful to think of options for moving in four categories: *moving yourself; hiring professional movers; hiring amateurs* (friends, family, students, etc.); and *combining options*. Let's examine each category.

Moving Yourself

Unless you own a truck or trailer, or have no more earthly possessions than Jack Kerouac's freight-hopping protagonist in *The Dharma Bums,* you'll have to rent a truck and/or trailer and possibly a car-top carrier to do your own moving. But you can still do all the work yourself.

The question is, do you want to? Doing it all yourself means doing all the packing, the loading, the driving and the unloading—not to mention picking up and returning the rentals. It's a backbreaking assignment, and it's a hassle. But doing your own moving *will* save you a lot of money, more than any other option; when compared with hiring a moving company, moving yourself can save you thousands of dollars.

When we moved from our apartment in west Los Angeles to our house in Virginia, we compared the costs of hiring a moving company, renting a truck and renting a trailer and car-top carrier. With just the two of us and not an overwhelming amount of cargo, we opted for the trailer and the car-top carrier, loading the rest of our things into the pickup and the VW Rabbit. Though the work was hard, we saved money, and the move went off without a hitch. (Okay, so we did have a *trailer* hitch!)

We did learn, though, that there's nothing heroic about doing all the work yourself. Don't be a martyr. If you don't want to do it—and you don't have to—choose another option.

Hiring Professional Movers

No question, this is the first-class way to go. For a considerable number of your hard-earned greenbacks, a moving company will do it all: pack and load your belongings, transport them, unload them in the rooms where you want them and even unpack them for you. How can you beat deluxe service like that? Except for the dent it puts in your wallet, this option is the most painless way to move.

But even when you do some of the work yourself, moving companies don't come cheaply. When Myron and Carmen Misiaszek priced moving companies in Boston prior to their move to Newport, Oregon, the best quote they could find was just under $16,000. For that price, the Misiaszeks would also have had to do the packing and unpacking themselves. Instead, they opted to rent the two 24-foot-long Ryder trucks that Myron and his friend drove to the Misiaszeks' new home. The price: $5,500. Add the cost of fuel for the trucks—around $900—and the Misiaszeks still came out at less than half of what a moving company would have charged.

The "Spread"

A second factor to consider in thinking about a moving company is whether you can live with the "spread." The spread is the range of days—usually from two days to a week—within which the moving company promises to unload your cargo. This means that you will not be able to pinpoint the exact day the mover delivers your possessions to your new home. In moving your things to a small town, the spread can be even wider than it is when moving to a city because moving vans often bundle the cargo of two or more customers together. If two other customers are moving from Boston to Portland, Oregon, and you're moving to out-of-the-way Newport, chances are good you'll be the last customer served.

Separation Anxiety

A third factor to weigh is whether you're comfortable being separated hundreds or even thousands of miles from your possessions. In some of the moving-company ads, you see the comforting image of the moving van on a scenic highway followed by the happy family in their car. Unfortunately, it doesn't work that way. Unless you can somehow strike a deal with the driver to follow the truck day and night, you may have to live with some temporary separation anxiety.

Hiring Amateurs

Amateurs include family, friends, students and anyone else for whom a little knowledge about moving can be a dangerous thing! On the other hand, the price is right. And amateurs can sometimes make up in esprit de corps what they lack in expertise.

At one time or another, many of us have hired amateurs to do some form of moving, especially loading and unloading. In our own experience, hiring amateurs isn't a bad idea if either they or you know how to load a truck or trailer. If you do and they don't, you'd better supervise.

An appealing but not always desirable variation on this theme is prevailing upon friends and family to work for free. The obvious upside—the cheapest labor on earth—is counterbalanced by some fairly subtle downsides. Most "free" labor comes with the unwritten price tag that the favor be returned someday. And unless you're extremely careful, free labor is a breeding ground for resentment, an emotion that usually sets in fast well before the work is even finished. What's more, free labor may rob you of some of the authority you may need to do the job right.

If you're going to use free labor, dispense instructions as diplomatically as possible. And be as generous as old Saint Nick.

Think of some nice gifts for your helpers. Have some good meals prepared, or treat the crew to pizza and soft drinks. Above all, be generous with your time. Very likely, one of the reasons family members and friends want to help you is that they want to spend time with you.

Combining Options

Moving companies and do-it-yourself companies want your business any way they can get it. As a result, some have expanded their services and offer more options than ever before. Essentially, services are offered à la carte. For example, you can hire a moving company to do all or any portion of your work. Perhaps you might elect to pack the sheets and towels and hire professionals to pack breakables like lamps, chinaware and crystal. These days, some moving companies will even allow you to load their truck—under the driver's supervision.

The menu of possible combinations offers considerable flexibility for your schedule and finances. You can hire amateurs to pack your belongings, Ryder to load them, drive the truck yourself and amateurs to unload. If the idea of driving a truck terrifies you, you can do everything yourself but the driving. If loading and unloading is your thing, you can leave everything else to your support troops.

When Marie Olesen Urbanski, Wanda's mother and a retired professor, moved from her house in Orono, Maine, to within a mile of us, she saved over a thousand dollars from what she would have paid a moving company for loading, hauling and unloading by picking and choosing from a menu of possibilities.

After renting a 15-foot Ryder truck for $880.60, she asked friends to help her pack, hired knowledgeable amateurs (graduate students at the University of Maine) to load the truck and flew us to Maine to drive the truck and her car 1,100 miles to Virginia. Once she arrived at her new home, Marie hired amateurs to unload the truck and cart her belongings to the appropriate rooms in her exquisite, old, two-story white-frame farmhouse. She then hired a young neighbor to help her unpack and shelve her many books. Marie's move—difficult under any circumstances for a woman of seventy-something—was accomplished with ingenuity and a minimum of muss and fuss.

ROMANCING THE MOVING COMPANIES

After researching your options, you must begin narrowing down the possibilities. Start six weeks before the move. No less than that. And preferably longer in advance, if your schedule permits. Call two moving companies. Two is enough for starters. This is what we call the "blind-date" stage. What you're doing is getting your feet wet without making any commitments or even choosing the moving company option. You're scoping out what these companies have to offer while getting two cost estimates that you can use later for bargaining purposes, both with rental companies and other moving companies.

Don't call the cut-rate moving companies unless you're a gambler by nature. A cut-rate company probably will advertise on bulletin boards. Some of them abide by the rules of the Interstate Commerce Commission (ICC), the regulatory agency for interstate moves, and some don't. They may not give you an estimate sheet, and some will offer little or no coverage for damages. Their paperwork—all the forms and contracts reputable companies use—may be in short supply. And they may be reluctant to give you references.

If you do opt for a cut-rate company, maybe you'll get lucky. Maybe all your goods will arrive in one piece. Some cut-rate companies can beat the price of reputable companies by as much as 25 percent. Assuming all goes well, you'll probably come out ahead financially. But do you want to take the chance?

Stick with the big boys or companies with an established track record. Their trucks are well maintained; they offer you references upon request; after the move, they talk to you about what you liked and didn't like about their service.

You can usually find them in the Yellow Pages—Allied Van Lines, Atlas Van Lines, Bekins, Global Van Lines, Mayflower, North American Van Lines, United Van Lines, to name a few.

Invite two of them to give you estimates. (If friends have had good experiences with any of them, call those companies.)

From the ads, it's easy to get the impression that the moving van arriving at your door has been dispatched from Moving Company Heaven. Instead, a national company like Global Van Lines is an umbrella company for local affiliated agents. These local agents—who split their profits with Global—are the people you do business with. Often the drivers are owner-operators of the moving vans. And, in many cases, the people who help the driver load and unload are freelancers.

The Estimator

The local agent or his representative who comes to your home at no charge is called the *estimator,* or *consultant.* That's because he will rummage around your home trying to estimate (as perhaps you have now done yourself) the cubic feet of the belongings you plan to move. The estimator then calculates their estimated weight by one of several methods. Using a mathematical formula, some estimators multiply the number of cubic feet by seven to establish a weight estimate.

On average, according to Courtland Weber of C & M Transfer, it takes estimators an hour and a half to do their job. One veteran North American Van Lines estimator we spoke with prides himself on being able to reach an estimate in one hour. No matter how long it takes, experienced estimators can make accurate weight estimates. Of course, the final cost estimate will depend on the number of extra services and the kind of coverage for damages you want. Theoretically, it will depend in larger part on the *tariff* or *base rate,* that is applied to the combination of total weight and total miles traveled in the move.

Base rates for interstate moves are fixed by the ICC. So it would appear that if you request the same services from each company, and if each company accurately estimates weight, you will wind up with comparable cost estimates, given comparable prices for additional services. But such is not always the case. In practice, the moving industry is highly competitive, and local agents who must abide by the base rates will often deliberately underestimate weight so that they can quote you a lower price. This amounts to a hidden discount.

Cost Estimates

There are two kinds of cost estimates—nonbinding and binding. A *nonbinding estimate* means that the moving company is not bound to its cost estimate, even though that estimate is in writing. Instead, when your load is weighed, you will pay for the actual, not the estimated weight. However, you should know that a moving company is not allowed to charge you more than the estimated cost plus 10 percent.

A *binding estimate* means that the mover is bound to the cost estimate made by the estimator, even if the estimate turns out low. You will not have to pay a penny more than the written cost estimate, even if the load weighs hundreds or even thousands of pounds more than the mover estimated.

How do you choose between the two? In general, it's better to go with a binding estimate if you have a lot of heavy items—books, appliances, heavy tools, etc. With a binding estimate, you can't be overcharged for all that weight. At the same time, particularly because some companies are making deliberately low weight estimates, you may wind up shipping a heavy load at a significantly discounted price. But if you think your load is relatively light, you're probably smarter to go with a nonbinding estimate. This way you won't fall victim to a high estimate, paying for weight that isn't there.

If you do choose a nonbinding estimate, however, be sure to get estimates from a number of companies to protect yourself against one or two deliberately low cost estimates. Multiple estimates will give you a better overall picture of the true weight of your cargo.

Insurance

Moving companies are required by law to provide a minimum of sixty cents a pound per article coverage for damage to your goods. But companies normally offer three kinds of *coverage* or *valuation.* All are based on weight, so you must know roughly how much your load weighs.

The first type of coverage, called *released value,* is that bare-bones sixty cents per pound per article coverage. If your cargo weighs 10,000 pounds, for example, and it is lost en route, you will receive $6,000 in compensation. Obviously this would be woefully inadequate compensation for valuable items. For an antique grandfather clock that weighs, say, 50 pounds, but whose value is $2,000, you would receive $30 in compensation. While this is the least costly way to go, it's clearly the riskiest.

With the second kind of coverage, *lump-sum value,* the moving company pays $1.25 per pound. But for every $1,000 the mover pays in compensation, you pay $5. Still, even though you have to pay in this scenario, it sounds like a better deal than released value. Yet a problem arises when only a fraction of your cargo is lost or damaged, but it's a valuable fraction. If your grandfather clock gets wiped out, you'll receive $62.50 under lump-sum value coverage. That beats thirty bucks, but not by much.

The third type of coverage is called *full-replacement protection.* According to industry professionals, this is the coverage of choice for the majority of people who hire moving companies. Again, coverage is based on weight. So if you want to recover roughly the full value of your grandfather clock, you multiply 50 pounds by 68, meaning that you want to replace your clock 68 times its weight, or 3,400 pounds. This also equals $3,400. Then, if your clock is destroyed, the moving company deducts the true weight of 50 pounds from the coverage weight of 3,400 pounds and gets 3,350. The mover then pays you sixty cents a pound of the extra 3,350 pounds, equaling $2,010. For each $1,000 of declared value of this type of coverage, you pay an average of $8.

An alternative to moving-company coverage is to take out a special insurance policy on a valued item or items, which normally requires an appraisal. When Jeff Jennings and his family moved from Fargo, North Dakota, to near Selah, Washington (pop. 5,110), he took out a special policy on a gun collection appraised at $35,000. (However, before you look into special policies—or before you ultimately sign on for a company's coverage—check your existing insurance policies to see what they cover.)

After all your options have been discussed, and when the estimator has made his initial cost estimate, he will draw up an *order for service*. Don't panic! Though some unscrupulous estimators might want you to think otherwise, an order for service does not obligate you to hire that company. It's not a contract. It's a way of recording what's been discussed during your session, and the moving company wants it for its files. You're entitled to a copy as well.

Tell the estimator up front that you'll be getting other estimates. Not only is it ethical, but telling him what you are doing lets the company know that you are looking for the best deal and are well-informed. As a result, company representatives may treat your concerns with more respect. And they may offer you a better deal, either now or down the road.

THIRTY BASIC QUESTIONS TO ASK THE ESTIMATOR

Copy these questions onto a notepad, or Xerox this page, and take notes copiously. Taking notes signals that you mean business. Don't hesitate to be politely skeptical when necessary.

1. How many years has your company been in business?

2. How many moving vans are in your fleet?

3. Has your company ever had problems with the ICC?

4. Could you provide me with references?

5. What services do you offer?

6. Why should I go with you if the estimates come out about the same?

7. Is your job performance better than that of other companies?

8. What kind of follow-up service do you offer?

9. Who is the driver and what relationship does he or she have to your company?

10. Who are the people who will do the loading and unloading?

11. How much experience do they have?

12. What priority will my goods have given the fact that I am moving to a small town?

13. What is your record of loading and unloading on schedule?

14. What sort of compensation do you offer if you are late either in loading or unloading?

15. Will my goods be loaded and unloaded before the end of a normal workday?

16. When and how do you expect to be paid?

17. Will everything that we agree on be in the contract, in writing?

18. Are there any hidden charges?

19. Do you sell boxes for packing?

20. Are they new or used?

21. Why should I buy your boxes?

22. What are the penalties if the driver has to repack?

23. Do you offer special handling on valuable items?

24. What kind of damage coverage do you offer?

25. Are there any deductibles or hidden waivers?

26. Why should I choose a binding or nonbinding estimate?

27. What's your ratio of damage claims to shipments?

28. How much time does it take to settle a claim?

29. If you refuse to settle a claim, where are disputes with your company normally resolved?

30. If there's an unresolved conflict between us, who is the person above you to whom I can talk?

PRELIMINARY WORKSHEET: USING A MOVING COMPANY
As you talk to estimators and consider hiring a moving company, use this worksheet to determine a preliminary ballpark figure for how much the entire move will cost you. (You may want to make a copy for each company.) As you look at your budget, this worksheet will help you decide about the affordability of a moving company and its various services. A final moving-company worksheet, provided later in this chapter when you have chosen a moving company, will reflect any bargaining you may have done, discounts, and other contingencies.

1. Moving company's binding or nonbinding estimate with all services (packing, loading, unloading, unpacking): _____
   a. If I pack _____
   b. If I load _____
   c. If I pack and load _____
   d. If I unload _____
   e. If I unload and unpack _____
   f. If I pack, load, unload, and unpack _____
   g. If I do other combinations of the above _____

2. Coverage, if I choose:
   a. Full replacement protection _____
   b. Special insurance _____

3. Other services _____

4. Senior-citizen discount _____

5. Boxes and packing materials if I:
   a. Buy them from the moving company _____
   b. Purchase them elsewhere _____

6. If I'm driving. Figure thirty-four cents a mile. _____

7. If I'm flying _____

8. If I'm taking the bus _____

9. If I'm going by train _____

10. Lodging. (Call the 800 number of your favorite motel chain to determine rates along your route. Multiply the

number of nights on the road times the average rate per night for two. To find the 800 number, check the Yellow Pages or dial 1-800-555-1212.) _____

11. Food. (Figure $35 a day for one person. Or make your own estimate, depending on what and where you like to eat.) _____

12. Storage. (See "Storage" section below.) _____

13. Contingencies. (Getting a flat tire fixed, etc. Figure $200.) _____

TOTAL COST _____

Talking to Rental (Do-It-Yourself) Companies

Even if you know you're going to use a moving van line, it's still a good idea to get a few quotes from Ryder and its ilk. Being able to quote the cost of doing it yourself can be a powerful bargaining chip when negotiating with moving companies. At the same time, now you have two quotes from moving companies to use with the rental companies. Already, you can start taking photocopies of these estimates to show the folks at Ryder.

Fortunately, learning the lingo of rental companies is simpler than it is with the moving companies. The first thing to do is collect and read the brochures. On a recent visit to our local U-Haul and Ryder agents, we found the U-Haul brochures to be slightly more comprehensive than Ryder's. But both offer clear and basic explanations of most of what you'll need to know in doing business with them.

Start with at least two companies. A third company to consider is Penske-Hertz, and there are others. Our own experiences with both U-Haul and Ryder have been satisfactory, but prices and services do vary. It pays to shop around.

What Size Equipment to Rent

The first and most important thing to know is how much truck and/or trailer space you'll need. You may have already determined the total cubic feet of the possessions you'll be transporting. If you haven't done that job, do it now. It's handier to lump your items whenever possible. If you have three items with the same number of cubic feet—say, three bookcases, each with 20 cubic feet—multiply by three. Your bookcases have a total of 60 cubic feet.

In their brochures, the rental companies provide simple formulas for translating total cubic feet into the right-size truck and/or trailer and/or car-top carrier. Rental companies also provide cubic-feet estimates based on the number of bedrooms in your home and the average type and number of possessions. But because your home may not be "average," it's usually better to go by your own cubic-feet estimate.

Weight Capacity

Another important factor to consider in choosing a truck is its weight capacity. Prior to his move from Boston to Newport, Oregon, Myron Misiaszek determined that U-Haul's and Ryder's rates were competitive. But with heavy possessions to transport, he learned that Ryder's largest truck—a 24-foot rig—could carry 3,000 pounds more than U-Haul's truck of equal size. For that reason, he went with Ryder. If the brochure fails to provide information on weight capacity, be sure to ask the agent.

Maintenance and Repair Service

Ask the rental company how often the trucks and other equipment are serviced. And be sure to find out what sort of on-the-road repair service the rental company offers. Especially if you are moving to an out-of-the-way small town, it's important to know what to do if the truck breaks down or if there's trouble with any of the other rental equipment.

Rental Equipment

In addition to trucks, trailers, hitches, car-top carriers and utility carriers (open-air luggage racks), rental companies normally rent hand trucks, moving dollies, furniture pads, side-view mirrors and tow bars and tow dollies for towing your car behind the truck. They also sell myriad boxes, mattress bags, tape for packing, rope and locks for loading, and hitches and light connectors for towing.

Other Services

If you want a rental company to do the packing and loading, U-Haul will send a crew to do those jobs in many cities. But such additional services are not available in most small towns, so chances are you'll have to do your own unloading and unpacking or hire amateurs. U-Haul asks that you reserve a crew at least twenty-four hours prior to moving day. Free estimates are available upon request. U-Haul will give you a list of things to do before the crew arrives (defrosting the refrigerator, disconnecting gas appliances, etc.). The U-Haul crew brings its own packing materials, for which you will be charged. In the event of damage to your goods while packing and loading, U-Haul maintains that it will settle most claims on the spot.

Insurance

Rental companies normally offer three kinds of insurance: for the truck and equipment; for your cargo and personal accident insurance, covering the driver and passengers. Before taking out any of these policies—which tend to be pushed hard, with dire warnings, by the salespeople who encourage you to cover everything with them by initialing an "Accept" blank on the rental agreement—be sure to determine from your insurance agent what your present policies cover. In some cases, your policies will provide sufficient overall coverage. In many other cases, your policies will provide coverage for some but not all of these contingencies.

Typical of the rental companies' coverage, Ryder offers full coverage for damage to the truck and other equipment. For one-way, long-distance rentals, Ryder will insure your cargo—as long as it is inside the truck—for up to $25,000, less a $100 deductible. Ryder also offers personal accident insurance covering the renter and passengers for loss of life, medical expenses and ambulance expenses. The Ryder plan includes personal injury occurring while you (but not your passengers) are loading or unloading the truck. Ryder will pay a maximum aggregate coverage of $80,000 for any one accident.

Rates

Unlike moving companies, which charge by a combination of weight plus miles, rental companies base their rates on the number of days rented and—in the case of rental trucks—the size of the truck and the number of miles traveled. Rental rates can also be affected by what is convenient for the rental company. According to U-Haul spokesperson Janet Cooper, when moving to a small town, a customer can sometimes get a lower rate by dropping off the rentals at a busy U-Haul dealership in the city nearest the small town.

Bargaining

If you're certain by now that you want to go with a rental company, and if you know what equipment and services you want, don't talk turkey with the rental agent yet. Instead, get three more estimates from moving companies, then return to the rental companies you've visited and show them your lowest estimate among the five you've obtained. If possible, talk to the head knocker. Say to her, "Okay, Forty Acres and a Mule Van Lines is asking just $3,000 and they're doing the packing, loading, hauling and unloading. You're asking $1,800, and I'm doing everything." The point is, the head knocker wants your business—especially if business is slow. She may come down on the mileage rate. Or you may be able to negotiate a lower fee for everything but the truck. True, this approach will take a bit more of your time. But it could save you a nice piece of change.

Of course, when it comes to bargaining, there's more than one way to go. When Myron Misiaszek started talking to a Ryder agent in Boston during the peak season in 1993, the agent wanted $7,500 to rent two 24-foot trucks like the ones Misiaszek and his friend drove to Newport, Oregon. Since he was not ready to move then anyway, Misiaszek walked. By February 1994, when Misiaszek talked to the agent again, the price dropped to $6,100.

Then Misiaszek played his trump card. He pointed out that he was renting two trucks, not one. He added that he was traveling a lot of miles. Having walked away once, Misiaszek made it clear that he was happy to do it again. He was able to get the price shaved even more: The final amount was $5,500.

Misiaszek did another smart thing. He determined that the Ryder 24-foot diesel trucks got better mileage than the gas-powered trucks of the same size. And, at the time of his move, the cost of diesel fuel was slightly lower in most states than that of gasoline. So, to save fuel costs, he rented diesel trucks, which averaged ten miles per gallon. Misiaszek's fuel bill for crossing the country was $900—considerably less, he insists, than what he would have paid using gasoline trucks.

FIFTEEN QUESTIONS TO ASK A RENTAL COMPANY

1. How long has your company been in business?

2. What services do you offer?

3. Are there any hidden charges?

4. What is the weight capacity of your vehicle?

5. What kind of insurance do you offer?

6. How often is your equipment serviced?

7. What kind of road service do you offer?

8. Do you offer any compensation for time delays and extra expenses due to equipment breakdowns?

9. Do you offer unloading service in the town to which I'm moving?

10. If the members of your packing-and-loading crew damage my goods, on what basis would a claim be resolved?

11. If there's an unresolved conflict between us, who is the person above you to whom I could talk?

12. If there's a conflict with the head person, where are disputes with your company usually resolved?

13. Do you sell boxes and packing materials?

14. Why should I buy from you if I can find boxes and packing materials cheaper elsewhere?

15. How many miles per gallon do your diesel-powered trucks get? What about gasoline-powered trucks?

Preliminary Worksheet: Using a Rental Company
As you talk to rental companies, use this worksheet to determine a preliminary ballpark figure for how much the entire move will cost you. As you look at your budget, compare this worksheet with your preliminary worksheet for a moving company. A final rental company worksheet, provided later in this chapter when you may have chosen a rental company, will reflect any bargaining you may have done, discounts, and other contingencies.

1. Rental company's quote with all services (packing, loading, unloading, unpacking): _____

    a. If I pack _____

    b. If I load _____

    c. If I pack and load _____

    d. If I unload _____

    e. If I unload and unpack _____

    f. If I pack, load, unload and unpack _____

    g. If I do other combinations of the above _____

2. Insurance, if I choose:

    a. Truck and equipment coverage _____

    b. Cargo coverage _____

    c. Personal accident coverage _____

    d. Special coverage _____

3. Boxes, if I:

    a. Buy them from the rental company _____

    b. Buy them elsewhere _____

4. Packing materials, if I:

    a. Buy them from the rental company _____

    b. Buy them elsewhere _____

5. If I or someone else is driving my car(s). (Figure 34 cents a mile per vehicle.) _____

6. If I or others fly _____

7. If I or others take the train _____

8. If I or others take the bus _____

9. Fuel for the truck. (Divide the total miles of the trip by the mpg of the truck to get the number of gallons you'll burn. Multiply that figure by the current average price of gas or diesel per gallon.) _____

10. Lodging. (Multiply the number of nights on the road by the average cost of your favorite motel chain for two people per night.) _____

11. Food. (Figure $35 per day for one person.) _____

12. Storage _____

13. Contingencies. (Figure $200 for the trip.) _____

TOTAL COST _____

Decision Time

You're doing well. Perhaps by now you've gotten the five estimates from moving companies. If not, round up the other three and make a decision. Compare the worksheets. Think about the trade-offs: time versus money, one kind of stress versus another. Do you want to go with a moving company? If so, choose one now.

Alternatively, perhaps you've weighed the trade-offs and, with your lowest moving company estimate in hand, bargained with a rental company and made your best deal. If not, do so now.

Making your decision between a moving company and a rental company is half the battle. It's the biggest decision you'll make while moving. Now that you've done it, take a deep breath. There's still plenty to think about.

MARRYING A MOVING COMPANY

If you chose a moving company, prepare to be married. For the next month to six weeks, you, your family and your possessions are going to be wedded to that moving company, for better or for worse, in sickness and in health—till at your new home do you part. From now on, everything you do—the negotiating, the packing, the loading, the shipping, the unpacking—will be done in the context of this relationship, with each party holding the other accountable for its actions.

If you make your wishes clear, if you leave as little as possible to chance, it can be a relatively happy marriage. Perfection is too much to hope for. But you should do everything in your power to make the process work.

Not only have you chosen a moving company, but by now you've decided whether you want a binding or nonbinding estimate. You've also discussed with the estimator/consultant what kind of insurance best suits your needs and made a decision. You're ready to talk schedule and sign the contract.

Pinpointing the Loading and Unloading Dates

This process is a negotiation, and the negotiation begins with you. In the best-case scenario, you give the moving company the exact dates you want it to pick up and deliver your goods. Sometimes this works out—more likely in the off season. But just as often, the moving company tells you those exact dates are unavailable. You then negotiate the dates that are mutually satisfactory.

But there's a catch there, too. Yes, the moving company, if it is honorable, picks up your cargo on the appointed day. But more than likely, it will deliver that cargo within the "spread"—the grace period of days, normally ranging from two days to week, but varying from company to company and by time of the year—within which it is entitled to deliver.

Unfortunately, there's nothing you can do about the spread unless you're willing to pay extra. Some moving companies offer service options, among them so-called expedited service. By paying for this option, you obligate the company to load and deliver your goods on specified dates.

But whether you choose that option or not, leave no room for ambiguity about the dates you desire. Never say, "As soon as possible." Agree on specific dates, including the spread—and make sure you have them in writing in the contract.

Be clear as well on what the penalties are when a moving company fails to deliver on time. Most companies offer compensation. When Jeff and Holly Jennings and their two small boys moved from Fargo, North Dakota, to near Selah, Washington, they collected $125 a day for eleven days from North American Van Lines because the shipment was late, forcing the Jennings family to live in a motel. Companies normally cover food and lodging expenses. Be sure your company does—and be sure it's in writing.

Signing the Contract

The contract you must sign is usually called the *bill of lading*. Read it carefully. Many horror stories originate in one's not having read the contract. Make sure everything in it corresponds with the verbal agreements you've made. The bill of lading should also match the description on the order for service, which you received from the estimator on the estimator's original visit. If there are discrepancies, refrain from signing. Ask the mover to take a second look at the bill of lading, and get in touch with the estimator/consultant. When everything checks out and you have signed, hang on to your copy for dear life until everything has been delivered. Should goods be damaged or the shipment be late, you'll need your copy to file for compensation.

THE FREDERICK FAMILY: THE MOVE FROM HELL

W hen Jane and Ed Frederick hired a moving company to haul their belongings along with those of their son, Darryl,* from Fort Lauderdale, Florida, to a town in northern Virginia, their move resembled one of those Chevy Chase Na-

*Names have been changed

tional Lampoon movies, where everything goes haywire for the entire family. Theirs is a cautionary tale—a primer in how not to make your move.

Having decided to go with a moving company because it seemed easier to do, the Fredericks got four estimates they were told were binding: from United Van Lines, $2,869; from Admired Movers, $2,428; from Graebel Van Lines, $3,346; and from Eastern Van Lines, $2,210. Because of the low estimate, the Fredericks chose Eastern Van Lines, even though its weight estimate of 6,727 pounds was significantly less than the other weight estimates, particularly Graebel's, which came in at just under 10,000 pounds. Though puzzled by the discrepancy, the Fredericks were assured by Eastern Van Lines—verbally—that the estimate was binding and figured they were getting a great deal.

"We didn't feel there was any need to bargain with them," Jane Frederick says. "It was such a low estimate."

Because the Fredericks did not carefully read the contract before they signed, they failed to realize that theirs was not a binding estimate. When the truck was weighed in Fort Lauderdale, their goods weighed nearly 10,000 pounds, very close to Graebel's estimate. They then realized they would have to pay a rate dictated by a nonbinding estimate. Outraged, the Fredericks tried to call the deal off and demanded that the mover unload their goods. Fine, replied the mover. He would do as they wished—for $750.

"We felt they were crooks," Frederick says. "I think they deliberately gave us a very low estimate to get our business. Once they had all our stuff in their truck, they had us over a barrel. What could we do?"

Not much. They were stuck with Eastern. After the mover drove off, the Fredericks tried to cool down by stopping at Disney World for several days on their drive north. Another mistake still haunted them. On moving day their four-year-old son, Darryl, collided with a man loading the truck, which left a large bruise on his head. Jane Frederick was wishing now she'd kept Darryl out of harm's way that day. His bruise reminded her not only of the painful collision but also of the family's bruised relationship with the movers. The Fredericks now worried that their belongings were in the hands of untrustworthy people. And, as it turned out, their travails were far from over.

"Until the day of the move," Jane Frederick says, "we had told them we wanted a specific delivery date. But when we signed the contract, I noticed that they had two or three weeks' range to deliver. I complained about it. But they said, 'Oh, don't worry, we'll be there when you asked us to.' Well, they wound up coming a week later than they said they would. This was a big problem because we couldn't get unpacked, we couldn't get started to work, and we had to eat all our meals out."

Even the Fredericks' final payment was torturous. When the mover finally arrived, it was late in the evening, and the mover demanded payment by cashier's check. "It was too late in the day to get a cashier's check," Jane Frederick says. "Then they demanded cash. They threatened to drive the truck back to Florida, with all our stuff in it. Ed got so disgusted he just said, 'Let them take it.' But we had irreplaceable stuff on the truck, like our photo albums." The Fredericks wound up paying with a credit card. But, Frederick says, "They just dumped all our stuff in the living room." She had assumed that the movers were obligated to unload their goods in the appropriate rooms. But again, the contract did not specify that—she had merely assumed it.

And about that "bargain" price. Rather than the $2,210 estimate, the Fredericks paid their moving company in excess of $4,500, more than double the original price they had anticipated.

To add insult to injury, "They scuffed a lot of our stuff," Jane Frederick says. "We found out we had a $500 deductible on our coverage and didn't recover for any damages."

JANE FREDERICK'S LESSONS FROM MOVING COMPANY HELL

1. Read the contract carefully.

2. Don't assume anything—get everything in writing.

3. If they say they'll deliver on a certain day, don't count on it. Be sure to leave your schedule flexible within a week to ten days if possible.

4. Demand that they deliver during normal business hours.

5. Check your coverage for deductibles.

6. Know how they plan to unload your goods.

Finding Boxes and Packing Materials

You're going to need plenty of boxes. Even for a small house, figure on well over one hundred boxes minimum. All the boxes should have lids.

In general, packing materials and new boxes are more expensive when you buy them from moving and rental companies. Whether you're using a moving company or doing your own moving, you can usually save money on boxes and packing materials by rounding them up yourself at places like liquor, furniture, appliance and grocery stores. (Be sure to examine these boxes carefully for insects and other pests.) Myron and Carmen Misiaszek got many of their boxes free at liquor stores—liquor boxes being particularly sturdy. They also purchased boxes from Boston storage companies, where, they report, prices were cheaper than at Ryder. There are also stores like Postal Plus that specialize in boxes and packing materials. Alternatively, you can divide your purchases among rental and moving companies, specialty stores and other outlets, and you can often buy used boxes at a cheaper rate.

Holly Jennings did the latter with much success. Jennings, who used a moving company but did her own packing, bought flat, 24 by 18 by 12-inch boxes in bulk quantities at an office supply store, which she put together herself. But Jennings supplemented this purchase by buying used boxes from her moving company, North American Van Lines, and from U-Haul. She estimates that this combination of boxes bought flat and in bulk and used boxes saved her several hundred dollars.

By looking in the Yellow Pages under "Packaging" and "Boxes," Bonnie and Peter Templeton were able to buy used wardrobe and mirror boxes for three to five times less than what they would have cost new, depending on the store. "Whatever you do," they insist, "don't buy new boxes from a moving store."

If you know that many of your goods will be in storage for a long period of time, consider plastic boxes. After their house sold in Oakland, and prior to moving to near Dobson, North Carolina, the Templetons and their three boys moved most of their possessions into storage while they rented a house. Many of these possessions remained in storage in North Carolina while the Templetons built a house on their new property. Concerned about the long-term effect of humidity and bugs, the Templetons bought five different sizes of plastic boxes (with snap-on lids), at Wal-Mart, that ranged in price from $5 to $8. Some of the largest boxes were being used to store Peter Templeton's extensive tool set. The majority of boxes were 24 by 18 by 12 inches—a standard size with moving companies.

For their packing materials, too, the Templetons shunned their moving company—North American Van Lines—instead buying from a specialty packaging store. For around $250—with a minimum purchase of $100 required—they bought 1,500 linear feet of bubble wrap, sold in rolls. Among other things, this bubble wrap covered their extensive art collection and framed photographs, which were then packed in boxes.

From Carmen Misiaszek's supervisor at the Boston hospital where she worked, she and her husband, Myron, learned that they could buy end rolls from newspaper companies to use as cheap but effective packing materials. The fifteen end rolls the Misiaszeks purchased for $2 per were each approximately 200 feet of virgin paper—paper stock on which newsprint had never been inked because the paper was at the outside edges of the roll. These end rolls were better than newspapers, the Misiaszeks say, because there's no print to rub off on dishes and other smudgeable items.

Another tip for fragile as well as smudgeable items comes from Marilyn and Tom Ross, authors of *Country Bound!:* "One trick we learned," they write, "was to use extra sheets and towels as the packing material for good dishes and other breakables."

Packing

When moving and rental companies do the packing for you, they usually charge on a per-box basis—and they don't come cheap. Packing charges of $1,000 or more are not uncommon for families of four. This is why—if you have the time—it pays to do as much of your own packing as you can.

But you need to know what you're doing. Moving companies have standards for packed-by-owner (PBO) items which you must meet. If, after inspection, you don't meet those standards, the mover is entitled to repack at your expense. Because those standards will vary slightly from mover to mover, if you do hire a moving company be sure to find out what that company's standards are. Normally they include such basics as not overloading boxes and bureau drawers, thorough taping of boxes, and not packing combustibles, such as flammable liquids and aerosol cans. The company's brochure should specify its do's and don'ts.

In addition to boxes, you'll need the following materials to start: labels; packing materials (end rolls, newspapers, Styrofoam chips, etc.); rope and/or heavy string; heavy tape; scissors; knife; inventory sheets; pen.

Fifteen Tips for Packing Perfection

1. If you get your boxes from liquor stores and the like, often they will be missing their lids. Be sure to get boxes with lids, or make

your own by cutting a piece of cardboard the size of the box and taping it on securely to close.

2. To reduce clutter, pack one area or room of your house at a time. Start with the least-used areas: your basement, garage and closets holding seldom-used things.

3. Pack little-used items first, like Christmas ornaments and shell collections.

4. Pack items last that you will be using right up till moving day, such as your coffeemaker, a few key pans and your microwave.

5. Whenever possible, use small boxes, especially for heavy items like books.

6. Always position the heaviest items at the bottom of the box.

7. Unless you plan to hire the Incredible Hulk, whenever possible, don't pack boxes with more than fifty pounds of cargo.

8. Pack items to the top of boxes, but don't overpack. Don't create bulges.

9. Pad boxes liberally, particularly boxes containing valuables. Wrap fragile items individually. Stack dishes side by side, not flat, and embed them in padding.

10. Put valuable clothing in wardrobe boxes.

11. Take breakables out of drawers.

12. Pack like items together.

13. Don't scrimp on the strapping or sealer tape to close the boxes securely—otherwise the mover will come behind you, charging you for both labor and materials.

14. Once the box is ready to go, label what's in it and to which room it is going, preferably on all sides. If you abbreviate the labels, make them intelligible for other handlers besides yourself.

15. Label appropriate boxes "Fragile."

And More Jobs

Before you committed to a moving company, you started on at least a dozen jobs designed to tie up loose ends before the move. You've finished many of them by now.

What to Do Two to Three Weeks Before the Move

1. If you're traveling by car or truck, call the 800 numbers for motel and hotel chains to make overnight reservations.

2. Get your car or cars inspected to avoid on-the-road difficulties.

3. Set a date on which utilities will be shut off.

4. Arrange to have the utilities turned on at your new home.

5. Get your appliances ready for shipment. (Call the people who service your appliances or the moving company for help.)

6. Return all borrowed items.

What to Do a Week to One Day Before the Move

1. Fill out a change-of-address card at the post office.

2. Close out your bank accounts.

3. Obtain the cash and/or traveler's checks you'll need to carry you through the trip.

4. Scour every corner of your house for items you don't want to leave behind.

5. Strip the mattresses (unless you plan to box or cover them).

6. Dispose of your trash and recyclables.

7. Compile all moving documents and keep them within easy reach, preferably in your pocketbook.

MOVING PETS AND PLANTS

As living things, pets and plants require special attention when you move. For good reason, moving companies are not allowed to transport pets. And, in general, it's better to transport plants yourself as well, because the same life-threatening extremes of heat or cold in the moving van can endanger them, too.

TRAVELS WITH MORRIS (AND FIDO)

Because pets are subject to inspection upon arrival in some states, your pet may need a health certificate less than ten days old issued by a veterinarian, along with an inoculations record. In some states you will also need a permit—if in doubt about your destination state, call the state veterinarian, whose office will normally be in the state capital. You'll also want to know the pet ordinances in the small town to which you are moving. Call the town clerk for information.

If your pets are traveling by plane (they're prohibited on trains and buses), check with the airline for its regulations. If pets are traveling by car, call the 800 number of the motel chain you plan to use to learn its requirements, or call the individual motels along your route at which you plan to stay. As you travel, be sure to have an ample supply of food and water.

HAVE PLANT, WILL TRAVEL

Three weeks before moving day, plants in clay pots should be repotted in unbreakable plastic containers. Make sure the new pot has ample room. Two days before moving day, experts say, plants should be watered normally—then packed the day you move, or the night before. Anchor them securely in the box, using soft paper to cushion branches and leaves. Punch air holes in the sides of the box and fasten the lid loosely to allow air flow from the top as well. If you haul the plants in your car, avoid putting them in the trunk. If possible, postpone watering plants until you arrive at your destination.

Having a Yard Sale

A week before we left Los Angeles, we had an all-day yard sale of used furniture, kitchenware, books and all sorts of odds and ends in which we netted over $400. There are as many theories about how to hold a yard sale as there are friends and neighbors, but we offer a baker's dozen of tips from our own experience and from people who've conducted them successfully.

1. If you can, do it with someone else. The more items spread out for sale in a limited space, the more inviting it seems for people off the street. "With other sponsors calling on friends and relatives to support the effort, you are certain to draw bigger overall crowds," writes relocation expert Nan DeVincentis Hayes.

2. Try to hold your yard sale in a location that can be seen from some distance and in a place with easy parking.

3. Take inventory before the sale and write down each sale.

4. Don't stint on advertising. Place a want ad in the local newspaper and post signs on nearby streets the night before.

5. Open early in the morning to catch the early birds.

6. Try to keep it to one day. The good stuff invariably gets taken that first day. Mark down prices as the day goes on, but not before three o'clock in the afternoon.

7. Before you price your items, get a sense of the market by visiting other yard sales.

8. Put price tags on items *before* the sale.

9. Let the customer haggle first. Don't volunteer a lower price. If someone's asking for a substantial bargain, ask him to come back after three o'clock.

10. Talking with the customers will help enhance sales. Don't be a statue.

11. Find out what room your customer is furnishing so that you can suggest a related item.

12. Have a separate table for your plants and price them to sell.

13. Take the leftover items to the Salvation Army or battered women's shelter and donate them. Or call them and ask them to come pick up the unsold merchandise.

Saying Goodbye: Countdown to "M-Day"

One of the jobs that can begin as early as several months before the move and extend to "M-Day" itself is saying goodbye. For adults, saying goodbye to friends and associates, as well as to familiar places, can be one of the most difficult aspects of moving. When Art and Dee Dee Rosenberg moved from San Diego to Galax, Virginia, each had emotionally wrenching farewell parties with co-workers and friends. "I was reading all the cards and I got totally choked up," Dee Dee Rosenberg says, "But, we still keep in touch. In many cases, I probably communicate with my friends now more than I did back then. When you're living in the same city, you often tend to take your friends for granted."

Rosenberg's perception strikes a responsive chord in us. With our closest friends in Los Angeles, bonds are as strong or stronger now than they were when we lived there. And a surprising number of our friends, intrigued by our new small-town lifestyle, have come to visit—a number of them repeatedly. To paraphrase the famous line from the film *Field of Dreams,* build a compelling new life and they will come.

Throwing a party with your friends can also be fun, especially a party with some creative touches and an accent on the positive aspects of moving to a new and desired life. Shortly before we left California, and just a few days from St. Patrick's Day, we threw a "Green Theme" party in which everyone wore green or used the word "green" in a toast or read a passage from a book in which the word appears. It was an exhilarating experience, a way of thanking our friends for their friendship and inviting them to come visit the greener pastures of southwest Virginia. It also saved us the time, wear, tear and expense of breaking bread individually with all the people to whom we wanted to say goodbye. With our closest friends, of course, we found time for individual farewells. But we were determined not to exhaust ourselves in the process.

"For kids," says Philadelphia clinical psychologist Suzanne Scott, "particularly school-age kids, there's a powerful sense of separation and loss when they move." If you have school-age children, be sure to schedule time for them to have meaningful, reassuring farewells with their friends.

Before Holly Jennings left Fargo, North Dakota, for Washington State, she and her seven-year-old son, Sam, made a list of eight special friends with whom Sam wanted extra time for saying goodbye. "We made an occasion with each friend," Jennings remembers. "Maybe we all went out to eat, or we had them over to our house. I wanted Sam to know that he could say goodbye to his friends, that they weren't just going to disappear. And I held out the possibility that we'd be coming back to Fargo to visit."

Of equal importance, never conceal the move from a child— no matter how young. "Let kids feel hurt," advises psychologist Scott. "Listen to them, and allow them to feel. Take time to be a little sad, and talk it out. The tendency is for parents to minimize what's going on, to reduce the significance of it. At the same time, don't magnify the event either. Try to tell it to a child as calmly and as straightforwardly as possible."

When the Rosenberg family moved from San Diego to Galax, Virginia, five-year-old Aaron got the straight goods from his parents right from the start. "When we decided to move, we told Aaron everything that was going on," Dee Dee Rosenberg says. "He knew everything we knew. After we described everything that would be happening—that he'd be flying on an airplane, that he'd be living in a place where it snowed, that he'd be involved in a lot of new activities—Aaron began to see it as a great adventure."

COPING WITH THE STRESS OF A MOVE

❧ ❧

Why is moving so stressful? "Moving, in and of itself, involves the excitement of change," says Suzanne Scott. "But the other side of that equation is that change is frightening. You're used to all these things in your life, and all of a sudden you don't have them anymore. You're leaving a lot of the props behind, and it may seem as if you're making the nuclear family the sole source of support. Even if you're familiar with the place to which you're moving, there's still a lot of uncertainty, there's fear of the unknown."

From our own experience, as well as from the recommendations of Suzanne Scott and others, we offer the following ten tips for stress reduction during the moving period:

1. Plan every step of the move carefully. But don't be rigid; expect some things to not go exactly as planned.

2. Start early; don't wait till the last minute.

3. When packing, pace yourself. Don't try to get it all done in a short period, no matter how long until moving day.

4. Learn the ins and outs of dealing with moving and rental companies. Knowledge is power.

5. To reduce anxiety about the unknown, familiarize yourself as much as possible with your new town. If it takes several visits to do that, spend the time.

6. Be honest about the difficulties, both with yourself as well as your kids. Accent the positive. Look at the move as an adventure.

7. Get help. Ask for friends' advice in deciding what to keep and what to take, etc. Avoid those who can be overbearing in their opinions.

8. Talk with your partner. Keep open the lines of communication. And don't blame anyone—including yourself—when things go poorly.

9. Keep all documents related to moving in one place.

10. Both for yourself and your kids, take reassuring, transitional things or pets with you on the journey. When Carmen Misiaszek moved to Newport, Oregon, she taped a picture of her horse on the dashboard of her car. Even Dorothy, when she visited the Land of Oz, took along her dog, Toto, as a companion. Do yourself the favor of having something dear and familiar close by.

The Big Day
At last it's here—the day you've long wanted to see. Yet, very likely, your feelings are mixed, your heart a little heavy. If you're able to, before the moving van arrives, take a few moments for contemplation. Have a cup of coffee; or, if your appliances are all disconnected, take a walk or drive to pick up a cup at the neighborhood store. Put all the details you'll need to think about out of your mind temporarily and give yourself a few moments to reflect on this major life change.

Then get down to the business of the day.

As we mentioned, some moving companies offer you the option to do your own loading, under the driver's supervision. If this is the option you selected, remember that you're no longer the boss. The driver is responsible for the delivery of the load. Do what he instructs you to do.

More likely, the loading will be done as you watch. If you decide it's better for your child to experience the tangible reality of moving than to be at a baby-sitter's (experts say that it is), keep the child out of harm's way.

If you haven't signed the bill of lading (contract), you'll have to do it now, before the first item is loaded. Remember, the bill of lading should list all services provided and the charges for those services. Double-check to make sure that the mover is required to unload your goods in the appropriate rooms.

Next, while inspecting your goods for their current condition, the mover will do an inventory of all your goods and, most likely, tag them. He will then present you with a copy of the *inventory papers*—a complete listing of what is to be transported—for you to sign. Read the papers carefully. Has he omitted anything? Do you agree with his assessment of the condition of your goods? Does the information on the inventory papers match the information on the bill of lading? If there are discrepancies, resolve the problem with the mover or call the moving company office and ask to speak with the *origin agent,* who may be the estimator or someone else. (Normally, the origin agent is ultimately responsible for the packing and loading of your goods. This person may or may not be present on moving day.) Resolve the discrepancy as quickly as possible and then, if everything looks good, sign the papers, and attach your copy to your copy of the bill of lading. Tuck those papers into a handy and secure place; you'll need them when your goods are unloaded.

Ask the driver how he wants to be paid when your goods are delivered. Don't count on being able to pay with a credit card or personal check. You may have to pay with a cashier's check, money order, or cash. Before the goods are delivered, however, you'll have to put down a deposit, up to 10 percent of the cost estimate. Be prepared to pay this with a cashier's check, money order or cash as well.

Weighing

Regardless of which kind of estimate you chose, your goods will be weighed. There are two methods of weighing: *origin weighing,* in which the truck is weighed soon after your goods are loaded; and *destination weighing,* in which the truck is weighed once it arrives at its destination. In either case, the driver determines the *tare weight*—the weight of the truck without your goods—and the *gross weight*—the weight of the truck with your goods—to calculate the net weight of your goods.

You have the right to be present at the weighing, which occurs at a weigh station. If you wish to do so, make arrangements with the driver. If you think the net weight of your goods is not accurate, you can request a second weighing at no charge. The average cubic foot weight of household items is approximately forty pounds. You can get a rough idea of how many pounds your load should weigh by multiplying the number of items on the inventory sheets by forty. Collect the weight ticket, which should show place and date of weighing, the truck's ID numbers, your name and shipment number and the signature of the person responsible for the weighing.

Before you part company with the driver, make sure he knows where to reach you in your new home. Make sure, too, that he's aware of the road conditions where you'll be living. "If you're moving out in the country, down a narrow road somewhere," says Jim Huth, director of corporate communications for Atlas Van Lines, "it's important to let the driver know before you move. He may need to make arrangements to unload into several smaller trucks." Also, ask the driver how you can contact him. Remind the driver that you will be at the destination when he arrives, and that you expect to see him within the agreed-upon range. And—just in case of trouble—jot down the truck's license number.

Jobs for Moving Day
In addition to dealing with the mover, here's a reminder of what you'll need to do:

1. If you haven't done it by now, pack your car.

2. Make a final inspection of your house to make sure nothing valuable is left behind. (When Wanda was fifteen and moving with her mother and sister from Lexington, Kentucky, to Orono, Maine, a final inspection of their duplex revealed that she'd left a small box of

valuable jewelry, including her grandmother's heirloom 10-karat gold bracelet, on a windowsill. Given the landlord's subsequent dirty dealings, it's clear that had this final inspection not been made, she would have lost forever what is now one of her most precious possessions.)

3. Turn everything off as needed.

4. Lock the windows and doors.

5. Turn over your house keys to the appropriate person.

6. If you've picked them up by now, make sure you have the keys to your new home.

7. If you're traveling with children, make sure they have toys, books, puzzles and snacks to keep them interested and busy.

Unloading in Your New Home

By car, truck, bus, train or plane, you've reached your new home. Eureka! Now where the heck is the moving van?

When you move from a city to another sizable city, in most cases, upon arrival you deal with what's called the *destination agent*. This local person supervises the delivery and unloading of your goods. But depending on the size of your small town, you may not have a moving company representative with whom to work. In some cases your representative will be your driver. Be sure you know with whom you can deal in case of problems. It may be the driver, the origin agent, or someone at the head office of the moving company.

As the Frederick family learned, in the worst-case scenario you can become a prisoner in your new home, unable to get on with your life until the mover arrives. With luck, this period will last only a matter of hours, not days. But be prepared for a modified version of house arrest. It does help somewhat that most moving companies will notify you as much as twenty-four hours ahead of time when they expect the truck to arrive.

If the mover delivers your goods later than the date specified in the contract, remember that you are entitled to per-diem compensation.

According to Global Van Lines, its drivers are required to unload before 6 P.M. This should be the standard required for all moving companies. Unfortunately, given road conditions and the idiosyncrasies of drivers and the unloading crew, it doesn't always work that way. Be prepared to unload late into the evening.

Be prepared, as well, for extra charges for what are called *long carries*. With Global Van Lines, for example, if the truck has to park more than twenty feet from the door, you'll be charged for long carries. You'll also be billed for each flight of stairs on which items must be carried. Before unloading, the mover will inspect your new home and require you to sign addenda to the bill of lading to cover extra charges. Movers will not unload unless you sign.

If you want washer and dryers, VCRS and the like hooked up in your new home, you'll probably also be charged for *special handling*.

You've done well if, in your contract, the mover is required to unload goods in their appropriate rooms. But that job won't begin until you pay the balance of your bill. If you don't pay, the driver cranks up the truck and hauls away your goods, eventually storing them at your expense.

If you think there are mistakes on the bill, start by talking with the driver. If that gets you nowhere, you'll need to get on the phone with the agent or whomever you've been dealing with. If you pay the driver and later find a mistake in the bill, write a letter to the mover and back up your argument with photocopies of relevant documents.

Be sure to examine your goods when they're unloaded. If anything is missing or damaged, take note and prepare to file a claim. After the mover leaves, you'll have more time to examine your goods carefully. You have nine months to file a claim—but why wait that long? If the moving company fails to cooperate, you have several recourses. You can file a claim at the courthouse in your new county, which may qualify for small claims court. You can also notify the ICC, which, though it can't resolve claims, can bring pressure to bear on a moving company. Additionally, some moving companies abide by the decisions of dispute-resolution programs.

FINAL WORKSHEET FOR USING A MOVING COMPANY

1. Total moving company charges _____

2. Cost of additional labor _____

3. Boxes _____

4. Packing materials _____

5. Cost of transportation _____

6. Cost of lodging _____

7. Cost of food _____

8. Cost of storage _____

9. Contingencies _____

TOTAL COST OF MOVING _____

Going with a Rental Company
We have already covered what you'll need to know in selecting and handling a rental company. However, you'll also need to know how much of a deposit is required, plus how to load, weigh, drive and unload your rentals.

Deposit
According to Janet Cooper, spokesperson for U-Haul, a deposit of $80 is required before you can drive away in your U-Haul truck. Ryder requires the same amount.

Loading

Here are some of the basics:

1. Park the truck as close to the house as possible but with enough room to extend the loading ramp.

2. Pull the hand truck up the ramp; don't push it.

3. Lift heavy objects by bending your knees and using your leg muscles.

4. Load the truck or trailer one-quarter at a time, as solidly as possible from floor to ceiling. Tie off each quarter with a rope.

5. Load the heaviest items, like appliances, first.

6. When loading a refrigerator, put the hand-truck strap between the coils and box. Never put the strap on top of the coils.

7. Put heavy boxes on the bottom, lighter boxes on top.

8. Load long items—mattresses, box springs, sofas, tables—on the sides. They can be placed on their ridge against the walls and tied down.

9. Load mirrors and framed art or pictures upright, either tying them to the walls or placing them between mattresses and box springs.

10. Place odd-shaped items either along the walls or on top of the load.

11. Never load flammable or potentially explosive substances.

Weighing the Truck

Though it's an inconvenience, weighing the truck when you have finished or almost finished loading is necessary for two reasons. First, if the truck weighs more than its gross vehicle weight limit, and you are insured by the rental company, the rental company relinquishes responsibility for your claim in the event of an accident. Second, rental trucks are required by law to stop and be weighed at truck weigh stations.

Many rental companies have their own scales. If yours doesn't, ask the agent where you can find one. They are usually not hard to find. Myron Misiaszek weighed his Ryder trucks at a neighborhood chemical company in Boston.

Driving the Truck and/or Trailer

Rental companies will give you written tips on how to drive with a truck or trailer. Take a good look at them—even if you've done it before, driving a truck or towing a trailer is trickier than you may think. Trailers are particularly difficult to back up, and making turns can be treacherous. Trucks are much slower than cars in accelerating, and take longer to pass, more room to change lanes and longer to stop.

For us, perhaps the trickiest part of driving the Ryder truck with Wanda's mother's possessions from Maine to Virginia was using the passenger-side mirrors, a small mirror within a large mirror that, together, theoretically eliminate the "blind spot" alongside the truck. If you have a little time to practice with your truck on some familiar roads—as we did on some roads in Maine—it will help develop a comfort level with its daunting size and other characteristics, as well as with using the mirrors.

Know the overhead clearance of your truck. And once you hit the road, be careful with service station and motel canopies, drive-throughs, low bridges and tree branches. Because it's more difficult, driving a truck is more tiring than driving a car. This is no time to be macho; stop for coffee and use the rest areas liberally, and, if possible, drivers should switch every two hours.

If you're driving a rental vehicle and your own vehicle in tandem, work out a game plan and a communications system ahead of the trip. This is particularly important when vehicles become separated by other vehicles, when driving at night and in heavy traffic. Then, it can be difficult for the driver of the truck to see the car, so the car must be sure to stay close to the truck. On our trip from Maine to Virginia, the truck set the pace and stayed directly ahead of the car except when the passengers in the car wanted to pull off the road. The car would then pull ahead of the truck and give a turn signal for the truck to follow.

Unloading and Returning the Rentals
When you reach your new home, you'll first want to relax and celebrate your arrival. But when you're ready, park the truck and/or trailer with the loading door as close as possible to the entrance door. If you're using a truck, then pull out the loading ramp and, if possible, place it on your new home's highest step. After you've unloaded, make sure the truck is completely empty. Be sure to sweep it as well—anything you've tracked into the truck, front or back, might cost you an extra cleaning charge. Then return it to the local agent. If you're not sure where to take it, look in the Yellow Pages.

FINAL WORKSHEET FOR USING A RENTAL COMPANY

Total rental company charges _____

Cost of additional labor _____

Cost of boxes _____

Cost of packing materials _____

Cost of transportation _____

Cost of lodging _____

Cost of food _____

Cost of storage _____

Contingencies _____

TOTAL COST _____

Storage

If your new living space is smaller than what you had in the city, or if you move into temporary quarters, you may want to consider renting storage space. Because of its cost, renting storage space is not a permanent solution to the problem of having too many things for your space—it's better to pare down, preferably before you move. But it does solve the problem temporarily, giving you time to organize a sale or perhaps arrange a move to a space large enough to accommodate all your possessions.

Storage space is usually available in the mini-warehouses that are common these days even in small towns. Look in the Yellow Pages to find out what's offered in your small town. Before you take a look (and if you haven't done so previously), measure the items you plan to store for width and height.

If you have a choice (in some small towns, you may not), there are five important factors to consider when you look at storage facilities. The first is *size*. Is the storage space large enough? Do your own measuring if you're not sure about its dimensions. You'll pay more for a larger space, but you may need it.

The second and third factors are *cost* and *location*. Even in small towns you may pay more for a certain location, as well as for size. Is a safer, more accessible location worth the extra cost?

The fourth factor is *how well the facility is run*. If problems arise, will they be addressed? Are the storage facilities clean and free of pests? It's a good idea to ask the owner or manager for references.

The fifth factor is *protection against theft*. What kind of security system does the facility offer?

When you choose a storage facility, get the terms in writing. You don't want to get off on the wrong foot in your new town with a misunderstanding.

Then move in. As you did when you moved from the city, take inventory, and map where you are stacking things in case you need to take something out.

Have the floor covered before you stack—old rugs or mats will do. Leave room around the walls for your things to breathe.

Stack heaviest things first, lightest last. Leave walkways for easy access.

Check your insurance policy to see if it covers your stored goods. If it doesn't, ask the owner or manager of the facility about insurance; some (but not all) storage facilities offer it.

GETTING SETTLED IN YOUR NEW HOME

Ready or not, here you are: in your new home, in your new town, starting your new life. It sounds exciting, and it *is* exciting! But look at all those boxes! And there are so many other things that seem to need doing all at once: getting a telephone connected and the utilities turned on (if you haven't done it prior to the move), settling the kids into school, meeting the neighbors, getting your vehicles registered, transferring your driver's license, registering to vote, finding the best stores; the list goes on. It's amazing how many details there are in daily living—details you may have taken for granted in your old life.

There are two things we learned from getting settled in our new home. The first is, be realistic about the time it takes to settle in. Allow oodles of time—we're talking months, not weeks—to get it all done. Don't get bent out of shape thinking it all has to be done in three days. Think of these months as the last stage in a long and necessary period of transition. Your patience will pay off in spades.

The second lesson? Prioritize. Make a list or lists of what needs to be done, and in what sequence—allowing yourself plenty of time—and then follow the list. Working with a list, with written jobs that can be crossed off when they are finished, creates a sense of order and a common language for everybody involved. And it offers you daily satisfaction and a feeling of progress, especially if you can cross off one or two jobs a day.

A word about unpacking. As much as possible, do it one room at a time, unpacking first the items you need right away. Unpacking one room at a time (just as you packed a room at a time) is the most efficient, as well as most orderly, method. The alternative—unpacking here, there, and everywhere—creates an "after-the-earthquake" feeling that your entire living space is in disarray. With so many other things to contend with beyond your home, that's not a feeling you want.

One last thing. Take some time off. You don't have to be purposeful every moment. Take some walks around town. Breathe in that small-town air. Catch a sunset or a softball game and smell the roses. You've earned it. After all, you didn't move to a small town merely to continue the furious pace of urban life.

No, getting settled shouldn't be rushed. But it won't be long before a feeling of contentment about your private life extends to your new, larger life as a member of the community.

CHAPTER SIX

Making a Place for Yourself

"Staying comfortable is largely a matter of culture. Informal or core culture is the foundation on which interpersonal relations rest. All of the little things that people take for granted . . . depend on sharing informal patterns."

—EDWARD HALL

THE ART OF CROSSING CULTURES

The rules governing small-town behavior are no more Byzantine or benighted than those of city life or corporate culture. Though small-towners often get a bad rap for rigidity and intolerance, city critics let themselves off the hook when they move to a town and expect their behavior, their individuality, to be accepted—no matter how eccentric, alien or off-putting—without extending the courtesy of understanding the culture of the small town and putting forth an effort to adapt to it.

In order to make a successful adjustment to a small town and carve out a place for yourself, you, the newcomer, must first recognize that each town (no matter what its size) has its own unique identity and culture that should be respected as that of a foreign land.

This chapter tackles that most difficult and delicate challenge that awaits you in moving to a small town—making a place for yourself in this "foreign land." It is a task that will prove essential to the outcome of your move.

Once you move, you'll want to hit the ground running. Your early days, weeks and months are crucial to your eventual adjustment, acceptance and success in a small town, unlike in the city, where you can take your time getting your bearings and tailoring your urban persona. In a small town, you're making your debut from day one, and this "coming out" will continue for months, if not a year or two. People will be sizing you up as a new community member, businessperson, churchgoer and potential friend. Everything from your dress and demeanor to your attitude and speech patterns will be carefully weighed.

Succeeding at this stage will help you determine whether your dream of a new life in a small town will take root and flourish or wither and die. After scouting your new location, transplanting your family and career and settling into your new home, you've already invested heavily in your plan and have a lot at stake. So why falter at this final stage?

"I've heard some folks who've moved here say, 'Obviously you have to be born here to make it.' But that's not at all true," says Tanya B. Rees, executive director of the Surry Arts Council in Mount Airy, North Carolina. "People are respected for coming in and doing their own thing. What's important is their level of sincerity. The folks who've been successful have simply been true to themselves."

Folks who are successful need not only be true to themselves but to behave in a culturally sensitive manner. Newcomers need to take in the new culture, oftentimes putting their individuality on the back burner and letting it emerge gradually. You needn't clobber people over the head with your identity or try too hard to impress them right off the bat. Try to relax, although that can be challenging because it is precisely when they are in flux that many people most need to assert their personalities.

Indeed, intercultural consultants to Fortune 500 companies assert that "cross-cultural adjustment" poses the greatest stumbling block for Americans when trying to make successful transitions overseas. More than one-third of Americans who move abroad for jobs or study return home "prematurely," writes Craig Storti, author of *The Art of Crossing Cultures*. "[M]any, perhaps, most . . . genuinely want to adapt to the local culture." The majority, he says, do not.

Why such a high rate of failure?

The author holds "cultural blindness" responsible. "True cultural adjustment and effective cross-cultural interaction are more elusive than we might imagine."

Since Americans share a common language and national (political and media) culture, we tend to minimize the difficulties of cross-cultural adaptation *within* our own country. But differences of customs, attitude and pace of life between regions of the country are compounded by *even greater* differences between the generic cultures of major metropolitan areas and small-town America. (Although tens of thousands of towns in the United States exist and no two cultures are identical, there's enough in common among small towns to establish cultural characteristics that accompany small-sized communities, particularly those that are primarily self-sustaining, not mere bedroom communities of major metropolitan areas.)

Cracking the Small-Town Code

This chapter will give you the lowdown on making the adjustment—and ultimately the commitment—to the culture of your small town. But don't expect to take to small-town culture like a duck to water; and don't expect adaptation to happen overnight. It takes time to advance through the typical and predictable stages of adjustment. These stages range from what Gretchen Janssen, author of *Women on the Move: A Christian Perspective on Cross-Cultural Adjustment,* describes as the "fascination-honeymoon" phase; the "subtle-irritations" phase; the "frustration-culture shock" phase; the "coping" phase; to the final "adaptation" phase. As you overcome these internal hurdles, you'll also be making more tangible progress: cracking the small-town code, building a network of relationships and a bedrock of trust and convincing people you're no fly-by-nighter—that you really are digging in your heels and staying.

"You really have to work at it, make it a real project," says Mary Lou Rich Goertzen, who in 1975 moved from Berkeley, California, to Deadwood, Oregon (population 150), with her husband, three teenagers and a foster child.

Although the length of time it takes to feel accepted in a rural community or small town depends on the size of the town and the degree of transience among its residents, Goertzen estimates that it took her ten years to establish her legitimacy as a player and a stayer. "We've been here for twenty years," says Goertzen, sixty-five. "I've become more like a country person (than a city person)."

Likewise, Kathleen Norris, the poet and essayist who in 1974 moved with her husband from New York City to her mother's hometown of Lemmon, South Dakota (population 1,871), fixed the date of passage from being a newcomer to a long-hauler at ten years. However, in larger towns with a higher degree of transience, this number is likely to be lower—perhaps as low as three to five years.

We've found the number of times that locals inquire about whether we're really here for good has diminished with each passing year. After ten years of residence, the questions have changed from: "Will you stay?" to "Do you ever miss L.A.?"

A Period of Personal Growth

If you're willing to make a commitment to change, to stretch your known capabilities and strive to uncover new ones, your early years in your new town will be exciting. The move to a small town can kick-start a period of tremendous personal growth—one in which you forge bonds with members of your new community and discover new strengths and skills within yourself.

"I thought I knew who I was when I came, but, once here, I learned much more about myself," says Norris of her adjustment to Lemmon. "I found out what I could and couldn't do in various situations." One of the things she found she *could* do is to write deeply felt essays about a carefully observed life in her corner of the world—a book that after an initial printing of 2,500 in hardcover became a surprise bestseller. The town of Lemmon served as a kind of cocoon, enabling Norris's "voice" to emerge. Whether or not you're a writer, your small town can serve the same purpose for you, providing roots to anchor you and wings to let your spirit fly.

What's at the end of the road (or at the corner of Main and Maple streets) may be your first genuine community, the first time in your life you've actually had a hometown to call your own. This chapter will lay out effective modes of small-town behavior and show you how to observe this often conservative code while still being true to yourself. It is about learning how to win in a small town. And while not everyone who moves to (or lives in) a small town subscribes to the following prescription for success, those who do invariably come out on top.

SIXTEEN SKILLS FOR CROSS-CULTURAL ADAPTATION

In his book, *Survival Kit for Overseas Living*, L. Robert Kohls writes that there are "certain skills or traits which you may have—or, with a little effort, develop—that will facilitate your rapid adjustment" into a new culture. These include the following:

- Tolerance for ambiguity

- Low goal/task orientation

- Open-mindedness

- Nonjudgmentalness

- Empathy

- Communicativeness

- Flexibility ; adaptability

- Curiosity

- Sense of humor

- Warmth in human relationships

- Motivation

- Self-reliance

- Strong sense of self

- Tolerance for differences

- Perceptiveness

- Ability to fail

LETTING GO OF THE CITY

No matter how much you disliked the city or how eager you were to decamp and start life anew in a small town, the city was nevertheless your home for however many months or years. Now that you've arrived in your small town, you'll need to unhook the old connection.

"City Fixes"
The best way to begin your psychic withdrawal from the city is to go at it gently. Give yourself some time to pull out, while reminding yourself that you *can* go back periodically for "city fixes." Because change is gradual, taking two steps forward (advancing into small-town life) and one step back (maintaining ties with old friends and keeping up with city news) is healthy. So is planning

excursions to the city to shop for presents and stock your cupboard with exotic food items and delicacies or taking in art galleries, opera and symphony music, French pastry and Vietnamese cuisine. If urban energy beckons, you may want to revisit a city periodically just to feed on the intensity of a cultural polyglot, to keep your city juices flowing.

When Monica Hinton first moved to Cullowhee, North Carolina (population 4,029), from Chicago, she used to drop down to Atlanta every several months just to "ride public transportation," she says. And she treasured her trips to New Orleans where she could walk on the sidewalks at 2 A.M. But once she made the adjustment to the slower pace and the commitment to her new life, such urban urges began to dissipate and today have all but vanished. "Now I'd *pay* someone to go [to the city] in my place," says Hinton.

When Kathleen Norris and her husband first arrived in Lemmon and were struck by cabin fever, they'd likewise hit the road. "We'd get the Bismarck paper and read about a first-run movie and drive 125 miles to see it. Gas was cheaper then," she explains. "We'd have a meal out, spend the night in a motel, do some shopping and come home. It was our big expedition." Though Bismarck, North Dakota (population 44,485), is a far cry from Manhattan, it did provide them with the feel of a *larger* town.

"Marooned on a Desert Island"
In part because Norris was familiar with Lemmon from spending many of her childhood summers there, the transition for her was neither shocking nor especially difficult. Discovering that some commodities they used regularly (like olive oil) weren't readily available nettled them at first. "Sometimes it was hard," says Norris, "but more often, it felt like an adventure, like being marooned on a desert island." She learned she could have her small-town cake and eat olive oil, too, by bundling her city errands and buying such items in bulk.

Developing new, unlikely skills helped to ease the transition as well. "I learned I liked to do a lot of things that I didn't have the time—or the inclination—for in the city. Like how to bake bread, can vegetables and make chokecherry jelly, jam and syrup," Norris says.

For others—because perhaps they moved to a small town under protest or as a trailing spouse—letting go of the big city proved more difficult. When Marie Garabed moved to Cumberland Center, Maine (population 2,015), from Detroit in 1969, she was appalled by the "vanilla-ice-cream, white-bread" mentality she found. "It was culturally a shock, the fact that no one understood what was going on outside [lily-white Maine]," says the native of Teaneck, New Jersey. She and her family had left Detroit in the midst of the civil-rights unrest and found residents of coastal Maine seemingly oblivious and their politicians completely out of touch. "I'd just come from the riots of Detroit and [Senator Edmund S.] Muskie was talking about how he understood busing because 95 percent of the kids in Maine were bused. And I thought to myself: 'That's kind of different.'"

Although Garabed's initial adjustment to the community was troublesome, after twenty-six years in the Pine Tree State, she's found a place for her multicultural point of view as a staffer at the Intercultural Press in Yarmouth. If she were to make the move all over again, she says she'd handle it differently. Instead of grousing about the provincialism of Mainers, Garabed says she'd be "more realistic" and more proactive. "I'd try to find a way to work around and through the parts that weren't okay," she says. "You can meet a need that might be unfulfilled in a small town." She cites the work she does on refugee resettlement as an example. Had she signed on for such work when she first arrived, it might have enabled her to make her peace with the place more quickly.

Don't Expect Too Much Too Quickly

As you're making the transition to small-town life, it's a good idea to pat yourself on the back, to congratulate yourself on your small steps and private victories. Recognize the first time you reach for the *Comstock Daily Bugle* instead of the *Cleveland Plain*

Dealer. Be proud when you are able to tell out-of-towners for whom your town was named and convincingly answer their follow-up questions. And you can outright celebrate the first time you tell a native a fact about her town that she didn't know.

Once you begin to make a successful adjustment to a small town—once you're integrated into the rhythms of community life and find a contribution you can make—you'll discover that your appetite for city fixes diminishes. And when you've established your presence in a small town—watch out!—your city friends will troop in by the dozens to get their vicarious taste of small-town life.

The Learning Curve

The minute you set foot in town, you've embarked on a major learning curve. You're taking in new people, scenery and sensations; new shops, customs and rhythms. Listen to the music of the place, the way people talk, the expressions they use, the cadences of their speech. Listen to their stories for what they reveal about themselves and the local culture. Whether you're oriented toward pen and ink or computer screen, start a journal of random musings about your new life, jotting down the things you hear (and overhear) that intrigue you, along with your own perceptions. Dig up the notes you took when scouting a new location and review them. The best way to get yourself acclimated to your new hometown is by gaining some depth of knowledge.

"Start by learning the history of the town," suggests Ken Munsell, of the Small Town Institute. "Make connections with the people who were there before. You need to get a feel for the economy, geography, land, what kinds of plants there are. Eventually, they interrelate. Pick up that information so you can feel a sense of connectedness early on."

Realize going in that learning a small town takes time and effort. You can begin to understand the town and the area by reading books and historical accounts; that way, you'll get a feel for the passions and proclivities of the people. However, refrain from touting your knowledge.

"Reading helps," says Kathleen Norris, "but if you start regurgitating everything you've read, you'll scare people off. It's a delicate balance."

PRINCIPLES OF SMALL-TOWN LIVING

People-Centered World

The first thing you need to understand about small-town life is that it's people-centered—far more so than any city. In a small town, people come first; this is both the greatest strength and the greatest limitation of small-town living.

You may reason that since there are more people per square mile in Manhattan than in Manhattan, Kansas, the former would be more people-oriented than the latter. Not so. In big cities, the sheer mass of humanity depersonalizes human beings, allowing for easier polarization, class categorization and stereotyping by race, gender, ethnicity and sexual orientation. Although the demographic composition of a city may demonstrate far greater ethnic and racial diversity than a given town, the actual *experience* of small-town living is likely to thrust you into regular and personal contact with a far greater range of people of differing age groups, economic categories and educational levels.

Because people who live in big cities tend to know others by industry or occupation, their interpersonal dealings are likely to be more stratified. In fact, you could make the case that prejudice of any form takes root more easily in a large city, where people are judged by externals, such as their skin color, ethnicity, gender, age and income. In a small town, you're more likely to know the individual or know of him or her, so these superficial factors become far less relevant. (See box, "Are Small Towns Right for Minorities and People of Color?")

If you're Lutheran, for instance, in some small towns there's likely to be only one church of that denomination. That's where congregants would mingle, whether they're factory workers or factory owners. The same holds true for public schools. In rural America, assert Marilyn and Tom Ross in their book, *Country*

Bound!, people are "measured not so much by the size of their wallets, what they wear, or what work they do, but rather by their personal qualities, such as promptness, honesty and resourcefulness."

The meaning of the classic film *It's a Wonderful Life* comes into full focus only after you've lived in a small town long enough to perceive the way in which friendship and relationships—"human capital"—can be even more valuable than money in the bank. Likewise, the film underscores the inordinate importance of one single caring and dynamic person in a small town. When the George character (played by Jimmy Stewart) comes back to Bedford Falls and sees how diminished life would be there had he never lived and built up a reservoir of good deeds, he learns from his friend Clarence, the angel, the ultimate wisdom that speaks volumes: "Remember, no man is a failure who has friends."

And, in small towns, these friendships overshadow all else. For instance, although small-towners tend to be more conservative politically and personally than residents of big cities, because people and friendships come first, their politics are often "compromised" by the code of intense loyalty to fellow residents or "members of the family." Even those with seemingly radical political ideas can be accepted and respected in their own hometowns. ("We bend the rules; that's part of small-town charm," writes Kathleen Norris in *Dakota*.) Norris points to an old "bohemian radical" in Lemmon, who used to work for a Communist bookstore in California in the 1930s who's now "one of the local characters, an irreplaceable old coot whom we love and hate."

After World War II, as early members of the United World Federalists, a group that advocated world government to prevent war, Frank's parents were hardly in step with the Republican majority in the small rural county in which we now live, nor with the conservative Democratic politics of nearby Mount Airy. Yet, they were constantly asked to address local churches, schools and civic clubs. And when Frank's mom, Miriam Lindsey Levering, died in 1991, a well-known Republican pronounced with personal anguish that "a great oak has fallen." What's more, the two senior Leverings were able to help establish a strong local chapter of a related organization, the American Freedom Association, which sponsors an annual trip to the United Nations and a speech contest for high school students promoting their ideas. Townsfolk of every political stripe have been only too eager for their children to participate.

Our Town: The Center of the Universe

It may be hard to fathom but it's true. Every small town is a world unto itself and the "true believers"—that is, the ones whose commitment to the community is absolute—are convinced that their town is the center of the universe. You can see this bias reflected in the column inches of newspaper stories, in which local news invariably overshadows state and national stories. The lead story may be: Fire Department Buys New Truck, with another, much shorter, story below the fold about less consequential matters such as a new trade agreement out of Washington or who's ahead in the presidential race. You'll see this personal bias everywhere and hear it in conversations at the drugstore, at the malls and at the town hall.

This is no case of soft brains or collective myopia. Rather it's a natural characteristic of every distinct human culture. "Every group of people, every culture, is, and has always been, ethnocentric," writes L. Robert Kohls in Survival Kit for Overseas Living. "[T]hat is, it thinks its own solutions are superior and would be recognized as superior by any right-thinking, intelligent, logical human being. It is significant that to each group, their own view of the world appears to be the 'common-sense' or 'natural' view."

Because ex-urbanites have deliberately chosen an off-the-beaten-track locale, this center-of-the-universe perspective can be especially difficult for many to swallow. And while it's certainly not a feeling that you can will yourself to internalize, it's important to recognize. Indeed, the famed New Yorker cover that shows the distorted perspective of Manhattan compared to the rest of America applies metaphorically to every small town in America. The smaller a community is (and the less likely it would *appear* to be the center of the universe), the more fiercely residents cling to this belief.

Community Service: You Can't Say No

In the city the attitude is, what's in it for me? In the small town, the attitude is, what's in it for my community? This may seem somewhat oversimplified, but there's an enormous amount of truth behind the statement. In the small town, about the highest compliment that can be paid to an individual is that he or she is "community minded." It means that that person puts community first. This isn't hokum; it's serious business.

Whereas community service is strictly voluntary in a big city, in the small town, it's gospel. A small town is like a family. Every member is supposed to contribute to the well-being of the whole, and community service is the way to go about it. Because of the anonymity in the big city, no one knows whether you're a good citizen, an indifferent one, or even a scoundrel, whereas in a small town, everyone knows who gives money, time and in-kind gifts to fund drives, benefits and volunteer organizations. They also know who shows up for blood drives and litter pickup and to bag groceries for the needy at Christmas.

"In Newport Beach, I was never solicited *one time* in fifteen years for charity," says Frank Crail, founder and CEO of the Rocky Mountain Chocolate Factory in Durango, Colorado, who in 1981 moved there from Southern California where he had a small but successful computer consulting business. "A two- or three-million-dollar business in Southern California was nothing," he says. "Now Exxon in L.A. was hit all the time. But the small ones, no one expected it. I didn't realize those needs were there, frankly."

If you're talented, wealthy or possess unique skills (as most newcomers discover they do), understand that the community will take note of it and expect you to contribute to the communal cause. The more accomplished you are, the more you will be asked to do, borrowing from the old adage, from those to whom much is given, much is expected. If in the city, you were used to having to fend off suitors for your time and purse, changing your automatic response from a no to a yes may involve a fundamental shift in your thinking. But giving time or money to community is a lovely way of being drawn into the community circle.

TWELVE AXIOMS OF COMMUNITY
From *The Search for Meaning* by Thomas H. Naylor, William H. Willimon and Magdalena R. Naylor

1. If you don't know where you are going, no road will get you there.

2. If you fear separation, meaninglessness and death, then unite.

3. The price of community is your own individualism.

4. There is no daddy and mommy, but if there were a daddy or mommy, he or she would be you.

5. Share power—one person, one vote.

6. Might doesn't make right.

7. There's no substitute for commitment and hard work.

8. Small is beautiful.

9. Keep it simple—always make molehills out of mountains.

10. Cooperate and communicate, if you want to survive.

11. Reduce tension; don't escalate conflict.

12. Grow spiritually, intellectually, and emotionally or die.

How to Behave

> "Don't complain and don't explain."
>
> —SMALL-TOWN MAXIM

A strong code of etiquette exists that will help guide you toward making (and maintaining) a happy adjustment in your new town. To retrofit your city mind-set and persona, you'll want to start on the inside—with your attitude. Adopting a mental posture of openness and expectancy will lead to discoveries large and small and will put you in the right frame of mind to build goodwill around town.

If you approach townspeople with the idea that they're unique treasures, you're likely to find individuals who will dazzle you, often in their small-town cover of plain brown wrap. You may encounter accomplished individuals who don't advertise their credentials. Don't be surprised to find a Ph.D. in molecular biology operating a dry-cleaning shop, a former performance artist from SoHo selling everlasting flower arrangements on Main Street or sharp-as-a-tack local businesspeople whose lack of a formal education has never detracted from their thriving enterprises.

While it's impossible to compile an irreproachable list of do's and don't's for small-town behavior, we will generalize about certain modes of behavior that are sure to please—or displease.

ATTITUDE

Probably the most common mistake newcomers to small towns make is in assuming that the community and its institutions are backward and that you, having come from the cutting edge of culture and life, naturally know better, have experienced better or simply deserve better. Even those of you who sought out small-town life may subconsciously harbor the feeling that you're stepping down or stepping backward. (Behavioral missteps are often made when one is trying to overcompensate for the feeling that moving to a small town means conceding some sort of defeat.)

This feeling is not surprising, given the deep-running societal prejudice—promulgated by big-city media—that cities are somehow superior to towns, that small towns are bastions of backwardness. (Witness a recent *New York Times* editorial, which begins with this inflammatory line: "Small-town cronyism is passable in small towns but dangerous when transplanted to Washington." Such condescending assumptions lurk behind much of the generic press about small towns, as if cronyism doesn't get by in Washington, D.C., New York City—or even, dare we mention it?—in the sacred halls of *The New York Times.)*

Nothing rankles the small-towner more than being prejudged by uppity city folks. The view that big cities are superior to small towns is not only erroneous but downright offensive. To try to erase this view, check yourself any time such a thought crosses your mind and censor yourself if you begin to speak it.

"Small-town people are so used to being exploited, misunderstood and stereotyped that any willingness to not do that will be appreciated and rewarded," says Kathleen Norris.

"I just really feel that you have to bend over backward so people don't think you think you're better than they are," says Mike Goldwasser, an Illinois native and one-time law student at the University of Pennsylvania in Philadelphia, who started a cattle farm in rural Carroll County, Virginia, in 1973. Goldwasser developed his community-sensitive philosophy in part after working as a Peace Corps volunteer teaching math and physics in Tanzania and Uganda in the late 1960s, where he was one of only a handful of Caucasians. He learned that "whenever you're from outside the community—if you're more educated or more white—you have to display more sensitivity, to bend over backward to not only *not* offend but to let people know you respect their way of life. There's going to be an assumption by people that you don't respect their way of life," he says, "so even if you *do* respect it, the burden is on you to demonstrate your respect."

Goldwasser, who served as a cross-cultural trainer for Peace Corps volunteers, applied this thinking to the mountain culture of Appalachia when he and his then fiancée moved to rural southwest Virginia. Although a fish out of water, he has remained in the area long enough to see his philosophy bear fruit. Respected and admired in the community for his thriving cattle enterprise, he serves on numerous local boards, was named Virginia Cattleman of the Year in 1989 and is one of one hundred representatives nationwide on the Cattlemen's Beef Board, an industry group for the promotion of and research on beef.

But he cautions any newcomers following in his footsteps: "You can only be sensitive to these things if you really believe in them."

Don't Prejudge

Never come into a new community with preconceived notions about the school system, medical care, the arts community or recreational facilities. Not only are you likely to be proven wrong, but you're liable to alienate the very people you should be befriending.

"There've been a number of folks who've come into Mount Airy assuming the schools are terrible because it's a small town, being highly critical when they haven't even bothered to learn the facts," says Tanya B. Rees of the Surry Arts Council. Affluent newcomers are the worst offenders, she says. Before giving local schools a chance, many check out the private schools in nearby Winston-Salem. "Everyone's child is gifted," remarks Rees wryly. "There's one couple who moved from New Jersey whose children had such fabulous backgrounds; they told me their children were so far superior to anything they'd likely encounter here. They wound up putting their children in our public schools. It turned out their children were of average intelligence."

Most former city residents are selectively guilty of this offense—ourselves included. Having met in a snooty, selective, creative-writing seminar at Harvard University, we didn't know what to expect when we team-taught our first class in creative writing at Surry Community College in Dobson, North Carolina. Some of our students had never been to college; others were high school English teachers with advanced degrees; some were retirees wanting to chronicle their stories for their grand-children; still others had compelling workplace tales to tell or pure yarns to spin but lacked the structural know-how. When the class finished, the group continued meeting on its own for several months. One of our students even sold a short story and an essay to two different national magazines. It inspired us to see her pure, over-the-transom talent prevail!

This experience and other similar ones taught us that *you can never prejudge the caliber of small-towners*. Check your diplomas, credentials, city-won accomplishments, and status at the town limits. Once you open yourself to discovering a small town, you'll be pleasantly surprised with what you see, feel and learn and, most of all, who you meet.

Don't Say You Know How Things Should Be Done

Prejudging often takes the form of assuming that you're doing small-towners a favor by bestowing your professional expertise or business acumen on them. Make this breach at your own peril.

Restaurateurs Jim and Fran Van Zandt, who moved to Santa Rosa Beach in the Florida panhandle from New York City in 1989 to start what is now the highly successful Santa Rosa Beach Cafe and Bakery, have watched other newcomers follow them—and fall flat on their faces for precisely this reason.

Not long ago, a pair came down from Atlanta to this small resort town about sixty miles east of Pensacola to establish a table-cloth restaurant serving entrees ranging in price from $18 to $25. "They went around town saying, 'No one here knows anything about food,'" Jim Van Zandt remembers. "'We'll show you what it's like.' They lasted one season. They got zero support from the locals."

"If you don't get local support, you're dead," adds Fran Van Zandt. Word of mouth is critically important in a small community. "It's easy for people to say, 'bad attitude'" and write you off entirely, she says. Indeed, the Van Zandts' cafe, which has become the local equivalent of the *Cheers* bar and watering hole, now employs forty-eight locals. "On our shirts, we say, 'Friend-liest place in town,'" says Fran Van Zandt. "We tell our staff, 'If you don't like a customer, be friendly anyway. They're gone in half an hour.' But you'll be glad they come back."

Jim Van Zandt says the attitude in Santa Rosa Beach toward know-it-all outsiders is best summed up by "a standard bumper sticker that says: 'We Don't *Care* How You Did It Up North.'"

What's more, says Van Zandt, people have "no curiosity" about his Manhattan years. "When you mention something about New York, it's surprising how many people who live here say, 'Too bad you had to live there.'" End of discussion. If Van Zandt were to give a single piece of advice to city people moving to a small town, it's this: "I'd be real low-key. Don't tell them how important you were. Nobody cares."

Don't Expect Amenities from Your City to Be Found in Town

Don't judge a small town's amenities by big-city standards, or gripe when you can't find cured Italian ham on Main Street, the way you were used to getting it elsewhere. "Don't try to bring New York City to Altoona," says Floyd Nelson, associate director of International Program Coordination for Habitat for Humanity in Americus, Georgia, who moved from Atlanta. "Accept it for what it is. Just as when you're at an Italian restaurant, you don't complain that there are no tacos."

Wanda was dumbfounded when she met a newcomer to Mount Airy one day at a Rotary lunch who, when asked how he liked it, complained that shopping here left something to be desired. He couldn't find any Gucci loafers or gourmet wines in town, he griped. Even though she's not a shopkeeper in town and is a relative newcomer herself, she could feel her defensive hackles going up.

Don't Be a "Cultural Monitor"

Just as you should never go around town strutting your stuff, be equally careful about criticizing—or even verbally sizing up—the local culture. If you feel compelled to remark upon your new hometown (especially if your comments are in any way critical), call and unload on your out-of-town friends.

A letter written by Pam Parrish of Advance, North Carolina, published January 18, 1995, in the *Winston-Salem Journal,* expresses the silent agony of hometowners when obstreperous newcomers make sport of an indigenous culture. "Recently my family and I attended a party [where] I overheard a conversation among several people who have recently moved to our area from points north," Parrish writes. "The conversation began with a discussion of the lack of multi-culturalism in North Carolina. As the conversation began to degrade into a North Carolina–bashing session, I left the room. Being reared a well-mannered Southern lady, I did not say anything. However, I feel the need to say something now.

"For our recent additions from the North, I have a few questions. How would you like it if I moved to your home state and took about a million of my best buddies with me; then, while living and working in your state and taking advantage of all it has to offer, begin making comments that characterized all Northerners as loud-mouthed, pushy, crass and with the table manners of barnyard animals?

"I . . . have been called a racist, a bigot and a red-necked hick. In my own home state, I am treated as if I lack something in the intelligence department because I speak with a Southern accent. To top it off, I am automatically closed-minded, intolerant and homophobic because my religion is Baptist. . . . Just who appointed you cultural monitors anyway? Why should we embrace your cultures or make any attempts to understand you when you turn up your noses at us and our culture and act as if we are so stupid that we can't even tell when we are being insulted?"

Realize that comments that might seem insightful, engaging or merely truthful to you may be easily misconstrued. If a native asks you what you think of Galesburg, do not take this as an opening to unload your woes, inmost doubts or postpartum moving blues. Understand that this kind of question is akin to a parent asking how you liked his or her child in a dance recital. This is not the time for gut-wrenching honesty. (You'd never say: "Well, it's obvious Jennifer will never make it to the American

Ballet Theater.") When people ask you what you think, this is the time for specific, positive feedback. A good response might be something on this order: "I'm amazed and delighted at how clean and litter-free the streets are." Or tell a story about someone in town who went out of his or her way to welcome you or perform an act of kindness.

Cultivate a Giving Attitude

Though this may seem commonsensical, in fact, cultivating a giving attitude may be more of a stretch for you than you realize. In the city, most people develop thick skins and with them a wariness about being taken advantage of. This coping mechanism may well be a healthy adaptation to the often predatory jungle of city life. But in a small town, it's healthy and wise to practice giving. Small-towners say that giving will come back to you in ways you can never anticipate.

By giving, we mean finding ways to give financially and of your time and of yourself for the greater good. By giving, we mean being able to rise above the win/lose of a specific encounter or exchange and take a broad, long-term view of the situation. We know of one urban expatriate who moved into a small town, established a small service business and developed a relationship with a local nonprofit agency in which its clients received a special discount. So concerned was the businessman about being taken advantage of that he began demanding freebies of the agency and made a point of giving discounted service for the price. In the end, he antagonized the very outfit that could have lent him greatest support. This is a classic case of penny wisdom and pound foolishness. His concern for the short-term bottom line jeopardized his long-term goodwill.

"Having a giving attitude in a small town is going to get you further than having a taking attitude," observes one small-towner who's seen a parade of city people move into her town (and quite a number move on down the road). "It will be noticed and will accrue to you in the long run. It's not being hypocritical; it's being wise."

WHAT YOU HEAR AND WHAT YOU SAY

> "The wise man knows what he says; the foolish man says all
> he knows."
>
> —UNKNOWN

Be a Good Listener

Emanating from your attitude are the words out of your mouth.
The first rule of thumb for any newcomer is to *be a good listener.*
Listening more than talking is essential in a small town—especially for the newcomer. There's a whole slew of expressions for
what we're recommending you do in your first six months in
town: hold your tongue, zip your lip, shut your mouth, *fermez la
bouche,* seal your lips. (The abundance of expressions for what's
desired here may reflect the relative scarcity of the practice.)

If any single pearl of wisdom holds doubly true for newcomers, it's this one, from Stephen R. Covey's book *Daily Reflections
for Highly Effective People:* highly effective newcomers need to
relearn constantly "the anatomy lesson that we have two ears and
one mouth, and we should use them accordingly," he writes.

Although you don't want to appear to be a stone-faced enigma
when conversing with small-towners, you *do* want to practice verbal
self-restraint. In conversation, you'll want to divulge some information about yourself to show that you're present, to reflect your
personality and aspirations, but never, *ever,* talk beyond the point
of audience interest. Think of listening as paying your dues.

Choose Your Battles

When you have to fight, choose your battles. Whether it's a
church or any other organization, don't jump into the fray when
heated issues are being discussed, even if they are seemingly inconsequential things such as the style of lights hanging in the
church sanctuary, or what colors to repaint the bathrooms, or
which plumber to give the contract to or what day to hold the
parade.

"I pick my fights and look at which things are really going to matter," says Kathleen Norris. "There's so much divisive talk in general in America. If we'd all listen more, rather than feel the need to spout our views on everything, we'd be better off."

Seek Input of Old Guard

Sonia Black, the head of an arts guild in a small Kansas town, says she's been appalled by the frequency with which newcomers—particularly those hired into leadership positions—come in and go on about how they're going to shake up the town without first seeking the input of the old guard. One such outsider, originally from Des Moines, came in with grand plans for his new job as school-system recreational director. Although Black's arts guild is responsible for arranging arts programming as well as bringing in visiting artists, the new man started telling Black and others what great, glorious plans he'd made for his new post: classes he'd start, special projects he'd undertake, artists he could deliver. His plans overlapped with much of what the guild already did. Instead of soliciting Black's input about what holes needed to be filled, he came out with his own agenda.

"Before you go out telling people what you're going to do, consider listening to what has already been done," advises Black. "If something hasn't been done, there may be a reason." A related point: you need not only listen respectfully but tread delicately on others' turf.

Sometimes newcomers make the mistake of moving in too quickly on positions of power and alienating the long-standing interests of the natives. Again, by coming in with their own agendas and by not taking into account the concerns and interest of the old guard, they may wind up alienated from their new communities.

Philip M. Burgess of the Center for the New West says that he's noticed for many small towns, tourism and economic development are hot-button issues, with newcomers often leading the charge against further development. Burgess recently spoke at the governor's conference on tourism at the University of Idaho in Moscow. During the question-and-answer period, a Sun Valley area economic development director agreed that a new breed of outsiders is coming to town and getting elected to city council or the library board. Many of these newcomers are "a problem," she said. "They often have different values and their own agenda. Sometimes they take over. Now we're having a big fight in our community because we want to spend money to buy porta-toilets and picnic tables for hikers and mountain bikers. But the lone eagles who've gotten into powerful positions don't want public money spent to encourage summer tourism, even though it's a major source of income for many old-timers in our community."

Don't Be the First Voice to Speak

> "I'd rather remain silent and be thought a fool than open my mouth and remove all doubt."
>
> —ABRAHAM LINCOLN

Marion McAdoo Goldwasser, who grew up outside Philadelphia and received her master's degree in English and education from Stanford University, taught in the Carroll County, Virginia, schools for more than twenty years. There she learned to discard some of her urban verbal habits the hard way. She had to work on "not being the first voice to speak out at a meeting. In Carroll County, people are more reticent; they take time to mull things over." However, their motives aren't entirely Olympian, she says. People weigh their words carefully so as not to "burn bridges or have their words come back to haunt them."

Indeed, we recommend a hearty diet of listening when you arrive in town, and if this evolves into a lifetime habit, so much the better. Remember that among those who are well established in a small town, the top achievers tend to be hearty practitioners of the big-ear, small-mouth approach.

Take Care in Choosing Words

Not only do you need to be sparing in what you say, but you should be *careful* about the content of your remarks. You do this because everyone's related (by blood, friendship or business) and everything's interrelated; you're liable to put your foot in your mouth if you utter a disparaging word about the car dealer with whom you just spoke (who turns out to be somebody's daughter, uncle, cousin or friend). Even if they happen not to know the person in question or the situation you're discussing, remember that your *attitude* will be gauged by small-towners. If you criticize someone from their town (or even someone from your old city), your listener may well leap to the conclusion that he or she will be next on your verbal chopping block. Remember that criticism tightens people up; praise loosens them. Although this holds universally true, with the long memories and extended "mulling" time in small towns, this truth rings even louder here.

If you have blabbermouth tendencies, hold this image in your mind before you go out and about or pick up the telephone: Imagine that you're on the stand in a court of law and every word you utter is being taken into court record. This *can* be the case with small-towners when drawing their first impressions of newcomers from the city.

Avoid Directness of Speech

In a small town, you should avoid directness of speech. Never tell someone: "Get to the point," when he is obscure or talking around a subject. He is speaking his mind in circular fashion. You may have to listen carefully to get what he's driving at and you may have to settle in for a long wait. Try to mirror the way the other person speaks in a manner that's not incongruent with your verbal style.

It's not always easy. Even small-town natives, after living for a spell in the city, have to work to avoid being brusque. Says Laurie Moorefield Forbes, a financial communications manager in Boston, who returned to her hometown of Mount Airy after living away for almost two decades, "I do check myself to see if I'm being abrupt." Several times since her return from Bean Town, she's gotten the impression that her direct manner and speech have put off some of the folks she grew up with. On occasions, when she's spit something out in a group setting, "it's like a pin drops. No one says anything, and people look at me, and it's like, 'Oh,'" she says. "I don't weave all that language around and soft-pedal it and spoon-feed it. Now I try—before I say something—to make sure they're going to understand it. The person I'm speaking with may be saying the same thing. Sometimes they just take longer to say it."

The "N" Word

Get ready to learn—and then unlearn—a new dirty word: the "N-word." Indeed, "no" is a no-no in a small town and suffers from being too abrupt. If there's any way you can get around it, avoid saying "no."

Likewise, it's a mistake to shoot down people or their propos-als. In a small town, consideration is the order of the hour. You protect others from rejection by saying, "Let me think about it," or, if you disagree with something, by saying as little as possible, or couching your differences as gently as possible.

Marie Lewis Judson, a friend from Mount Airy, told of a re-cent faux pas committed by a woman new to town from Detroit. When the newcomer, whom we'll call Paula, was introduced to some women at the country club, one extended the hand of friendship by saying: "I'll just drop in sometime, and we can have a cigarette."

Paula put her feelings right out front and center: "I don't smoke and I don't permit it in my home."

Her directness put off everyone, including the nonsmokers in the group. Judson recommended an alternative approach that would have achieved the same result. Paula should have graciously accepted the offer and when the caller came and pulled out her cigarettes, she should have mentioned that because of her allergies she could only allow smoking outside. (This would have encour-aged the caller's friendship and saved the woman's face in public.)

"That way, no one's feathers would have been ruffled," says Judson. "And she wouldn't have missed out on the opportunity to make a new friend."

Ask for Help or Advice

Everyone likes playing the expert. Small-towners are no exception. Asking for help or advice is one of the easiest ways of getting the verbal ball rolling with strangers, engaging them in your story and your transition into small-town life. It's a classic win/win exchange. The person you've met gets a chance to impart information, and you usually come away much the wiser. It can also be the first step to a new friendship.

From the newcomer's perspective, even the most "ordinary" person you encounter is someone special, the one holding the cards of knowledge about his or her home turf. Think of it this way: If you're lost on a two-lane highway, anyone you meet who can point you in the right direction has a leg up on you. During this brief encounter, that person is your superior and you his or her subordinate.

When you're a newcomer in a small town, you're in the same position. You might ask people where they shop for groceries and why; a good place to buy a car; which third-grade teacher would be best for your hyperactive son. If you need to, take notes. Ask follow-up questions and listen attentively. Be a sponge. Never make the mistake of asking someone's advice, then launching into a rebuttal. Always thank that person after advice is given. If she tells you something you already know, treat it as a new revelation.

When you next see the person, relate the impact his or her pearl of wisdom has had on your life—even if it's incredibly minor. (Remember, no detail is inconsequential in the context of small-town life.) Mention that after you talked, you went directly to the Kroger's on Lebanon Street and were amazed to find your favorite ice cream there. People enjoy knowing that they've touched your life in some small way, and that you've remembered them and their advice.

You will need to be more discriminating about soliciting physical help than verbal advice. Don't flag down your neighbor to ask him to help you move the new sofa into your den. The best way to ask for this kind of assistance is to do so indirectly. Say to him: "Do you know of anyone I could hire to help me move my sofa?"

More than likely, he'll offer his brute strength at no charge, but phrasing it delicately gives him an out that stops short of having to resort to the dreaded "N" word. He may say: "I'd like to help you, but I'm due downtown at three o'clock. If you haven't found anyone by the time I get back, give me a buzz." It also gives him the opportunity to feel generous by refusing money.

A note of caution. Even with the friendliest of neighbors, be sure never to impose on their generosity. Always thank people for their trouble, even if they merely point you in a direction to find help.

Effecting Change

A move from the city to town is one of the greatest catalysts for creative inspiration and will often spark a stream of new ideas— not only for rearranging your life but on how to improve things in your new community. When you do have suggestions about new ways of doing things, be sure to couch them in a positive, nonthreatening way. Don't come out and say: "I can't believe you've never tried this." Or: "How in the world could you have overlooked this possibility?"

Instead say: "Would you like to hear about what we did in Dallas?" Or: "There's an innovative new method of displaying Christmas ornaments that I noticed in Denver that you might like learning about."

When scouting a new small town in the Southwest, one big-city resident noticed that the local chamber of commerce gave out its promotional brochures stuffed inside a telephone book. After selecting that town, he joined the chamber, and when the time was right, suggested that new folders be printed to give the town "a more professional presentation." His approach made all the difference: Instead of condemning the chamber for its backwardness, he proposed a better way in a positive context—a suggestion that chamber members readily embraced.

"When I joined the women's group at church, I sat and listened for the longest time," says Kathleen Norris. "After you've listened for a while, they're willing to listen to you."

As a (witting or unwitting) agent of change, you're smart to introduce ideas gradually. Consult with others and win them to your side. When the time is right to take a stand, be sure to think your position through *before* speaking out. "You need to say something that's halfway reasonable—not the most drastic change in the world—and get people to try it," advises Norris.

This go-easy approach enabled Norris to become what she calls "a good subversive" in Lemmon. When a controversy erupted over the pastors of her Presbyterian church—whom she believes were mistreated and scapegoated for the farm crisis of the 1980s—Norris forced herself to hold her tongue, "which I don't normally do. Emotionally, I was very upset. My instinct was to jump into the fray and get vocal about defending them. But the church congregation was divided. I decided speaking out was the worst thing I could do."

Although she did venture to express some opinions, she managed to refrain from getting emotional. "Everyone knew I was friends with the pastors," she says. "I'd say things in support of them. But I wouldn't get caught up in the bitter, crazy fighting."

The reward for Norris's self-restraint?

"I was asked to be on the search committee for the next pastor, partly because I hadn't joined in taking sides. I was one of the first people to be nominated, which surprised me. I was able to effect change that way [in helping to select the new minister]."

"Effecting change involves patience and time—those things that we don't value in America," says Norris.

Use Code Language

> **"Where seldom is heard a discouraging word"**
> —*Lyric from* "HOME ON THE RANGE"

The small-town code of conversation evolved over the years as townspeople sought to protect each other's feelings, to look out

for the general good and to save face for those who might otherwise lose it (as well as for their relatives, friends and associates).
Because the small-town credo forbids vicious gossip and direct
put-downs (especially for newcomers with whom a level of trust
and confidentiality has yet to be established), shades of meaning
and truth are often marbled into what might seem to an outsider
like innocuous or surprisingly upbeat talk about "sad" stories and
"defeated" souls.

When we first moved back to Mount Airy, we became acquainted with one of the saddest sad-luck stories of them all. A
brilliant graduate of a prestigious southern university, whom
we'll call Pete, had destroyed his high-powered international
banking career by abusing drugs and alcohol. He was then forced
to move back into his parents' home in Mount Airy. He bounced
from job to menial job—jobs that family connections helped him
obtain. Pete couldn't hold the fast-food job, was fired from the
clothing store when caught imbibing in the stockroom and eventually died in a tragic workplace accident at a hosiery mill. What
struck Wanda was the subdued and charitable way people discussed Pete's plight—right up until his death.

"Things never seem to work out right for Pete," people would
say, before relating his latest job disaster. "Bless his heart," they'd
say and then go on to to bless the hearts of his long-suffering parents. Frank's mother, Miriam, suggested Pete's "beverage problem" was responsible for his fall from grace. (She never would
use the word alcohol.) "It's gotten hold of him," she said, as if referring to some beast that had quite literally sunk its teeth into his
flesh and refused to let him loose. "If I'd ever started drinking,
I'm sure that would have happened to me," she added, so as not
to sound judgmental. "That's why I never took it up."

The emotion people displayed when relating sad tales convinced Wanda of their sincerity. They weren't sticking a knife in
Pete's back; they derived no pleasure from it. Their concern was
genuine. She never once heard anyone descend to cruelty or a
lack of compassion by saying something like: "That slobbering
drunk has shot himself in the foot again." Or: "If I were his par-

ents, I'd throw the bum out of the house." This humane approach to discussing problems was revolutionary to Wanda, who'd grown up in a let-it-all-hang-out household of confrontational truth-telling.

Ascribing the best of intentions to a troubled soul is a leading feature of this charitable, small-town code. We often hear things like, "Mary means well, but things never seem to work out right." (Translation: Mary invariably messes things up. Her marriages have failed, ditto friendships, and she was caught shoplifting.) As with Pete, the phrasing lets Mary off the hook by condemning an agent outside herself for her troubles. It's not hypocritical. The generous language leads to a generosity of spirit.

If you hear: "Joe is never able to hold on to a job," the translation is: Don't ever hire Joe; he's a lousy worker.

Code language is often used out of respect when applying labels to people. A dear friend told Wanda that whenever people first meet his mother—a well-known and little-liked battleax—they describe her as a "character." What they mean, he said, is that she's a bitch. Another man in town, when discussing his cousin whom we know well, described her as "a free spirit." What he was really saying is that his cousin is a flake. In Mount Airy, we've noticed that whenever anyone communicates a critical idea about a person, it's always accompanied by a disclaimer. "Now don't get me wrong. I like Emily, but she has a ways to go in the truthfulness department."

Another common practice in small-town parlance when saying something harsh is to include oneself (and/or all of humanity) under the umbrella of fault or susceptibility. Miriam Levering, a minister's daughter who grew up in the small Pennsylvania towns of Coraopolis and New Kensington, was a master of this approach. She'd say: "Like myself, Nancy has a hard time keeping the pounds off." Or: "Like the rest of us, Ronald never likes to surrender center stage." The message is communicated that Nancy eats too much and Ronald talks too much but never once does the listener get the feeling that he or she is participating in a verbal lynching. You come away seeing your humanity linked with the foibles of these two people; you relearn the lesson that all of us suffer from common weaknesses.

Indirect Criticism

If you put your foot in your mouth (and who among us hasn't?) or repeatedly say or do the wrong thing, how are you going to find out about it so you can amend your errant behavior?

For all the reasons related above, small-towners are unlikely to come right out and directly criticize you or cite any behavioral transgressions you may have made. But if you listen closely to what they say and don't say, you're likely to hear what's on their minds—including feedback about your own performance.

Indeed, foreigners' indirect criticism of visiting Americans is strikingly similar to the phenomenon we've observed in small towns. "If you are with a group of Japanese," writes Craig Storti in *The Art of Crossing Cultures,* "or Thais, and they offer an offhand criticism of Americans in general, chances are they have just given you a piece of personal feedback on something you've done. If they should go on to specifically exempt you from the criticism—'But you aren't like most Americans'—then you can be *sure* the criticism is aimed at you." (Italics ours.)

By the same token, small-towners who are skeptical of your behavior will often make generalizations about city slickers, Johnny-come-latelies or Yankees (if you've moved to the South) that you *should* consider taking personally.

If you're starting a new business in town, for instance, and you've been running around trying to round up inventory and close the deal with a rental agent, an official at the chamber of commerce may remark: "Some people try to come in here and move too fast." Chances are, he's commenting on you. It's a good idea to review your behavior; try to pinpoint what made him say that.

To give another example, let's say you stop at a yard sale in town and attempt to drive a hard bargain on a used lawnmower. Let's say you make a bid that seriously undercuts the tag price and that you keep hammering away on why it's in the seller's interest to bite. Perhaps he might say something like: "I like dealing with you. A lot of city folks are too aggressive." What he's really telling you is that you are, too.

A casual remark can often signal constructive criticism, should you pick up on the cue. Once, after Wanda's thrice-weekly swim in Galax, Virginia, she got to chatting with the lifeguard. Wanda said: "It must be tedious sitting up there, watching the lap swimmers go back and forth, up and down the pool."

He said: "Usually I look at swimmers' strokes and go over in my mind how they could be improved."

Wanda realized that he was using code language to signal that he had ideas about improving *her* stroke, but that he'd offer advice only if she wanted to hear it.

Her response was: "How could I improve mine?"

This was the license he needed to launch into a critique of her stroke. He detailed how her right arm was dominant in the stroke but that she wasted energy by splashing it into the water rather than cutting it in neatly; he went on to say that her left stroke was sluggishly inefficient (a surprising revelation, since she's a southpaw).

Although the lifeguard's suggestion may sound trivial, the way in which he broached it is significant; it demonstrates the small-town approach to offering both criticism and advice. Small-towners will let you know what's on their minds, but only after you reassure them that you wish to hear it, often after you prod it out of them. No matter what they say—even if you vehemently disagree—always remember to thank them for their ideas and opinions.

DISCIPLINE

Self-Discipline

It takes effort to be an active listener and a disciplined conversationalist. Although these skills bear cultivating in places urban as well as rural, they're especially important in the context of small towns. Exercising self-discipline—whether by holding your tongue when every cell in your body is aching to speak out, restraining yourself from blasting someone when you feel you've been crossed or simply in sublimating the emotion of the moment—is a survival skill in a small town. Failure to do so will cost you dearly.

"Instinct Override"

One of the best ways to cultivate a disciplined approach is to suppress the impulse to speak or act out of turn and to develop the skills of observation. It's an ability that cross-cultural trainer and author Craig Storti terms "instinct override." It means simply that when in a new culture, you should override your first instincts and approach the locals with what he calls "caution and circumspection," which will enable you to "sidestep some of the more obvious cultural traps."

Day-in and day-out self-discipline may prove difficult for many former city residents to achieve. It can be especially challenging to Baby Boomers who were raised to believe that self-discipline was square—perhaps even obsolete—or, at the very least, less important than such goals as self-expression and self-fulfillment.

No More "Throwaway" People

Over the last few generations, the character of all Americans, but particularly Baby Boomers—and especially *urban* Baby Boomers—has begun to resemble that of the careless consumer. If a friendship, relationship, or marriage wasn't working, people became accustomed to wadding it up, throwing it away and replacing it as quickly as possible. Using discipline to maintain personal relationships was all but discarded.

When you're in a city, it is easier to "throw away" people than it is in a small town. In the city, you can date someone until he starts to seem ordinary or until his weaknesses emerge and then dump him in a proverbial heartbeat. And you may never see that person again. There are few (if any) social consequences to pay.

Such tactics will backfire on you in a small town—and not

only on the dating circuit but in every arena of life. You *will* see that "throwaway" person again and again—at the market, at the post office, in line at the bank. It's important to part as amicably as possible. The cardinal rule in a small town is to treat everyone fairly.

No Burning Bridges or Holding Grudges

A disciplined approach in a small town requires you to hang in there with others through the tough times—theirs, yours and theirs as they affect yours. You'll need to rise above not only the petty slight but the major transgression to stick it out for the long haul. In a small town, you should never burn bridges behind you or vent your anger carelessly.

"It doesn't do any good to hold grudges," asserts Frank Crail, founder and CEO of the Rocky Mountain Chocolate Factory in Durango, Colorado. Crail himself has the grounds to hold a few if he chose to, having received scant support from the local financial and economic-development communities when his company needed infusions of cash. But he and his wife and their seven children have made a commitment to stay in Durango, and they realize that the only way to flourish is to rise above past slights and get on with the business of succeeding.

If you're convinced that no malice was intended when you were wronged, you're well advised to let go of your grievances. We know of an instance in a small midwestern town where a young woman's physician, who was also a close personal friend, made a serious judgment error which almost cost her her life. But because she was convinced that no malice was intended—it was a mere oversight—the subject was never spoken of again. However, the woman quietly sought the services of another doctor.

In a small town, you'll need to let go of the notion that being true to yourself and indiscriminately expressing your feelings is your highest priority. Making it in a small town invariably involves revisiting the notion that honoring your private lights should be your paramount concern. Honoring your new community and its mores and manners is the appropriate substitute.

You Make the Effort

Even if you're disciplined in your approach to establishing a base for yourself in your small town, don't expect everything to fall into place automatically for you. As the newcomer, the ball is in your court. You're still going to have to expend the effort to carve out a niche for yourself.

"I don't think community comes to you," says Frank Crail. "In a small town, everyone may be friendly, and it may be easy to meet people. But a lot of that is superficial. If you're going to get involved in community, *you* have to make the effort."

Let Your Individuality Emerge . . . Gradually

"Don't spring your differences on others before you get to know them," recommends one small-towner. "Tread softly." Let your character emerge gradually. Someone who wears well over time will make more of a lasting impression than a flash in the pan. As with good writing, it's best to reveal your character through your actions rather than broadcast it through your words.

BEHAVIOR

We've already relayed a whole host of suggestions relating to your attitude in a small town. Additional behavioral pointers to help ease the transition and adjustment to small-town life follow.

Slow Your Pace

Slowing your pace is a necessary adjustment for most high-strung ex-urbanites. The person in a hurry is viewed with wariness, even suspicion, in a small town. A quick step and rushed manner are the marks of an outsider, much as the slow-stepping skyscraper-gawker signals an out-of-town visitor to a New Yorker or a Chicagoan.

Be Punctual

A part of slowing your pace involves leaving yourself cushions of time when configuring your day so that you're not hurried or running chronically late. Slowing your pace allows you to have time to visit with people who might call or those you might run into in town.

In most small towns, people are punctual, if not early, for just about everything. Arriving late at a dinner party or an appointment is considered a major faux pas. We learned the hard way. Once we arrived at a wedding that was scheduled to begin at 6 P.M. at one minute of. The processional had already begun.

Indeed, some small-towners even vie for the designation of early bird. This contest can carry an almost moral overtone, determining who is Earlier Than Thou. A friend of Wanda's—the owner of a local convenience-store chain who believes punctuality to be a virtue right up there with integrity—kindly offered to drive her to district court in Danbury, North Carolina, to help her fight a speeding ticket. Knowing his feelings about punctuality, Wanda arrived at the designated meeting place ten minutes ahead of time.

It wasn't early enough. He was already there, sitting inside his running vehicle. He might have been waiting an hour. She didn't ask how long he'd been there and offered no apology for being later than he. However, when they returned from the trip, she thanked him profusely for his trouble and offered to buy him lunch.

Adjust to the "DI's"

To avoid ruffling local feathers, city people need to make time for what Ann Moltu Ashman, an insurance salesperson in Elkin, North Carolina, calls the "DI's" (drop-ins). Ashman and her husband, Ron Ashman, had lived and worked in San Francisco, Washington, D.C., and Stamford, Connecticut, before moving to Elkin in 1983. In Stamford, not only did neighbors in their swanky neighborhood never drop in, but they were likely to refuse to open the door if you tried.

Ann Ashman remembers one holiday when Ron had gone door to door to distribute invitations to a neighborhood New Year's Day party they were throwing. "One lady wouldn't open the door to accept the invitation," she says. "A few close friends came, but the party was not well attended. We got the message that Stamford wasn't the place for us."

When the Ashmans moved to Elkin, where Ron Ashman took an executive position with a textile manufacturer, the couple was confronted with the opposite problem: a surfeit of neighborliness.

"The community was very embracing, largely due to Ron's boss," Ann says. "They could not have been warmer. I almost couldn't believe the extent to which we were welcomed." That initial welcome phase seemingly never ended, and people continued to drop in on the Ashmans—especially on Ann, who was at home preparing for the birth of their first child. Now that Ann is working full-time, the problem has abated, but they still chuckle over drop-in guests.

"We call them the 'DI's'," says Ann. "They never call. They assume their schedule is yours. I used to get uptight about it. I've changed."

She's come to accept dropping in as a part of the social culture of Elkin and as an act of friendliness rather than one of insensitivity. While it did take some jaw-setting discipline to let go of the tightly scheduled, DayMinder approach she'd pursued in the city, today, after twelve years, she's embraced the "DI" practice and is a hearty practitioner of it. "Now *I* drop in on other people to let them know how it feels," she jokes. "Seriously, I've changed in a positive way."

Avoid Discussing Education/Elite Cultural Tastes

If you come into town with designer diplomas and elite or esoteric cultural tastes—and the educational level of the community is low or people don't sit anywhere near the cutting edge of city-defined culture—you're wise to downplay these subjects.

Jim Van Zandt, a restaurant owner in Santa Rosa Beach, Florida, for instance, makes it a point never to discuss education with employees. "You can't come in and say, 'Go on to college,' or 'How come you didn't graduate high school?'" he says. "In the big picture, they understand the message, 'Stay in school.' But I don't get into conversations about what people shoulda, coulda, woulda done." For Van Zandt's employees who remain in school, he does his part to encourage them to stay—and keep their grades up. He and his wife check their student-employees' report cards. "They can't work if they get anything below a C," he says.

By the same token, in most instances, it's unwise to broadcast your own college degree, or advanced academic or professional credentials (unless you're hanging a shingle as an attorney). If your degree is from a prestigious university or an Ivy League institution, unless you are asked directly where you went to school, by all means keep it to yourself. This is especially true in the infancy of a relationship. Once people get to know you and realize you're a regular Joe (or Josie), you can dribble out more and more personal information.

Remember that the last thing you want to do is get people's backs up and stir any latent feelings of inadequacy. Small-towners are sensitive to anything that smacks of condescension or superiority; some may fear that because they haven't seen the world as you presumably have, or because they've never tested their wings in a big-city job market, that they're somehow out of your league. These are feelings you'll want to dispel if you want to establish a comfort zone.

"Some of the people who never left are very self-derogatory," says Virginia Emerson Hopkins, who returned to her hometown of Anniston, Alabama, in 1991 after more than a decade of practicing law in Washington, D.C. "They commuted from home to the local university, graduated, got married and stayed. They're self-derogatory about never having left." When confronted with others' feelings of inadequacy, Hopkins's tack is to be jokingly self-deprecatory. "I just say: 'Some people like me are slow learners. It took me a long time to come back.'"

DEVELOP A WEB OF FAVORS AND DEPENDENCIES

One surefire method of ingratiating yourself to others in a small town comes from the old adage that if you want a friend, you have to *be* a friend. We've noticed that small-towners develop webs of favors and dependencies. There's no reason a newcomer can't work her way into these webs by spinning some fibers of her own. One of the best web-weavers we've met in Mount Airy is a

State Farm insurance salesperson named Janet K. Edwards. In 1988, she moved to Mount Airy from rural southwestern Virginia, without knowing a soul in town. In just seven years, Edwards has managed to develop a wide circle of friends, place herself at the center of community activity *and* build a thriving business.

How?

By old-fashioned good-deed-doing and extending a helping hand to those in need. Edwards volunteers to squire around the elderly mothers of friends and clients on historic house tours. She celebrates friends' achievements, remembers birthdays and holidays with greeting cards and bottles of wine or boxes of chocolate. She participates in (if she doesn't organize) activities ranging from chamber social hours to Rotary fund-raisers. She purchased a ticket to go to Oakland with 55 Mount Airians to cheer on town presenters competing for the 1994 All-America City designation. Edwards knocks herself out to be useful, and, in so doing, has endeared herself to her adopted community.

Just as you should develop a giving attitude, you should also follow Edwards's lead in doing as many favors as possible and saying "yes" as often as you possibly can. Yeses will help build your "community bank account" of goodwill with each person for whom you've done a favor, and, in turn, they will help spread a favorable buzz about you around town. Eventually, these deposits will accrue to you with interest. Remember that the value of your friendships and of being known as a community player are significant components of your "wealth" in town.

One final caveat. Don't be too eager to demand quid pro quo or take credit for what you've done. People will remember what you've contributed, even if they don't always have the good manners to thank you or return the favor.

Embrace Conspiracies of Kindness

Among the most touching phenomena we've witnessed since making Mount Airy our hometown—something we never saw in Los Angeles—are what we call conspiracies of kindness.

These arise when ad hoc cabals form to help protect someone from his own blunders and gaffes, to shield that person from the naked truth or to spare him unnecessary suffering.

This phenomenon came into focus for Wanda after she saw a program at the Mount Airy Rotary Club in July of 1993. A district official for the Salvation Army drove an hour and a half from Charlotte to give the program at the regular Tuesday lunch meeting. The man opened by saying how happy he was to be in "Andy Griffin's hometown." He mentioned the actor by name several times, and though the actor's name is not Griffin but Griffith, each of the seventy-odd people assembled stifled the urge to say: "If you're going to drop someone's name, at least get it right."

But this was a minor matter compared to the fiasco that followed. For his program, the man played a videotape about the Salvation Army's Hurricane Andrew relief and cleanup efforts. That was fine . . . except for the fact that the club—an assemblage of high-powered business leaders and executives—had already viewed the tape several months earlier in a previous program. What amazed Wanda was that the *entire* group sat politely through the presentation again, and not one person nodded off or left impatiently. Come the question and answer period, someone even raised his hand and posed a courtesy question. And even though the speaker had done his homework poorly, he was graciously thanked by the club president, given the standard souvenir pen and sent on his way with his head held high, his dignity intact.

From our interviews, we found that this dynamic is fairly common among small towns. These collective acts of benevolence, conspiracies of kindness, rarely occur in cities. If the same scenario unfolded in Los Angeles—or even in Charlotte—you can bet someone would grow impatient and storm out, or speak up: "We've already seen this one. You're wasting our time."

Forgive: It's the Ultimate Healer
Of all the suggestions and rules outlined throughout, the one key to keep in mind about the small-town mentality is that people are

ultimately forgiving. Just as you can't afford to blow others off, neither can they you—even if you've committed some transgression.
Even if you violate the small-town code (and everyone is guilty of a
misstep now and then), rest assured that people will cut you some
slack. Usually people come around in the end.

And once you've established yourself as a community player,
even if you get into serious trouble, they'll let you off the hook.
"After a few years, they'll accept just about *anything* you do, as
long as it's not some heinous crime," asserts Laurie Moorefield
Forbes. "Small-town folk are, in general, very forgiving because
they know a person's history and mitigating circumstances. We
often don't give people enough credit for that. Say someone
cheated the IRS and got caught. In a few years, they'll say: 'He
got into some trouble with the IRS. But he's a good fellow.'"

ENDEARING YOURSELF TO THE LOCALS AND BUILDING GOODWILL
Patronize Local Merchants
Nothing engenders goodwill as quickly as buying from local
merchants rather than giving your business to chain stores or
buying out of town. For anyone who wants to be part of a community, this is perhaps the quickest way to score points; and it's
doubly important if you're trying to set up your own business.
Unless you're positively strapped for cash, it's worth it to spend
the extra money on merchandise acquired locally, including big-
ticket items, such as refrigerators, washing machines and vehicles. (Remember, local merchants will also feel responsible to
replace or repair if problems arise. And, because you're right
there in front of them, they can't shirk accountability.)

Tanya B. Rees says she buys "100 percent of what I wear on
my body" at her husband's clothing shop, The Addition, in
downtown Mount Airy. "Gene is extremely committed not
only to Mount Airy but to downtown. He's like, 'Get it downtown.' He would not even *consider* going out of town to buy a
car. It's a given he'll buy it here." Even if you end up paying

something of a premium for the product, "You'll get it back," declares Rees. "Because in a small town, no one forgets."

While you're buying, get acquainted with the salesperson and/or owner. Take an interest in the establishment: How long has it been in business? What is it known for? Take this opportunity to tell them what you're doing in town.

Never Say Things Are "Quaint"

The things you think are quaint or quirky may be the very things that the locals despise, such as antiquated machinery or pre-computer-age methods. Maybe you're charmed by a post office where you have to walk upstairs to get to the post office boxes (while the locals and the postal workers hate the inconvenience but have never been able to find the funds to build a new one). If you think something is quaint, hold your tongue. What you say might sound patronizing.

"Outsiders always come here and say, 'Look at the nice dirt lanes that go into the woods,'" says Jim Van Zandt of Santa Rosa Beach, Florida. "Locals can't stand them. They go nuts over dirt lanes. When it rains, red clay gets on their cars. Out-of-staters think it's quaint to have people down on the docks cutting fish. Locally, they're called 'fishheads.' If someone gets mad at you, he calls you a fishhead. Fishheads are the people you don't want your kids to hang out with."

Find Common Ground

Instead of always accenting your own individuality, or the differences between you and others, work to find common ground in conversation. Let's say you're a rabid Democrat and you meet up with an equally vehement Republican. Do not get into political tussling right away. Instead find common interests in sports, children or community history—even that old standby, the weather. If you work at it, you'll always be able to find common interests and avoid potentially inflammatory material.

By all means, avoid proselytizing about any subject. If people agree with you, they'll be bored. If they disagree with you, they'll be put off by having to listen.

Always Donate Things

When asked, contribute what you can. If a community group is trying to raise funds for a worthy enterprise, by all means, chip in. In a recent money-raising campaign in which Wanda participated to market Mount Airy after it won the All-America City designation, businesses were asked to contribute $250. Obviously, some businesses couldn't go that far, but the smart ones responded with encouraging words and more modest contributions.

Fran Van Zandt says that she and her husband have made it a policy to be yeasayers whenever any worthwhile community group solicits a contribution. They give gifts in-kind, such as a catered party for fifteen, a full sheet cake, whole fillets of beef, breakfast for two, lunch for two. "Because of the business we're in, it's easy to meet people," she says. "We say yes to a lot of people we might not have before. We're soft touches but there's also a payback to it."

Likewise, at the Rocky Mountain Chocolate Factory, Frank Crail says that his company makes it a policy to respond to "every worthy organization that calls" with gifts of cash or chocolate. It recently donated $25,000 to a concert-hall campaign, and overall giving "runs in excess of $50,000 to $100,000 a year," says Crail. For the last eight years, the company has thrown an annual Christmas party for 150 underprivileged children. "It's a very high priority to give back to the community in any area that will help. We have a high social conscience." This giving spirit has helped make Crail and his company a well-loved winner.

Join Clubs and Volunteer

Don't sit at home waiting for the phone to ring. Remember that small-towners may be intimidated by you and may be afraid to ask you to join a club, committee or enterprise. So step forward.

Although you don't want to join *every* club in town just be-

cause it's there, you should select the one or ones that complement your interests. Then join and be a doer. The best way to
demonstrate your commitment is to raise your hand every time
the club calls for volunteers. Offer to sell hot dogs at ball games
and give out pizza slices at the walkathon fund-raiser. Clean up
after parties or luncheons and offer to try to recruit guest speakers for programs. You can type the minutes and take out the
trash. Make yourself useful. Nothing will earn you credibility so
quickly as pitching in.

Issue Compliments Liberally

No social lubricant works so effectively to grease the wheels of
goodwill and positive feelings than conferring praise on others.
Although you never want to be disingenuous, you do want to
give praise when it's called for. Look for ways in which you see
people excel and hand out specific praise. It's free; it's uplifting;
and it does wonders for the spirits of those around you, which in
turn accrues to you. At the Mount Airy Rotary Club, members
are big praise-givers. They compliment everything from percep-
tive questions to striking apparel to mentions in the local newspaper.

Make it a Point to Socialize with Natives

Like college freshmen, some newcomers fall into the trap of un-
wittingly forming separatist cliques that exclude natives. Although hanging out with fellow newcomers whom you meet will
allow you to compare notes, air grievances and express homesick-
ness, doing so exclusively will deprive you of the opportunity to
mix and mingle with longtime residents and natives, which is essential for full integration into the life in the community.

"Some outsiders come in and make their own society," grouses
one longtime small-towner about the behavior of newcomers.
"They don't even try to get involved." Failure to engage with the
locals will give off the message of a certain skittish noncommit-
ment on your part to the town and could set up a vicious cycle in
which you become excluded from local goings-on.

Although in many places you'll be welcomed by natives with open arms, dinner invitations and such things as squash casseroles and peach cobblers, if you don't find a Welcome Wagon knocking at your door, you'll need to take the initiative and invite others over for a meal or cake and coffee.

Join a Church

Linda T. Lastinger, a physician specializing in internal medicine who moved with her physician husband from North Carolina's Research Triangle to Galax, Virginia, in 1980, advises others following the same trajectory to join a church (or synagogue or mosque). Aside from the spiritual rewards, church membership is enormously beneficial in bringing you into the church family and community. Church life is often fun, with youth groups and religious study for children and teens and day-care preschoolers. It's also a way of meeting people when they're at their most generous.

Join a Country Club

Belonging to a country club can also promote your integration into the life of a community—provided you can afford it. (Rates should be considerably lower in small towns than in big cities. Annual dues at the Lastingers' Galax club cost just $300 a year.) Little works better to get the social juices flowing than rubbing elbows with someone out on the putting green, at the club lounge or playing a round of tennis.

Deal with Gossip

There's no way around it. When you move to a small town, you're guaranteed to be the subject of gossip. "It's the fun of a small town, to hear the gossip!" exclaims Marie Judson of Mount Airy.

"For a newcomer to get angry about gossip is really naive, like moving to New York City and complaining that it's dirty," says Kathleen Norris, whose home in Lemmon, South Dakota, is just three blocks south of the North Dakota state line. "No one would recognize a small town if everyone—and especially newcomers—weren't raked over the coals. Newcomers are a wonderful toy chest. Why did they move here? What's wrong with them? Even if you do everything by the book, people will be trying to peek under the shades."

As a newcomer (though not exactly outsider), Norris is well-acquainted with the workings of the rumor mill. When she and her writer husband, David Dwyer, arrived in town in 1974 and moved into Norris's late grandparents' home, Dwyer looked for work as a bartender at a "beer bar" in town. Even though he had the entree of being "Doc Totten's grandson-in-law," his long hair and New York accent made him somewhat suspect. "The woman who owned the bar said some people had told her David was a drug dealer. Others said he was a federal narcotics agent," Norris remembers with a chuckle. "She told him, 'I figured I couldn't lose.'"

And when a limited edition of Norris's book, *Dakota: A Spiritual Biography* was published by Ticknor and Fields in January 1993, "wild rumors started to fly" about its contents.

Out of town when the book was first published, Norris heard the townsfolks' reaction through the grapevine. "People were saying I used real names, and they were all prepared to get hysterical," she remembers. "People were talking about the book but it turns out that none of them had *read* it. When they started reading it, they discovered it wasn't as bad as they thought."

Norris was amused by those individuals who didn't recognize themselves in some of the thinly veiled, more cryptic portraits; some even complimented the book. "They didn't recognize themselves and said what a great book it was!" she chuckles. Now the town has developed "a kind of wary pride" in *Dakota*. The book is being sold at the chamber of commerce, the newspaper office, the dimestore and drugstore, since there is no bookstore in town.

Linda Lastinger says the best way to avoid gossip is simply to detach yourself from the grapevine. If people talk about you, at least you won't know about it. "People in town really respect my privacy," she says. "Maybe they know I'm interested in respecting other people's privacy." By refusing to provide a receptive ear to gossip or an active mouth to spread it, you'll diminish its effect on your life.

However, it's *impossible* to avoid the small-town grapevine altogether. "Len loves to tell the story about how he pronounced a fellow dead at the hospital," says Linda Lastinger, "and I knew about it before he got home five minutes later."

RETURNING TO THE HOMETOWN OF YOUR YOUTH

If you're returning to the hometown of your youth, you're in a special position, beset by the advantages and disadvantages of being a native daughter or son. You've got names, contacts and common history with others. You may have family in town or, at the very least, common memories and reference points with those who live here. By the same token, if you're like most people, you've got a certain amount of baggage, as well—personal and familial.

It will be almost impossible to start with a completely clean slate. You're still Jimmy, the kid who knocked a ball into the plate-glass window of the Woolworth's downtown, or Dori, the girl who threw up on stage during the premiere of the class play. Or maybe you're Angie, the homecoming queen, or Rick, the boy who broke the school record for the 100-yard dash, or Thomas, the heartthrob.

But unless you had a terrible reputation or committed a crime, in most cases, having a history in town will work to your advantage, provided you don't attempt to rest on your laurels. But be forewarned: you do run into the danger of being typecast from the past; in some cases, people may think they already know all they need to know about you, without bothering to learn about the new person you've become.

"As people know your family, they think they know you," says Laurie Moorefield Forbes, who moved back to Mount Airy from Boston in 1988, after having lived there almost twenty years.

Followed by the Family Name
In Frank's case, he had a family name that was widely recognized locally. The Levering name was associated with a high degree of abstract (but not practical) intelligence, eccentricity and political idealism—not sound business judgment. This perception posed an obstacle to Frank when he set the goal of pulling our orchard business out of debt and making it profitable. When he behaved contrary to his father's style, some locals resisted, yearning for the good old days. For example, when attempting to collect a bill on the spot as opposed to "carrying" someone on credit, Frank might hear something slightly accusatory like: "Mr. Sam didn't do me this way." It proved a challenge for Frank to establish a set of rules and behaviors independent of his parents. When he was able to pull it off, he was able to step out of his father's shadow and establish his own individual identity.

Being Your Own Person
Although Kathleen Norris was neither an insider nor an outsider (having vacationed for summers at her mother's hometown), she nevertheless felt the weight of family expectations descend on her when she moved to Lemmon, South Dakota, in 1974. Her grandfather had been everyone's doctor and her mother a high-minded Presbyterian. "If people go back with preconceived roles from family history, it can be a hovering ghost or confining straitjacket," says Norris. "If they try to fit themselves into a mold, it might not work."

She was able to separate herself from preconceived expectations by picking and choosing what she wanted to do. "I was supposed to join the fanciest ladies' club in town and turned them down nicely, gently. I wasn't supposed to know who my sponsor was (but I did). I said, 'Lucille, Grandmother would be disappointed.' But I didn't feel I could step into my grandmother's shoes."

Norris did, however, join her grandparents' church. At first, she felt as if she were "putting on [her] grandmother's role. After a couple of years, I realized it was something I wanted to do for me, too."

Don't Expect It to Be the Way It Was

Several friends of Laurie Forbes's—also members of Mount Airy High School's class of 1965—moved back to town, expecting life to be the way it had been back then. "They were disappointed," she says. Those who were made short work of their stay and moved on.

Get this straight: moving back to your hometown is "*not* like stepping back in time," says Virginia Emerson Hopkins, who returned in 1991 to her hometown of Anniston, Alabama, after living in the Washington, D.C., area for more than ten years. "You're a different person and guess what? So's the town! Maybe there aren't five hundred new buildings, and they haven't torn up the streets, but the town *has* changed. There's a new mayor, new high schools have been built, people have left, moved in, died, divorced. Anyone who thinks they can step back in time to the place they left is going to be disappointed. It's kind of like going back to college after you've graduated. The buildings—maybe the teachers—are the same, but it's not the same. It's a different world."

Often, you'll have nothing in common with the people you went to high school with, except the past, which gets old fast. And often, the friends you expect to be there for you won't come through, while new ones will unexpectedly appear. Like other newcomers, you'll go through the "honeymoon stage" of buzzing around reacquainting yourself with old friends and meeting new ones, before settling into friendships with the people who will count.

Strong Sense of Self

If you had problems with the town while you were growing up (and who among those who've fled hasn't?), be sure you've resolved them and feel strongly enough established in your own identity before you return.

"If you don't have a strong sense of self, you'll feel like you have to act and play a role (to conform to the small-town code)," advises Forbes. "But if you're a strong person, you have yourself anyway and are not threatened by not doing what the natives do."

Timing Is Everything

The time to return to your hometown is at that moment when your yearning for the town outweighs your apprehension about moving back. One thing most returnees agree upon is that their tenure in the big city prepared them for the return, making it feel like a voluntary effort rather than an obligatory move. City life broadened them and enabled them to come back to small-town life with a newer, more cosmopolitan perspective—to feel not saddled but rather uplifted by it.

"If you like the present, you shouldn't throw stones at the past," says Hopkins. "I didn't need to come to Anniston straight out of law school." And she shouldn't have. She came at precisely the right juncture—when she wanted to lay down roots for herself, her husband and her two sons and spend time with her aging mother.

Ironically, often it is precisely those who were most eager to escape their hometowns who find themselves called back home. When Mount Airy native Burke Robertson graduated from Presbyterian College in Clinton, South Carolina, in 1969, he had the option of returning to join the family business. But, he says, he categorically ruled it out. "Mount Airy was not the place I wanted to live under any circumstances. I wanted something different. So I went to Atlanta—that was the big city at the time—to make my way." Twenty-two years later, the town Robertson felt compelled to flee lured him back.

Likewise, after Mount Airy native Robert Merritt graduated from Mount Airy High School in 1944, he said, "There's a country-western song that could have been my theme song back then: 'Happiness Is Mount Airy in the Rear-View Mirror.' I thought everything important and significant in the world was happening somewhere else. Growing up, I always thought of Mount Airy as a one-horse town—provincial and quaint." By 1953, when Merritt returned with his wife, Cama Clarkson Merritt, he'd come to realize that the rest of the world was a one-horse place, too. Mount Airy looked better than ever as a place to start a family and grow a business.

Though returning sons and daughters may start out with advantages, ultimately, like everyone else, they're on their own to clear a path. Laurie Forbes describes those whom she knew from before as being very welcoming when she first moved back with her Boston-bred husband. "They were very accepting and helpful. That's real nice. But after that initial couple of months after you've come back and everyone's seen you, everyone goes on with their lives."

After the initial welcome, it's up to you, the returning native daughter or son, to pick up the ball and carry it. To prove once again that you can play by the rules governing small-town life and forge a new place for yourself.

ARE SMALL TOWNS RIGHT FOR PEOPLE OF COLOR?

Your most immediate response to this question might be no—especially in those small towns which have negligible minority populations or are located in areas of the country long thought to be racist, such as the South. But think again. In fact, a small town may be the *best* place for people of color—even if you find one in which there may not be great numbers of people from your particular racial or ethnic group living there.

A recent editorial in *Small Town* dispels the notion that small towns are poor places for minorities. "Many small towns have the capability to heal wounds caused by discrimination. . . . Simply knowing somebody, knowing their family and knowing what they go through forces people to understand."

"If you have to interact with someone who is not like you,

often you find out that they're not the stereotype," says Ken Munsell, editor of *Small Town.*

YOU STAND OUT AS AN INDIVIDUAL

Understand that as an educated and motivated newcomer of color or ethnicity, you *will* stand out in the crowd. Once people have processed the fact of your race, the good news is that you'll be noticed as an individual. Assuming that you follow the small-town code, you're more apt to be viewed as an individual than merely as an African-American, Asian-American or Hispanic. This individuation will happen more quickly and more completely than in a city in part because of the enormous curiosity about you. If you play your cards right, in some respects, you, as a minority member, may even be ahead of the game.

This was precisely the case for Esther Nettles Rauch, who, as an extroverted, savvy and highly educated African-American, moved to tiny Castine, Maine, with her WASP husband, retired Navy Admiral Charles F. "Chick" Rauch in 1981. Esther threw herself into community life; she joined the Episcopal church and the Castine Scientific Society of the Wilson Museum and took a last-minute, full-time, fill-in job teaching freshman composition at the Maine Maritime Academy in Castine. (In true small-town fashion, she got the job after their *realtor* told the dean about the qualifications of his new client, who was then working toward her Ph.D. in English.)

The interracial couple quickly became the toast of the town. Why?

With their social skills, easy empathy and piquant backgrounds, Esther and Chick would have been welcomed no matter what their race. But her being black created an added incentive for the many Castiners who'd never been close to an African-American.

"They were curious about why a black woman would want to move to a small Maine town," says Rauch. "They wanted

to know: Would I stay?" (The couple has lived in Castine and
now nearby Orono, Maine, for a total of fifteen years. Today
Esther Rauch is something of a local legend.)

THEY'RE SEEKING DIVERSITY (TO KEEP UP WITH THE REST OF AMERICA)

Don't for a moment think that small-towners are oblivious to
the larger society as it's changing around them. Small-
towners are aware of the need as a society to become more
multicultural and inclusive, to bring women and people of
color into the inner sanctums of power. When Wanda attended high school in Orono, Maine, from which she graduated in 1974 in a class of eighty-three, there was only one
black student at the school, a year younger than she. The girl
was hot stuff—the Oprah Winfrey of Orono High. A gifted
athlete, a good student and universally liked, she had it all
over everyone else. It was hip—if not politically correct (before the term was invented)—to be her friend. We've known
other African-Americans, like this girl, for whom race was an
advantage in the context of scarcity.

Living in Americus, Georgia (population 16,512), Habitat
for Humanity's Floyd Nelson is far from being the only
African-American. However, the former Atlantan, who grew
up in Milwaukee, has been pleasantly surprised by the fabric
of life in a region of the country that was once overwhelmingly
racist. He advises other African-Americans moving to the
small-town South to come with "an open mind. Don't assume
anything moving in."

"The South has the factual reputation of being the bastion
of racism and segregation. But 1996 is not the same as 1956,
and people are different. Come and experience what was,
what is and what is to be all at the same time."

The social fabric of Americus is already changing for the
better and, in the future, Nelson envisions a more racially integrated society. "You're going to have more of a meshing to-

gether of individuals of different backgrounds, communities, families. Americus is both segregated and integrated. I go to a variety of churches—some white, some black, some intermingled. I tend to go to Baptist churches. In some white churches, I'd be the only black person there. I'd be treated with respect. Some people would feel uncomfortable. But I, for the most part, would be comfortable."

YOU'VE ARRIVED!

> "Commuters give the city its tidal restlessness; natives give it solidity and continuity; but the settlers give it passion."
>
> —E. B. WHITE, *Here Is New York*

Just as new New Yorkers give the city its passion, so do new arrivals to small-town America. As a newcomer, carrying the banner of change (along with elements of surprise and mystery), you're a charged entity, endowed with the ability to attract and repel. Coming in from the outside, you have fresh blood and insight, and the power to provide leadership for change.

What You Can Contribute

Once you've learned the lay of the land, mastered the code of small-town life, broken into "the club," and removed the "O word" (outsider) from your forehead, you'll be able to champion social change more effectively and significantly than you would ever have been able to in the city. You'll make a place for yourself—and take your place alongside the stalwarts of the town—once you determine what offering of your talents you can bring to the table, what is your signature "dish."

"You need to figure out what you can contribute to a community yourself," says Janet Topolsky, associate director of the rural economic policy program of the Aspen Institute in Washington,

D.C. "Small towns are intimate. Just as you can be miserable in a family, you can be miserable in a small town unless there's a piece of community to which you can contribute, and it can contribute back to you."

Chris Murray, the waterfowl carver in Castine, Maine, found out that he could not only contribute his pieces of artwork to local charities but that he could give to his community by volunteering to coach golf at the high school.

When she moved from Boston back to her hometown of Mount Airy, Laurie Moorefield Forbes was called upon to teach "assertiveness" to nurse-trainees and leadership development skills to scholarship students at Surry Community College.

In addition to her teaching, Philadelphia native Marion Goldwasser filled a community-service niche in Hillsville, Virginia, by periodically gathering together minivans of students to make the two-hour drive to Roanoke to hear authors read. She took groups to Charlottesville to tour the University of Virginia campus in the hopes of encouraging kids to apply there. (Oddly enough, it's a rarity in rural southwestern Virginia for college-bound students to even consider UVA.)

When he returned to his hometown of Mount Airy from Charlotte, real estate developer Burke Robertson worked to bring city hall closer to the chamber of commerce. He helped revitalize the downtown by renovating a dilapidated minimall near Main Street and chasing down new tenants for it as well as filling vacant storefronts downtown.

Professional dancer and choreographer Betsy Ogden, who moved from Manhattan to rural Washington state, found that she could bring her expertise to the town of Ellensburg in the form of dance classes.

Once you've figured out what you can give, you're en route to becoming a successful cultural transplant. You now understand two cultures, can walk two walks and talk two talks and can move easily between big city and small town; this ability gives you a fluency and flexibility that many small-towners lack. You can bring this outside expertise into the well of your small-town self and draw from it when bestowing your gifts on the small town and developing your perspective. Unlike some small-towners, who are here by default, you will be glad to know that you've tried both worlds and are here by choice.

Once you determine what "piece" is uniquely yours to contribute and carve out a niche that no one else fills, you'll be able to make the ultimate transition and commitment to your town. This final move—in which, in some important way, you take on as your own the identity of the town, while deciding what to give to sustain it—will likely correspond with the townsfolks' acceptance of you. It is at this moment that you've arrived. With the exception of native sons and daughters returning to their home-towns, this final transition into community life may take up to five years.

By now, you've assembled all the tools you need to make a place for yourself in your small town. You've learned (or are learning) a mode of behavior and a code of conduct that are very likely more livable, forgiving, and humane than anything you've ever experienced in the city. You may have discovered for the first time that precious element of life called community that many Americans never experience.

Living in a small town can be confining at times; it can, at times, feel like you're living in a fishbowl; and, yes, there may be occasions when you get possessive about your life, which is not entirely your own. Gossip about you may get back to you, and you may at times become overextended; but consider the rewards. You've got a place that you will come to know well, a community which you can help shape and influence, with people you will come to know over time in multiple contexts. The right small town may be the very best place in America in which to raise children and where seniors can age with grace and dignity. It may well be the best place in the world for you as an adult to develop your capabilities and career or to grow your business. It may be the best place for you to solve problems in the context of a community, to reconnect with humanity and to come fully alive.

It has worked that way for us. We feel more alive here than anywhere else, moving forward with a set of characters and a giant family we never had before. But probably the most significant and valuable lesson we've learned in our ten years living in a small town can be summed up this way: Learning how to live in a small town is learning how to live.

Acknowledgments

So many people have helped make this book a reality, it would be impossible to list everyone. We'd like to start by thanking the good people of Mount Airy, North Carolina, for providing the inspiration and context for the book.

Certain individuals and groups deserve special recognition, and they include the following: the members of the Mount Airy Rotary Club but especially Janet K. Edwards; Burke Robertson; Mike King; Robert Merritt; Jack Wilson; Brenda Goings; Monroe Watkins; Gary T. York; Pat Mangels; Gene Rees; David Swann; Laurie Moorefield Forbes; Teresa Yeatts; Cooper Adams; Eddie Hatch; Jim Grimes; Bob Moody and Dick Johnson; the members of Mount Airy's All-America City committee; Dr. Philip M. Burgess, president of the Center for the New West; Mary Sue Burgess; Milan Wall, co-director of the Heartland Center for Leadership Development; Christopher T. Gates, president, National Civic League; Mike McGrath and David Lampe, National Civic League; Dale Badgett, executive director, Greater Mount Airy Chamber of Commerce; Jim Grimes, former executive director Greater Mount Airy Chamber of Commerce; Yvonne Nichols of the Chamber; Frank Dobisky of Dobisky and Associates, Keene, N.H.; Tom Halicki, executive director, National Association of Towns and Townships (NATaT), Washington, D.C.; John Overton, finance director, City of Mount Airy; Ron Niland, Mount Airy city manager;

former Mount Airy Mayor Maynard Beamer; Gary Tilley, Surry Community College; Dr. Swanson Richards; Pat Gwyn Woltz and John Woltz; Hattie Mae Love; Lydia Steck, public information officer, American Medical Association; Sylvia Prokop of the Joint Commission on Accreditation of Healthcare Organizations; Bill Graham, North Carolina Commissioner of Banks; Robert Donnan, Southern Growth Policies Board; Rheta Grimsley Johnson, columnist *Atlanta Journal & Constitution;* Marion and Mike Goldwasser; Monica Hinton and Delos Monteith Center for Mountain Living; Janet Topolsky, Aspen Institute; Kathie deNobriga, Alternate Roots; Dr. Vaughn Grisham, George McLean Institute for Community Development, University of Mississippi; Dale Doyle, International Downtown Association; Charles W. "Chuck" Stroup, director of economic development and finance for the State of North Dakota; Robert Quick, National Rural Health Association; Abhijeet Rane, senior analyst, LINK Resources; Peggy J. Schmidt; Dr. Kenneth Stone, professor of economics, Iowa State University; Dr. Joel Worley, professor of management, Northwestern (Louisiana) State University; Carol Lyons, dean of career services, Northeastern University; Joanne Kroll, director of career planning and placement, Bowling Green State University; Morton J. Marcus, economist with the Indiana University School of Business; Dr. Charles F. Longino, Jr., Wake Forest University; Dr. David Hentzel, University of Missouri, Rolla; Bonnie and Peter Templeton; William L. Seavey, Greener Pastures; Dr. Larry Leistritz, professor of agricultural economics, North Dakota State University; Joanne H. Pratt, Dallas-based business consultant; Lisa A. Rogak; the New Road Map Foundation; Betsy Jackson; Suzanne F. Scott; National Main Street; Jim Schriner and Pat Watson, PHH Fantus; Howard and Nancy Smith; Dan and Mary Smith; John de Graaf; Liz Brody; Bonni Kogen-Brodnick; Norman Crampton; David Savageau; Kathleen Norris; Nicholas and Nancy Bragg; Tanya B. Rees; Floyd E. "Flip" Rees; Susan Ashley; Linda and Millard Fuller, Habitat for Humanity.

In a league of their own are supporters from the publishing industry. We'd like to thank Marilyn Abraham, formerly with Simon & Schuster, and Mitch Horowitz for their early support of the project. A huge debt of gratitude goes to our dear friend and agent Charlotte Sheedy for her guidance and faith, and to our editor, Laureen Connelly Rowland, for her enthusiastic response and exceptional editing. Even though Laureen works in mid-town Manhattan, it's clear that her heart still skips to the small-town beat!

Index

About the Authors

WANDA URBANSKA and FRANK LEVERING own and operate Levering Orchard, the largest cherry orchard in the South. In 1993, they founded Orchard Gap Press, specializing in books on fruit, simple living and small-town life.

They are consultants and speakers on rural relocation, small towns, and simple living. They welcome comments about *Moving to a Small Town,* which should be sent to: Rt. 2, Box 310, Ararat, VA, 24053.